SHERMAN MINTON

NEW DEAL SENATOR, COLD WAR JUSTICE

Linda C. Gugin and James E. St. Clair

INDIANA HISTORICAL SOCIETY
INDIANAPOLIS 1997

Printed in the United States of America

The paper in this publication meets the minimum requirements of American National Standard for Information Sciences—Permanence of Paper for Printed Library Materials, ANSI Z39.48-1984. ∞

Library of Congress Cataloging-in-Publication Data

Gugin, Linda C.

Sherman Minton : New Deal senator, cold war justice / Linda C. Gugin and James E. St. Clair.

p. cm.

Includes bibliographical references and index.

ISBN 0–87195–116–9

1. Minton, Sherman A., 1890–1965. 2. United States. Supreme Court—Biography. 3. Judges—United States—Biography. I. St. Clair, James E. II. Title.

KF8754.M54G84 1997

347.73'2634—dc21

[B]

97–3899

CIP

To David

To Jessica and Junior

Contents

Foreword

by Abner J. Mikva, former Chief Judge, United States Court of Appeals, D.C. Circuit, and counsel to President William Jefferson Clinton, 1994–95

This is a long-overdue biography. Sherman Minton of Indiana was the last appointee to the United States Supreme Court who had prior experience as a member of Congress. Congressional experience had been a common ingredient in the biographies of Supreme Court justices in prior times. When I clerked for Justice Minton in 1951 there were four justices who had been a part of the legislative branch of government. In addition to Minton, Chief Justice Fred M. Vinson and Justices Hugo L. Black and Harold H. Burton had been members of Congress. Justice Stanley F. Reed had served in the Kentucky state legislature, so there were five justices with prior legislative experience.

Such previous congressional employment affected the outlook and the work product of the justices. Even from my perch as an "inferior court" judge, I was constantly aware of how my congressional service colored my attitude toward the cases I considered. When it comes to Supreme Court cases, the impact is far greater.

Authors Linda C. Gugin and James E. St. Clair are fully aware of the experiences that Senator Minton brought to the Supreme Court as Justice Minton. Justice Minton's willingness to defer to the judgment of the elected branches of government put him at odds with the activists who dominated the Court and the Court watchers during the subsequent tenure of Chief Justice Earl Warren, but that characteristic put him very much in the mainstream of the Vinson Court when Minton commenced his Supreme Court service.

As the authors point out, it is impossible to overemphasize the importance of Minton's political experience to his role as a Supreme Court justice. Indeed, his appointment came from his close friendship with President Harry S. Truman during their days as seatmates in the United States Senate. The only opposition to the appointment stemmed from his contentious efforts, while in the Senate, to put through President Franklin D. Roosevelt's Court-packing plan.

No case better typified the attitude that the justices with congressional experience had toward the elected branches of government than *Youngstown Sheet & Tube* v. *United Steelworkers of America* (the *Steel Seizure* case). While only Minton and Reed joined Chief Justice Vinson's dissent in the case, which overturned President Truman's efforts to head off a strike by seizing the mills, the tone of the dissent set the pattern for the holding. The case remains a landmark because, like *Marbury* v. *Madison*, it used judicial power to arbitrate a dispute between the elected branches of government. Justice Minton found such an authority hard to square with his notions of how power was to be distributed in a democracy. Those notions were honed in the Congress of the United States, and while Justices Black and Burton voted with the majority in the *Steel Seizure* case, the other former members of Congress voted to let the president and the Congress fight it out.

It is the notion of deference that is clearly missing from the Court decisions since the last of the congressmen were appointed to the Court. Whether the decisions are perceived as "liberal" or "conservative," whether "activist" or "passivist," the Supreme Court is seldom perceived as deferential to the Congress. Sherman Minton never forgot his senatorial experiences. They were reflected in every court decision he made, and this biography faithfully tracks that role.

Minton was tagged as "Mr. Main Street" by one of his "elitist brethren." Gugin and St. Clair accurately chronicle the career that earned Minton that appellation. He considered himself a small-town lawyer who had been lucky in politics and had been blessed by the friendship and loyalty of two presidents—Roosevelt and Truman. He never thought that he was responsible for his own success. While not a humble man generally, he was very modest about his intellectual capacity. It never occurred to him that he possessed better academic credentials than any member of the Supreme Court. (He was the only justice with a master's degree in law. Justice Jackson, who was considered one of the scholars on the Vinson Court, had not even graduated from law school.) To Minton, the important credential that he brought to the Court was his status as an alumnus of the United States Senate.

What makes this biography so pertinent is its thorough examination of Minton's entire career. While his greatest claim to fame was as one of the 107 justices of the Supreme Court, he arrived there and operated there because of the many things he did before his appointment. Because none of the present justices had similar experiences (nor have any of the appointees since 1949, when Minton was sworn in), the book describes a direction on the Supreme Court that no longer exists and probably will not be replicated. The day when political experience is considered a plus in the selection of Supreme Court justices is over. While the shorthand terms used to describe Supreme Court justices and cases may not be impacted by this change in direction, the real substance of the Court's decisions, and the real role that the Court plays in our democracy, will be vastly affected. Gugin and St. Clair explain this in their very authentic description of the life and times of Sherman Minton.

Preface

Sherman Minton was at center-stage during two important periods of twentieth-century America: the New Deal and the Cold War. As a United States senator in the 1930s he fought vigorously on behalf of President Franklin D. Roosevelt and New Deal economic legislation and against an activist Supreme Court that consistently declared these laws unconstitutional. Minton's outspoken criticism of the Supreme Court and his ardent support of Roosevelt's scheme to pack the Court to get more favorable decisions propelled his rise to prominence. Minton believed the Court should be more deferential to the government's efforts to meet the economic emergencies of the depression era.

Similarly, when Minton became a member of the Supreme Court in 1949 he held to his view that the Court should be reluctant to interfere with legislative actions. This meant that during the Cold War he frequently sided with government policies that limited individual rights for the sake of national security, incurring the wrath of liberals, who, in a shift from New Deal days, had come to embrace judicial activism.

Although scholars have attempted to explain Minton's career as politician and jurist by using the terms liberal and conservative, he actually defies categorization. In truth, he was a pragmatist with no well-grounded political or judicial philosophy who focused on results rather than process. In times of national crises, such as the depression era and the Cold War, Minton advocated strong government action to serve the needs of the majority and had little concern for procedural matters.

In this biography, Minton's activities during these two critical periods in American history receive extensive treatment. Minton, however, was much more than a New Deal senator and Cold War justice, and this work presents a thorough study of a remarkable Indiana son. Born into poverty, Sherman Minton attained top positions in all three branches of national government, one of only a few to do so. His name and achievements, however, are not widely recognized, even in his native state. Thus, the authors' primary aim in this biography is to bring to the fore, without embellishment, the life and times of a public servant whose record merits examination and consideration.

From the early 1930s to the mid-1950s, when the great political issues of the day in Indiana and the nation were being debated and decided, Minton was often in the middle of the action and at the right hand of such powerful figures as Franklin D. Roosevelt, Harry S. Truman, and Gov. Paul V. McNutt. This volume details Minton's close relationships with these important leaders and how that closeness both helped and hurt his career.

In Minton these political leaders had an ideal disciple. He relished the tumult of partisan politics, repressed his own ambitions, if necessary, for the good of the Democratic party, and remained loyal to them regardless of the political climate. For his unwavering loyalty and partisanship, these men rewarded Minton whenever possible. McNutt gave Minton his start in public life, which led to his election to the United States Senate. Roosevelt helped engineer Minton's rapid rise to a leadership position in the Senate, gave him a safe harbor in the White House after his reelection bid failed, and put him on the federal bench. Truman, his longtime soul mate, elevated him to the United States Supreme Court.

Because of his intimate ties to his political benefactors, Minton was branded a crony and "rubber stamp," especially for Roosevelt, and he never completely shed the image of ward heeler, even as a Supreme Court justice. Minton, however, made no apologies for his hardball brand of patronage politics that he learned in machine-controlled Indiana of the 1930s. It was enough for Minton that the system was simple, orderly, and seemed to work. For the same reasons he defended the much-maligned Two Percent Club, which forced state government workers to contribute to the party's treasury. Minton thought the party system worked best and was more democratic when it received many small grassroots contributions. Otherwise, he felt, control of parties and the political process would shift to a few rich overlords, a prospect he found alarming.

Minton's views on politics, and on most things for that matter, were greatly influenced by his upbringing in the hills of southern Indiana. Childhood experiences planted the seeds of both liberal and conservative tendencies. His liberalism was most evident by his belief that the federal government actively had to help society's disadvantaged. Undoubtedly, this sentiment stemmed from the poverty and adversity in his youth, including the death of his mother at an early age. As a New Deal senator, Minton was able to put his liberalism to work as a spirited supporter of government programs aimed at improving the conditions of common people. Minton's childhood also left conservative markings. Because his youth was filled with chaos, he valued order and had a need for certainty. Accordingly, as a Supreme Court justice he believed that following precedents was essential for continuity and stability in the law. He also believed that preservation of order required strong government, and therefore he consistently upheld restrictions on civil liberties and individual rights.

Minton's hard-line approach in these two areas of law has been criticized by Court historians and undoubtedly is partly responsible for the low rating he has received as a justice. Minton was not one of the Court's great thinkers or writers, and the authors have tried not to make more out of him than what he was. Still, to label his service as a failure, as some scholars have done, is unfair. His tenure was a brief seven years, but during that time Minton worked hard and wrote more than his share of opinions. He wrote in every category of the law and wrote all the cases on tax liens heard during his time on the Court. Moreover, Minton played an important role in the school desegregation cases and in virtually all of the other civil rights cases in which he participated.

Although Minton's legal impact was minimal, his instinctive political skills allowed him to mediate between warring justices and make the Court more harmonious. By focusing on this aspect of his tenure the authors have attempted to show the Court as a human institution, not just a legal one, and that Minton, as always, was the consummate Hoosier politician.

Minton was first and foremost a politician who happened into a career as a jurist primarily because in 1940 the voters in Indiana denied him the pursuit of his first love, politics. Even as a judge, though, he was never far from political action, maintaining an active involvement in patronage matters at the state and national levels. As a justice he voted to uphold Truman in the steel seizure case out of loyalty to Truman, his old friend. Fittingly, on the eve of his retirement from the Supreme Court, Minton created a sensation when he injected himself into the 1956 presidential election. Minton, in the political vernacular of today, was just being Minton. For the authors, getting to know what it was like being Minton has been an exhilarating journey. He was a man with a great sense of humor, a wide-ranging intellect, sincere compassion, a love of country, family, and friends, and a true public servant.

The authors have written this biography for those interested in Indiana history, political history, and legal history. Whatever your interest, the authors hope you will share their belief that learning about Sherman Minton was worth the effort.

Acknowledgments

The publication of this biography represents the culmination of a long journey that was assisted at every juncture by the generous and unselfish support of so many. Before acknowledging these contributions we would first like to pay tribute to Shay Minton, the subject of our attention and fascination for the better part of six years. To us, he was endlessly interesting and lively, and we feel fortunate to have had the opportunity to study and chronicle his life.

The first major step in our journey was a program in October of 1990 that honored the one hundredth anniversary of Minton's birth, which was funded by a grant from the Indiana Humanities Council. As a result of that program, we met people who were critical to the success of this undertaking. These included Minton's three children, Sherman, Mary Anne, and John, and his former Supreme Court law clerk, Judge Abner Mikva.

We are especially indebted to Minton's daughter, Mary Anne Callanan, for opening her home to us, allowing us complete access to her father's papers, and patiently answering our many questions. Without Mary Anne's encouragement and support, this biography would not have been possible.

Judge Mikva, likewise, played a crucial role in the book's genesis and development. His address at the anniversary ceremony gave us valuable insight into Minton's judicial philosophy and character. Despite his busy schedule, Judge

Mikva unhesitatingly made himself available to us on numerous occasions for detailed discussions about Minton's Supreme Court service. And we deeply appreciate the fact that he so graciously agreed to write the foreword to this book.

We also are profoundly grateful that David J. Bodenhamer, a legal historian at a sister campus of Indiana University, agreed to be our editorial guide. His wisdom and advice were strong beacons that unfailingly kept us on course. He not only became our mentor, he became our friend. The penetrating and instructive review of this work by James Ely, also a legal historian, helped us to sharpen and strengthen the manuscript.

Harry L. Wallace, who served as a law clerk to Minton on the Supreme Court, deserves special mention and our thanks for sharing with us his unpublished biography of Minton, his memories of Minton, and his correspondence with Minton.

Others generously shared their memories of Minton with us. Because of his long and close association with Minton, New Albany attorney John Cody was a fount of stories that revealed Minton's warmth and wit. In much the same manner, Alan T. Nolan, whose mother and father were among Minton's closest friends, regaled us with anecdotes that showed Minton's human and humorous sides. The measure of Minton as a caring and compassionate man came through in our conversations with Frances Kelly, his faithful secretary from the Senate to the Supreme Court; Olyus F. Hood, whose official duty was as messenger to Minton on the Court, but whose role was so much more; Ruth Walts, who illuminated for us how the tiny town of Georgetown, Indiana, Minton's birthplace, was such an enduring force in his life; and Dilsey Scott, who cared for Minton during his final years and noted how he had been "a caring man all his life."

We gained additional insight into the life and times of Minton from the following: Raymond Gray, Richard T.

Conway, Larry R. Taylor, and Keith Mann, law clerks for Justice Minton; Robert H. Ferrell, Donald F. Carmony, and James H. Madison, Indiana University historians; Rayman L. Solomon, associate dean of the Northwestern University law school; Gordon Owen, a retired University of New Mexico communications professor who analyzed Minton's public speeches for his dissertation; John Hurt, a Martinsville, Indiana, lawyer with intimate knowledge of Hoosier politics; and Alice O'Donnell, of Washington, D.C., who was a secretary to Justice Tom Clark.

The Indiana Historical Society, of course, has been instrumental in this biography from the beginning. Our thanks to Thomas A. Mason, director of the Publications Division, who agreed to listen to our proposal in the first place, and then suggested we apply for a Society Clio grant, which we did and which we received. We also appreciate the help and encouragement from Robert M. Taylor, Jr., director of the Education Division, and the expert editing by Paula Corpuz, Shirley McCord, Kathleen Breen, and George Hanlin.

We gladly acknowledge the support that our own institution, Indiana University Southeast, provided in the form of summer research fellowships, a sabbatical leave, and grants that allowed us to hire student research assistants. The help we received from Kim Pelle greatly facilitated the progress of our work. We were also aided by John Ingle, Kory Wilcoxson, and Doris Cleek.

Valuable assistance was provided by numerous librarians and research assistants at the following: the Indiana Room of the New Albany-Floyd County Library; Harry S. Truman Presidential Library; Library of Congress; Supreme Court Library; Lilly Library at Indiana University; Indiana State Library; Indiana State Archives; Indiana Historical Society Library; Special Collections Department at the Margaret I. King Library at the University of Kentucky; and the Indiana University Southeast Library. Special thanks go to Jan Beckett and Diane Warren, librarians at Harlaxton College in Grantham, England.

CHAPTER ONE

The Last New Dealer Takes a Seat

On the morning of 12 October 1949, an unseasonably hot fall day in Washington, D.C., Hoosier Sherman Minton, who in eight days would be fifty-nine years old, stood on the portico of the White House by the Rose Garden to be sworn in as an associate justice of the United States Supreme Court. Nearly four hundred people were assembled in summerlike eighty-degree heat to witness the culmination of an odyssey that had a lowly beginning. Minton, who was born into poverty on a small farm in the hardscrabble hills of Floyd County in southern Indiana, lived a saga of only-in-America proportions: star athlete in high school and college; honors graduate of two law schools; World War I army officer; reform-minded utility regulator; populist United States senator; assistant to President Franklin D. Roosevelt; respected federal appeals court judge; and, finally, Supreme Court justice.

Through it all Minton remained true to his upbringing in rural, small-town America at the turn of the century. "It doesn't rub off when you're born in the Southern Indiana hills," Minton once said.[1] The values and beliefs that stayed with him a lifetime sprang from the hardships of his youth and were central to his successes and to his strengths when he suffered defeat. His father's struggles to eke out an existence from marginal land, the premature death of his mother, and the necessity of helping support his family at a young age taught Minton the lessons of persistence, hard work, cunning, and independence and gave him an affinity for the plight of common people. His humble beginnings also kept Minton unassuming regardless of his office or title. To most people he was always "Shay," the nickname he acquired in childhood because his younger brother pronounced "Sherman" as "Shayman." Minton was serious-minded, but he had a spirited streak as well that he displayed through exuberance, good humor, and occasional mischievousness. He attributed this dichotomy to an ancestral blend of New England Puritan and Virginia Cavalier. "There's swashbuckling but there's a ramrod up the back," Minton said.[2]

That ramrod helped Minton weather political and professional defeat and disappointment. Twice he lost in primary elections for the Democratic nomination to Congress, and he was defeated for reelection to the United States Senate in 1940. Losing the Senate seat was perhaps the most agonizing experience of his career. Minton, who by education and training appeared to be tailor-made for the judiciary, was a politician down to the marrow. Ever the loyal Democrat and New Deal senator, he thrived in the heat of partisan politics. He loved fighting and winning legislative battles, leveling opponents with sarcasm, and working behind the scenes to win political appointments for his friends. Not only did Minton love politics, he also excelled at it. Although he served only one term in the Senate he achieved positions of power normally reserved to those with greater seniority.

Minton never shed his political side after defeat at the polls led him into a career on the bench, nor did he think it was necessary. One of the glaring ironies of Minton's life is that his strengths as a politician both helped and hurt him in the consideration for judicial appointments. His passionate, forceful, and articulate advocacy of New Deal proposals brought Minton acclaim, visibility, and the good graces of Roosevelt. The president, obviously impressed with Minton's talents and loyalty, contemplated appointing him to the Supreme Court in 1937. Minton's no-holds-barred approach, acerbic manner, and partisan nature, however, raised questions about his tolerance and judicial temperament when his nomination to the Supreme Court finally came in 1949.

The prospect of Minton on the Supreme Court was first discussed when Justice Willis Van Devanter, also a native Hoosier, retired in mid-1937, giving Roosevelt the opportunity to make his first selection to the Court.[3] Supreme Court nominations are always significant, but this one, besides being Roosevelt's first, had added meaning since many of the president's New Deal initiatives had been struck down by the Court, and he had just suffered a humiliating defeat in the Senate over his controversial plan to pack the Court. His nominee, then, had to have more than just a good legal mind. Roosevelt wanted someone who not only was certain of Senate confirmation but also was an affront to those senators who had opposed him on his Court-packing plan. In other words, "He longed to give the Senate a bitter pill to swallow, yet make the rebellious legislators gulp it down."[4] In short order a list of possible candidates was pared from sixty names to three: Minton, Sen. Hugo L. Black of Alabama, and Solicitor General Stanley F. Reed. The choice came down to Minton and Black after the president concluded, according to Interior Secretary Harold L. Ickes, that Reed was "a good man but without much force or color."[5]

Both Minton and Black, however, could fill the president's bitter pill prescription. Since both were senators, the time-honored tradition of senatorial courtesy made confirmation a certainty. Both Minton and Black were loyal New Dealers and, in their zealous advocacy of the president's proposal to enlarge the Court, had venomously attacked its opponents. The president, according to Ickes, favored Black, in part because Black was facing reelection in 1938 and his prospects, after compiling a liberal voting record in the Senate, were not promising in conservative Alabama. Minton, on the other hand, with more than three years left in his term, was a rising star in the Senate who could be counted on to forcefully and eloquently plead the administration's causes.

The nomination of Black was sealed when Minton took himself out of the running for reasons that "exhibited a delicacy of feeling singular in a politician and job holder."[6] During the Court-packing fight Minton had vociferously attacked the Court and its "Nine Old Men," and he felt it would be personally embarrassing to be named to the Court at the time and that the sitting justices would take his appointment as a personal insult.

For the next twelve years the possibility that Minton would be named to the high court was raised and dashed a number of times. Though Roosevelt was to make seven more appointments to the Court, 1937 probably had been Minton's best chance to become a Supreme Court justice under Roosevelt. There was speculation, however, that Minton had the inside track for an appointment when Justice Benjamin Cardozo died in 1938. Minton said such reports were "wishful thinking on somebody's part," and he publicly advocated that the position go to Harvard law professor Felix Frankfurter, which it did.[7] Minton's prospects this time may have been affected by his efforts to help launch a presidential bid for his old ally, former Indiana governor Paul V. McNutt. In the late 1930s it was widely believed that Roosevelt would not seek an unprecedented third term in 1940.[8] When

Roosevelt did seek a third term, Minton, ever the loyalist, duly supported the president's reelection.

The president, rewarding Minton's loyalty and support, named him an administrative assistant in the White House after Minton was defeated for reelection to the Senate in 1940. Then in May 1941 the president appointed Minton to the United States Court of Appeals for the Seventh Circuit in Chicago. Throughout the early 1940s Minton continued to be under consideration for positions that would have thrust him back into the political maelstrom in which he thrived. In late 1943 he was offered the job as chairman of the Democratic party. He was tempted, but declined. For reassurance that his inclination to refuse the position was sound, Minton sought the opinion of an old friend from his Senate days, Lewis B. Schwellenbach, then a United States district judge in Spokane, Washington. Schwellenbach wrote a five-page reply detailing the reasons why Minton should decline the job. He said the "sacrifice they're asking you to make is a tremendous one and I agree with you that the answer should be 'no.'" Schwellenbach discussed several key reasons why Minton should decline, including the lack of party unity, prospects of Democratic losses in 1944, and Minton's apparent happiness in his work on the appeals court.[9]

The next year Minton's name was on a list of vice presidential candidates acceptable to Roosevelt, who would be running for a fourth term in 1944 and who had been convinced that keeping Vice President Henry Wallace on the ticket would be detrimental to the party.[10] More was at stake than the party's future, however, since it was evident in 1944 that the president's health was declining and he most likely would not live through another four-year term. The vice presidential selection would in effect be a presidential selection. Roosevelt, who was also considering others such as Justice William O. Douglas and James F. Byrnes, his War Mobilization director, gave his consent to Harry Truman after strong lobbying by Democratic chairman Robert Hannegan and other party leaders. Hannegan and the others persuaded Roosevelt that "Truman was the man who would hurt him least."[11]

After his nomination at the Democratic convention in Chicago, Truman, in a letter to Schwellenbach, wrote: "If the steam had been rolled up behind Minton he would have been nominated, and I think both of us would have been much happier about it, but I am going to try to do the job the best I can."[12]

When Vice President Truman became president in April 1945, speculation heightened that bigger things were in store for Minton. The two men had forged a strong friendship during their six years together in the Senate from 1935 to 1941. The elections of 1934 brought so many New Deal Democrats to the Senate that an extra row of desks had to be crowded onto the Democratic side of the chamber. As it turned out, Truman had desk number 93 in the back row and Minton had desk number 92.

However, the bond that developed between the two freshmen senators resulted from more than just their close physical proximity on the Senate floor or their support for the sweeping legislative reform agenda of Roosevelt's New Deal. Their backgrounds were similar in many respects: both were farm boys; both had served overseas in World War I as army captains; both were Masons; both were aided in their political careers by machine politics; both sought to stand up for the common man; both were noted for their salty language; and both, as fiercely loyal and rabid partisans, were willing to reward an old friend when in a position to do so.

Actually, the opportunity for one man to advance the career of the other first came to Minton during his brief role as an aide to Roosevelt in early 1941. Minton, in a memo dated 27 February 1941, recommended that Roosevelt support Truman as chairman of a senatorial committee that would investigate allegations of wasteful defense spending.[13] The president did, and the resulting favorable publicity Truman received from the Special Senate Committee to Investigate the National Defense Program, commonly known as the Truman Committee, helped put him in the national spotlight and boosted his stock as a vice presidential candidate in 1944. Minton later sent Truman his original typewritten memo to the president and in a cover letter wrote, "You can see from a perusal of it that your old seat mate was batting for you when he was down at the White House." On the memo itself Minton added a handwritten notation: "Here's how vice presidents are made."[14] When Roosevelt died only a few months into his fourth term and Truman became president, it was natural to assume that he would go to bat for his old Senate colleague Sherman Minton.

Rumors of Minton's ascension accelerated after he was Truman's guest for a Memorial Day cruise in 1945 on the Potomac in the presidential yacht and had lunch with the president the next day at the White House. Subsequent newspaper stories confidently predicted that Minton would be named to a cabinet position in the new administration, either as secretary of war or secretary of the interior. And when Supreme Court Justice Owen J. Roberts announced that he would retire on 31 July 1945 Minton, for yet another time, was mentioned as a possible successor.[15]

Throughout the summer of 1945, as the United States and its allies negotiated peace in Europe and pressed the war to its conclusion in the Pacific, Minton continued to be mentioned as the likely replacement for Secretary of War Henry L. Stimson or Interior Secretary Harold L. Ickes. However, the reports were unfounded. In early September 1945 Minton squelched speculation about becoming secretary of war. Minton, responding to a prediction by Drew Pearson, Washington columnist and radio commentator, that his appointment was imminent, said, "There's nothing to it. As of right now, I don't think I would take it, even if the appointment were offered to me."[16] Just a few days later Truman named Robert P. Patterson, who had been undersecretary of war, to the top post. Minton, likewise, did not get the job at Interior. Ickes stayed on as secretary until 1946 when he was succeeded by Julius A. Krug, former chief of the War Production Board.

Minton, recalling the Memorial Day cruise with Truman, said the only job possibility he discussed with the president that day was as solicitor general. Minton, who had been diagnosed with pernicious anemia in 1943, declined, saying, "I told the President my health was too poor to consider it."[17]

However, Minton apparently was more than willing to take risks to his health in pursuing the position he really wanted: justice of the Supreme Court. However, it was not in his nature to campaign for it or to ask Truman directly for the appointment. Instead, Minton asked Justice Black, the man for whom he had stepped aside eight years earlier, to intercede in his behalf. In a letter to Black dated 15 September 1945 Minton wrote that "it would be very helpful in my case if you would call Harry or go down and see him and express your views. I think you will agree with me it would be better to have Lew [Schwellenbach] on the bench than me, but he seems to have eliminated himself; and I believe if you would say a word to Harry it would just tip the scales in my favor. As you know, I have never done anything to further my interest in the past, and I rather hesitate to do it this time, but I suppose this will be the last chance I will ever have."[18]

After receiving Minton's letter, Black made an appointment to see Truman on the morning of 18 September.

In a letter to Minton on 19 September Black reported the bad news: "I went and did my best but it was not enough as you now know. Whether it would have been more effective had I gone earlier will remain unknown, but I wish that I had. While the party believes that the selection is a good one, the reason given why it did not go another way was 'health.' Unquestionably you stand very high in the respect and affection of the gentleman. You may entertain regrets but I doubt whether your regret equals mine."[19]

The previous day Truman had announced that his first appointment to the Supreme Court would be Harold H. Burton, a Republican senator from Ohio who had worked closely with Truman on the committee that investigated defense spending. Minton was nonplussed by the appointment of a Republican in general and of Burton in particular. In a letter to thank Black for his efforts Minton wrote: "Thanks a million. I thought the gang had sold him off the idea of appointing a Republican. I never thought I would live to see the day my Democracy would be used against me by my own party!! It is alright. While I don't agree with him as to the wisdom of appointing a Republican or his choice of Republican I cheerfully accept his judgment. He has the responsibility both to the Party & to the Court. The politics of it just doesn't make sense to me."

Minton ended by writing, "My hopes of ever coming back to Washington are long gone so I will reconcile myself to living most of my life in the spew of the Chicago Tribune & the filth that is Chicago."[20] He was wrong, of course, about his fate, but shortly thereafter the concerns in the White House about Minton's health proved prescient for he was stricken by a massive heart attack and remained hospitalized for nineteen weeks. Minton's health problems first surfaced in December 1940 when his legs buckled as he and his daughter Mary Anne were running to catch a train in Washington, D.C.[21]

It was the first sign of the anemia disorder that would plague him throughout the remainder of his life.

Minton's heart attack occurred in late September 1945 while he was in Washington in connection with a special assignment he had accepted in mid-June as chairman of a five-member clemency board. The board helped the War Department review court-martial convictions handed out during the war and to determine whether sentences should be reduced. The board was created after several members of Congress, complaining that many wartime sentences were too severe, demanded an investigation of the military justice system. This assignment required Minton to commute to Washington every other week. In addition, he normally commuted between Chicago and his home in New Albany every weekend. The strain of the special assignment, the regular duties of the appeals court, and all the traveling proved too much for the fifty-five-year-old Minton.

After nearly a four-month stay at Walter Reed Hospital in Washington and additional convalescence at his home in New Albany, Minton returned to his work on the appeals court in Chicago in the spring of 1946, presumably out of the running for future Supreme Court or cabinet appointments because of his health. Indeed, when the deaths of Chief Justice Harlan F. Stone in 1946 and Associate Justice Frank Murphy in 1949 created vacancies on the Court, Minton's name was not mentioned in speculation about possible successors. Truman, in making his second and third appointments to the Court, turned to two members of his cabinet, who were also his personal friends. He named Fred M. Vinson, secretary of the treasury, to replace Stone as chief justice, and Tom C. Clark, attorney general, to succeed Murphy.

Minton's health, however, had recovered to the point that in late March 1948 he again assumed a special presidential assignment, but this one was shorter and less arduous than the assignment in 1945. Truman appointed him to chair a board of three commissioners to investigate the coal strike that had idled most of the nation's mines. In a matter of a few days, the board had concluded its hearings and presented the president with a report that charged mine union president John L. Lewis with "inducing" the strike.[22] Minton then returned to the appeals court in Chicago, and as the year 1948 unfolded it seemed increasingly likely that he would remain there until retirement. Minton's chances for a high position in national government were becoming more remote because the reelection prospects of his benefactor in the White House were dimming almost daily.

Truman's troubles in the presidential election year of 1948 went far beyond the crisis in the coalfields. Not only did he have to combat a contentious Republican-controlled Congress, but he also had to confront fracturing of the New Deal coalition within his own party. On the right were unhappy southerners and anti-Communists and on the left were dissident liberals and progressives. Added to the turbulent domestic scene was the red-hot Cold War: the overthrow of Czechoslovakia by Communists; the Soviet blockade of Berlin; the Greek government battling Communist rebels; and the Communists on the verge of victory in China. As Truman's job-performance rating in the polls slid to 36 percent, some Democrats, worried that his unpopularity would mean disaster for the party in the fall, cast about for someone else, even a Republican, to head the ticket in 1948. Minton was approached by some anxious party leaders to talk to Truman about bowing out of the race, and he obligingly arranged a meeting with the president when Truman was in Chicago. Upon seeing his old friend, Minton inquired, "How ye doin'?" Truman was buoyant. "Oh, we're going to win. They're [the Republicans] wrong and we're right and the people know it," he replied. Minton was so taken with Truman's spirit that the thought of raising the withdrawal issue evaporated.[23]

The "dump Truman" movement fizzled, and the president was nominated on the first ballot at the party's convention in Philadelphia. Minton, in an enthusiastic letter to Truman shortly after the convention, congratulated him on his "rip-roaring fighting speech" and said it was the type of speech "you should make all over the country." Minton also wrote, "When you started stamping your feet and shaking your fists and telling off the 80th Congress, you hit a responsive chord."[24] Truman's "give 'em hell" style and his attacks against the "Do Nothing" Congress in the fall campaign hit a responsive chord with the nation as a whole, and he defied the odds by being returned to office.

Although his reelection was sweetened by Democrats regaining control of Congress, the heat was hardly off Truman in 1949. The Communist menace appeared even more ominous: the Soviets exploded their first atomic bomb, ending America's nuclear monopoly, and China fell to the Communists, an event that launched Sen. Joseph McCarthy into his roguish crusade to ferret out alleged Communists in the United States State Department and elsewhere in the national government. The Red Scare was rampant in the country, and Truman was pushed to prove he was not soft on Communism. In fact, it has been suggested that Truman looked for men who would provide "judicial support for the Administration's security and anti-Communist programs" when he made two additional Supreme Court appointments in 1949.[25] Vacancies occurred that year not only with the death of Murphy but also of Wiley B. Rutledge, which meant that the Court in a period of less than two months lost two of its most liberal justices.

While the need to demonstrate a hard-line approach to Communism may have influenced Truman's 1949

Supreme Court selections, the overriding factor, as with earlier appointments, was his close personal and political relationships with his two choices.[26] To replace Murphy, Truman turned to Tom Clark, a loyal friend and political ally. Their friendship developed when Clark, as head of the Justice Department's Criminal Division, worked with Truman's special investigative committee. Clark also supported Truman's vice presidential bid at the 1944 Democratic convention and was a vigorous campaigner for him in the 1948 election. Clark also had strong anti-Communist credentials. As attorney general, Clark's concern about subversive activities extended to supporting loyalty oaths and broader authority for the FBI to use wire taps, prosecuting aliens, immigrants, and leaders of the American Communist party, and issuing the first list of dangerous political organizations.

Truman also picked Clark to strengthen the hand of Chief Justice Vinson, who "had failed to influence the Court in the large way that the President had hoped he would."[27] With Clark, whose personality and conservatism were similar to Vinson's, the chief justice had "a handy and useful extra vote."[28] Although Clark won a comfortable confirmation vote of 73 to 8, his elevation to the Court was controversial. In particular, liberals were critical of his performance as attorney general in the areas of civil liberties and civil rights. A prominent critic, ex-Interior Secretary Ickes, called Clark a "second-rate political hack" and said it was "the worst appointment ever made."[29]

The storm over Clark hardly had time to subside when Rutledge died on 10 September 1949, creating a vacancy that gave Truman his fourth and final appointment to the Court. Constituencies of varying interests and philosophies weighed in with their advice: New Dealers of the Roosevelt era and Truman Fair Dealers wanted Truman to pick someone who would strengthen the liberal Black-Douglas faction decimated by the deaths of Murphy and Rutledge; conservatives argued for a nominee comparable to Frankfurter or Jackson; Republicans pressed for further representation in addition to Burton; women, becoming more politically active, believed they were due for recognition; many felt it was important to promote an experienced judge from one of the federal appellate courts; westerners wanted more representation; and Roman Catholics noted that with the death of Murphy earlier in 1949, no one of their faith was on the Court for the first time in almost seventy-five years.[30]

Typically, Truman did not pay a great deal of attention to his would-be advisers or spend much time ruminating about this decision. At a press conference on 15 September, only five days after Rutledge's death, he announced the nomination of Sherman Minton to the Supreme Court, a selection similar to Clark's in several respects. Minton was a trusted and loyal friend, who shared Vinson's philosophy of judicial restraint. In addition, Minton's national security record was grounded in his senatorial vote in 1940 for the anti-Communist Smith Act. His qualifications also consisted of impressive educational credentials that included a master's degree in law from Yale, graduate work at the Sorbonne, and eight years' experience as a federal appeals court judge. Truman, according to Minton, "always thought, when we served together in the Senate, that I was a good lawyer."[31]

Minton, who had not been mentioned in the early speculation about possible successors to Rutledge, was understandably reluctant to get his hopes too high when word leaked out the day before Truman's press conference that he finally would be elevated to the nation's highest court. Commenting on the rumors from his home in New Albany, where he was recovering from a broken leg, Minton said he would be "happy" to be

THE COURIER-JOURNAL

Sherman Minton at home talking to a friend after he had been informed of his nomination to the Supreme Court.

named to the Supreme Court. But, he noted, "Each time there's been a vacancy, they've talked about me but nothing's ever happened yet. You can't tell. If it's in the cards it might happen."[32]

Frances Kelly, Minton's secretary in the Senate and on the Seventh Circuit, had a premonition that this time it was in the cards. Even though the court was in recess, she said, "I made sure to be in the office in case the White House called. You never know—lightning strikes."[33] Sure enough, on the morning of 15 September the call came, and Kelly gave the White House Minton's New Albany phone number. Characteristically, Truman's offer to his former Senate seatmate was nonchalant: "I was figuring on naming you to the Supreme Court today. Will you accept?" Minton, recounting the conversation, said, "I told him I would and then we talked for a few minutes."[34]

As word spread quickly after Truman made his selection public at the press conference, the normally placid Minton household turned into bedlam. Minton was on the phone an average of twenty times an hour as well-wishers called all day and into the night. Friends and neighbors dropped by to offer their congratulations, and a parade of newspaper, magazine, and radio reporters and photographers marched in to capture it all. Minton, though hobbling around on a gold-tipped cane that Truman had given him, was ebullient. He granted all requests for interviews and said it was the first time "so much of a fuss was made over me. I love these calls. I don't mind telling you I feel pretty good."[35]

Minton was also humbled by the appointment and appreciative to those who had helped him along the way. Writing to thank Paul McNutt, who as governor gave Minton his start in politics, he said: "It is a long ways from the hills of Southern Indiana to the Supreme Court of the United States, and I know I have not traveled that road alone."[36]

GARY YOHLER/FREDERICK VOLLRATH, TIFFANY STUDIO, *INDIANAPOLIS TIMES* COLLECTION

Ira L. Haymaker (left), Indiana's Democratic chairman, and Frank McHale (right), a longtime Hoosier politico, celebrate with Sherman Minton his elevation to the Supreme Court.

Similarly Minton exhibited humility in responding to a letter of congratulations from Democratic congressman Winfield K. Denton of Indiana's Eighth District: "Well, the woods are full of lawyers better than I, I know, and judges far abler and more deserving, but I am gratified to know that the President of the United States has enough confidence in me to think I might measure up to this great responsibility."[37]

Indiana politicians of both parties hailed Minton's selection. Hoosier Democrats, naturally, were especially overjoyed that a product of the state party had attained such a high position. Democratic governor Henry F. Schricker said, "We Hoosiers have occasion to feel extremely proud. Judge Minton is a faithful and capable public servant. He has every qualification to bring dignity to the Supreme Court bench." Ira L. Haymaker, the state's Democratic chairman, called the appointment "a great honor."[38] Republican senator Homer E. Capehart of Indiana was disappointed that someone from his party was not nominated. However, since Truman did not choose to appoint a Republican, Capehart was "delighted to see a 'Hoosier' Democrat" chosen. Indiana's other senator, William E. Jenner, also a Republican, declined comment because he was a member of the Senate Judiciary Committee, which would have to approve the nomination. However, he foresaw no opposition to Minton.[39]

Hoosier newspapers, likewise, applauded the nomination. Even Republican papers that had been hostile to Minton in the past permitted parochial pride to overcome partisanship in praising Minton's selection. An editorial in the usually conservative, Republican *Indianapolis News* observed: "Unlike some of the President's personal appointments . . . this one has much to recommend it. Belatedly, the President has recognized the principle that the nation's highest court should be staffed by experienced jurists who have made their mark in the lower courts."[40] Minton's hometown paper, the *New Albany Tribune*, which had supported his Republican rival in the 1940 Senate race, grudgingly extended its congratulations in a brief and bland editorial. Some Indiana newspapers mistakenly claimed that Minton would be the state's first Supreme Court justice. Actually the honor belonged to Van Devanter, a native of Marion, Indiana, but a resident of Wyoming at the time of his appointment in 1911.

While his home state reacted with understandable pride, Minton's selection was received less enthusiastically elsewhere. His partisan reputation came back to haunt him. Other newspapers and national magazines, while conceding that Truman at least heeded the call to appoint someone with experience on the federal bench, nonetheless laced their commentaries with faint praise, criticism, and cautious optimism. The *New York Times* commented: "Judge Minton may, and we fervently hope will, prove to be a worthy addition to the nation's highest bench. The President certainly could have done much worse in filling this vacancy; and, we dare say, he could also have done better."[41]

The New Republic, meanwhile, criticized Minton's selection as yet another example of cronyism, charging that "the President was again reverting to his deplorable habit of choosing men for high posts because they happen to be friends of his, and not because of essential fitness for the jobs for which they are selected."[42]

Because of his friendship with Truman and his strong sense of loyalty, *The Nation* said that Minton "will start out with an enthusiastic sympathy for the Administration's aims and methods." It added: "What was needed was an appointment on a higher level of politics, one that would assure the country of an intellect and a will devoted to the constant refreshening of the Constitution in light of current social demands and yet jealously protective of the freedoms laid down in that document."[43]

The *Washington Post*, in an editorial that foreshadowed Senate debate on the nomination, said that "many in Washington will have an unfavorable view of the appointment because of the unjudicial qualities that Mr. Minton demonstrated in the Senate." It cited Minton's role in championing Roosevelt's Court-packing plan and his own impetuous bill that would have punished newspapers for publishing anything known to be false. However, the editorial cautioned against reading too much into Minton's senatorial actions. "It was the all-out nature of Senator Minton's New Dealism and the hot contests in which he became involved that gave an impression that his emotions sometimes ran away with his judgment," the editorial said. "Our information, however, is to the effect that Judge Minton has not carried his passionate crusades to the bench. His record is said to be that of a liberal-minded judge who has made a good impression on the bench and bar of the Middle West."[44]

The press, in attempting to predict where Minton would line up philosophically on the Court, mistakenly branded him as a progressive and a liberal who would ally himself with Black and Douglas. Ickes, for example, praised the nomination and said it demonstrated that Truman realized the importance of filling the vacancy "with a man of the general type of Justice Rutledge, to which type Justices Black and Douglas also conform."[45] In projecting Minton into the Black-Douglas orbit, commentators typically referred to his vigorous advocacy of New Deal legislation as a senator and the decisions he had recently written on the appeals court in antitrust cases against the Great Atlantic and Pacific Tea Company (A&P) and the Standard Oil Company.[46] They also assumed that the close personal relationship between Minton and Black and the congruence of their voting behavior in the Senate would spill over into a philosophical kinship. Minton unabashedly admired Black's record on the Supreme Court and urged Truman to name him as chief justice in 1946.[47] Minton, in reviewing a biography of Black by John P. Frank, lauded his record in civil rights and called him "a truly great judge."[48]

The political battles of the 1930s, however, left Minton and Black with different perspectives on the role of a justice. Black believed in activism, while Minton took a much narrower approach to judicial review. Had commentators examined Minton's record as an appeals court judge, they would have discerned "the disparity between the two men with regard to their respective legal philosophies."[49]

Although *Newsweek* also erred in predicting that Minton would align with Black and Douglas, it was more perceptive in observing that when confronted with cases where individual liberties conflict with the government, Minton's "party loyalty and New Deal background probably will push him over to the government side." The magazine noted that as a senator Minton "advocated judicial restraint where Congressional power was challenged and can be expected to stand by this position."[50]

For his part Minton said he had "no label, either conservative or liberal; I simply make decisions on the merit of a case."[51]

In the ensuing Senate debate over his nomination, however, Minton's judicial philosophy and eight-year record as a federal judge were all but submerged by the storm that swelled over his tempestuous and highly partisan senatorial conduct. In particular, Minton's vigorous support of Roosevelt's attempt to remake the Supreme Court in 1937 became an issue. The chairman of the Senate Judiciary Committee was Pat McCarran of Nevada, who, although a Democrat like Minton, had opposed Roosevelt's proposal. McCarran, en route to Europe on a three-week trip when Minton's appointment was announced, sent word that the hearing process would be handled routinely instead of by a speedier procedure often used when senators vote on promoting a current or former colleague. Both Black and Burton, for example, won quick confirmation, though they, unlike Minton, were still in the Senate at the time of their nominations.

Though it seemed unlikely that the Senate would reject Minton, his nomination nonetheless provided the ammunition for a brief but highly charged political skirmish. When the judiciary committee convened its public session on 27 September Republican members Homer Ferguson of Michigan and Forrest C. Donnell of Missouri led the attack against Minton. Scott W. Lucas of Illinois, Democratic leader of the Senate, who had volunteered to testify before the committee, was thrust into the role as Minton's principal defender. The issue of Minton's health was raised and quickly put to rest. Lucas, noting Minton's heart attack in 1945, said that "for the last 3 years he has been regularly attending to his duties on the circuit court of appeals."[52]

Committee Republicans then turned their aim to Minton's stormy six-year term in the Senate. The Republicans intimated that Minton lacked the judicial temperament required of a justice and that he had demonstrated disrespect for the Court and disregard for the Constitution, citing his often-belligerent style and his advocacy of proposals to alter the Supreme Court and to restrict press freedoms. Lucas tried on several occasions to steer the debate to Minton's eight-year record as a federal judge, but the Republican inquisitors kept returning to his activities as a senator.

Ferguson and Donnell recounted Minton's verbal assault on the Supreme Court after it struck down the Agricultural Adjustment Act as unconstitutional; his fight to enact Roosevelt's plan to reorganize the Court; Minton's own proposal that would require a two-thirds majority of the justices before a law could be declared unconstitutional; and his bill that would have made it a felony for a newspaper to publish anything it knew to be false.[53] Lucas responded by saying, "I am satisfied that the judicial branch of the Government on which he is serving has more or less calmed him down a little, and sobered some of his thoughts."[54]

In raising the freedom of the press issue Donnell read into the record newspaper editorials published in 1938 condemning Minton's proposal. The *New York Herald Tribune* wrote that Minton "has become notable in Washington for several things: rudeness to witnesses, extravagant remarks on the floor of the Senate, and unbridled and often pointless loquacity."[55]

The *St. Louis Globe Democrat* remarked that Minton "has shown himself no respecter of the Bill of Rights. He has proven himself to be a man utterly without the reasoning calm that makes for judicial poise. He has admitted himself biased in his contentions and views. He has little regard for argument by fact and deals in half truths."[56]

Lucas replied that the committee should not rely on newspaper editorials written eleven years ago "to make a determination upon as to whether a man has the judicial character and the temperament to make a good judge." He said the best witnesses to Minton's ability and judicial behavior were lawyers who appeared before him in the circuit court of appeals. "I have never heard any lawyer speak disparagingly of Judge Minton's ability, deportment, demeanor, or conduct while a judge," Lucas noted.[57]

Lucas, in summing up his support for Minton, said: "I cannot repeat too frequently that what you are considering here is the judicial appointment, and not what Sherman Minton did as United States Senator. If he had carried his beliefs to the bench of some of these so-called radical things that he advocates into his judicial opinions, that is another thing. I do not believe that has happened."[58]

The only other witness appearing before the committee was Henry J. Richardson, Jr., an Indianapolis attorney, who, speaking on behalf of the black National Bar Association, strongly endorsed Minton's nomination. He said the association, after a thorough investigation, concluded that Minton "qualifies in training, experience, ideals, and character" to be a justice of the Supreme Court.[59] After Richardson summarized Minton's achievements and abilities, Ferguson and Donnell resumed their drumbeat about Minton's senatorial career. Specifically, the senators questioned whether Minton, who had never publicly disavowed the Court-packing scheme, still believed in the idea. Richardson responded by saying, "I do not think that his record, or any statements or public speeches that he has made within recent years would justify any conclusions that it is still his opinion."[60]

Acting committee chairman Harley Kilgore, Democrat of West Virginia, recalling that Roosevelt's plan came at a perilous time, asked Richardson whether it was true "that there was a great deal of sentiment throughout the country that the Supreme Court in its rulings was stultifying or holding up the recovery program?" Richardson agreed, noting that even "some of the prominent bar conventions" were split on the issue. He added, "You had a state in America where the banks were closed and everyone was apprehensive and sensitive. We were kind of grabbing at straws to save America."[61]

After Richardson's testimony Kilgore read messages from the American Bar Association, National Lawyers Guild, and Senator Capehart endorsing Minton. Senator Jenner, a committee member, announced he probably would vote to confirm Minton, but would do so reluctantly. Jenner said it was "deplorable that this Senate is asked to consent and advise on . . . purely political appointments." He said that the Roosevelt and Truman administrations had destroyed the political balance in the federal judiciary. Jenner noted that with the addition of Minton there would be 8 Democrats and only 1 Republican on the Supreme Court and that of the 192 federal judges appointed since 1933, 184 were Democrats and only 8 were Republicans. "I consider it regrettable [in naming a successor to Rutledge] . . . the President did not return to the traditional custom of maintaining as equitable a balance as possible between the two major political parties," Jenner said. Still, Jenner was inclined to favor confirmation because Minton was a Hoosier and because "time and his judicial experience have tempered his judgment, and there is every indication he has abandoned his radical beliefs."[62]

The committee at the urging of Ferguson and Donnell voted 5 to 4 to ask Minton to appear for questioning in executive session before it acted on the nomination. While not unprecedented, the appearance of a Supreme

Court nominee before the judiciary committee was not standard practice. The first nominee to do so was Harlan Fiske Stone in 1925. However, every nominee since John Marshall Harlan in 1955 has appeared before the judiciary committee.[63]

Back home in New Albany, Minton, still recuperating from a broken leg, said publicly after the committee vote that he would be available for questioning, but privately he was still weighing his options. Clearly, though, he was disappointed that the committee did not vote to approve his nomination and that his Senate service dominated the hearing. Ever the politician, Minton saw the committee's wrangling over his appointment in terms of partisan politics. In a letter to Claude G. Bowers, a friend from Indiana who was then United States ambassador to Chile, Minton surmised that the Republicans wanted to grill him about his political views so they "might get some advantage out of it for the campaign, which they are struggling manfully to commence for 1950."[64]

In a letter, on the day of the committee hearing to Kurt Pantzer, eminent Indianapolis lawyer, political, civic, and cultural leader, and cofounder of the Bar Association of the Seventh Federal Circuit, Minton complained that his eight years on the bench had been largely overlooked in the debate over his nomination. He said it was not "a brilliant record but it will bear comparison with my brothers on the Courts of Appeals generally."

Moreover, Minton wrote, his approach to judicial matters was entirely different from his tough competitive nature in athletics and politics "where I had a 'team' to play upon." Noting that "there is a vast difference between a competitor & an umpire or judge," Minton stated that his prime concern as a judge was trying to "find the answer to the legal question presented on the record before me—no other consideration except the law in that record ever received any consideration."

Minton told Pantzer that he had not yet been "advised when the Committee will be ready to receive me if I choose to appear."[65] Given a few days to ponder his next move, Minton decided he should not appear before the committee. In a letter written on Saturday, 1 October, and received by the committee on Monday, 3 October, Minton indicated he would comply with the committee's request, but felt his appearance "presents a serious question of propriety, particularly when I might be required to express my views on highly controversial and litigious issues affecting the Court."

Acknowledging that the committee seemed concerned mainly with his support of Roosevelt's proposal to increase the number of Supreme Court justices, Minton wrote that at the time he was assistant majority whip in the Senate and "understandably, I strongly supported those legislative measures recommended by the Administration." He noted that his record as a senator was public and open to scrutiny by the committee as it was in 1941 "when I was unanimously confirmed by the Senate to the second highest court in the land."

Minton pointed out in his letter that three current justices—Black, Reed, and Jackson—also had supported Roosevelt's Court plan, and the judiciary committee "did not see fit to query any of these gentlemen on this matter." As he did in his letter to Pantzer, Minton drew a distinction between his competitive and partisan behavior in athletics and politics and his neutral stance as a judge. "I think no man can point to one of my more than 200 opinions in the past eight years and truthfully say it was characterized by partisanship of any kind," Minton wrote.[66]

On the day it received Minton's letter, the judiciary committee, with three additional Democrats present, voted 9 to 3 to rescind its earlier request that Minton appear for questioning, and then it approved his nomination by a 9 to 2 vote. Not surprisingly Ferguson and

Donnell cast the two opposing votes. Their anger at the reversal carried over to the next day when the full Senate considered the nomination. The two made a last-ditch effort on the floor to recommit the nomination to the committee. Wayne Morse of Oregon, then a Republican, supported the move, arguing that the Senate should insist that Minton be questioned. The vote to recommit failed by a vote of 45 to 21. At the end of a marathon session that lasted until almost midnight, the Senate voted 48 to 16 to confirm Minton's nomination as the eighty-seventh justice of the United States Supreme Court.

After the vote Ferguson and Donnell were still fuming that they would not have the chance to question Minton. Ferguson said the action was an example of how the executive branch exerted its power over legislators and that he continued to have serious doubts about Minton's positions on various matters. Donnell did not think "that sufficient information has been made available to me." However, Lucas, the Democratic leader, said that "nothing good" could come from cross-examination of Minton by the judiciary committee.[67]

Minton, who had been in Washington awaiting a decision on whether he would be called to appear before the judiciary committee, went to the White House on 5 October, the day following his Senate confirmation, to thank his old friend President Truman for the appointment. The president was watching the opening World Series game between the Brooklyn Dodgers and the New York Yankees, and Minton, who loved baseball and the Yankees in particular, joined Truman to watch the rest of the game. When the Yankees' Tommy Henrich came to bat in the last of the ninth inning in the scoreless game, Minton said to Truman, "Here's one of the most dangerous hitters in baseball!" Moments later Henrich slammed the ball into the right-field bleachers to win the game. Afterwards Minton said, "I expect the President hopes I know my law as well as my baseball."[68]

UPI/CORBIS-BETTMANN

Sherman Minton is congratulated by President Harry S. Truman and Chief Justice Fred M. Vinson after taking his oath as associate justice of the Supreme Court on 12 October 1949.

When Minton returned to the White House one week later on 12 October he was the center of attention as he stood on the porch just outside the president's office for his swearing-in ceremony. With him were his wife Gertrude, President Truman, and Chief Justice Vinson, who administered the oath of office after the president handed Minton a scroll commissioning him as the nation's eighty-seventh justice. Truman, in typical homespun fashion, said, "I am about to perform the most pleasant duty of my political career. . . . There you are, Shay."[69]

The crowd in the Rose Garden included members of the Court, the cabinet, about one hundred friends from New Albany, a forty-member delegation from the Indiana Bar Association, Hoosier political leaders of both parties, and members of the Minton family. After the ceremony Minton, who stood leaning on his cane, stayed at the White House for about an hour greeting and chatting with friends and family. He then went right to work, donning his new robe and taking the customary end seat of a new justice. His first official act was to witness the admission of seven lawyers from Jeffersonville to practice before the Supreme Court.

Although his new position was exalted and important, Minton remained plain and unaffected. When

GARY YOHLER/FREDERICK VOLLRATH, TIFFANY STUDIO, *INDIANAPOLIS TIMES* COLLECTION

Sherman Minton with his wife Gertrude at the Supreme Court the day of his swearing in.

a reporter asked, "What should we call you now? Mr. Justice Minton?"

"Don't you mister me," the Hoosier replied. "I'm Shay."[70]

Minton's rise to the pinnacle of the United States judiciary was certainly a remarkable achievement, but his tenure as a justice was neither long-lasting nor particularly distinguished. In less than seven years' time he retired from the Court because of failing health and returned home to Indiana to quietly and unobtrusively live out the remainder of his life. Although he was conscientious about his duties on the Court, he was not destined to become one of its most notable justices. Such distinction is reserved for those who by temperament and intellect are able to create a niche for themselves in the ever-changing tides of prevailing jurisprudence. Judicial assertiveness, a capacity for complex philosophical reasoning, and an ability to articulate fundamental points of law into memorable phrases are essential qualities of justices who are rated highly by legal scholars.

Minton was not that kind of man. For one thing he was not given to introspection, a consequence of his early years of poverty when all that mattered was getting by one day at a time. His political instincts and experiences were also influential in shaping his judicial behavior, but strategies well suited to legislative politics do not always transfer to the bench. Minton tended to view legal issues, as he had legislative matters, in black and white, with no shades of gray. Judicial issues seldom lend themselves to this kind of simplicity, but Minton approached his opinion writing as if they did.

By the time Minton reached the Court the era of the politician-justice was ending and the movement to "depoliticize" the courts was ascending. He was the last New Dealer as well as the last member of Congress to be appointed to the Court. Without the perspective of justices with legislative experience, it was inevitable that the Court would assert a more independent role within the political system, a phenomenon that disturbed both Truman and Minton.

Long an advocate of a passive judiciary, Minton sought to limit the intervention of the Court into legislative affairs, refusing to substitute his personal preferences for those of the elected representatives of the people. Those who maintain that justices must be activists in order to rein in the undemocratic tendencies of legislators and to protect the constitutional rights of individuals have legitimate reasons for finding Minton's judicial passivity troubling. To them the label "Mr. Main Street," given to Minton by one of his more elitist brethren, is an apt if not a particularly complimentary description. For those who thought that he was right in deferring to the elected branches of government, "Mr. Main Street" is a fitting tribute to a man who never forgot his origins or the people whom government is supposed to serve.

CHAPTER TWO

Poverty Was His Inheritance

There was no reason to expect that the third child born to John Evan and Emma Livers Minton in their four-room frame cottage on 20 October 1890 was destined for anything other than the hard, bare-bones existence prevalent in the small Floyd County farming community of Georgetown. Expectations soon changed though, when the boy, forced by adversity into early independence, demonstrated the potential to rise above his impoverished heritage. During his teenage years a luster began to appear as his rough edges were smoothed and his energies were directed. And by the time he reached adulthood there seemed little doubt that Sherman Minton would make his mark in the world.

Minton's ancestors, who migrated to southern Indiana in the early and mid-nineteenth century from Maryland, Virginia, and Kentucky, were typical of the pioneers venturing into the deep green forests north of the Ohio River. Landless in their native states, they came west seeking a better life by laying claim to a portion of largely untapped Indiana wilderness, a prospect made easier by the federal government's generous land credit policy.

Acquiring land was one thing; taming it was another. The enormous task of carving out an existence in an isolated section of the southern Indiana woods bred distinct characteristics, attitudes, and behavior in the early settlers that would be embodied in those of future generations.

The wide-open spaces and the absence of slavery and an aristocracy underscored the freedom settlers enjoyed and instilled in them a deep commitment to social equality. These pioneers were physically strong because the work of clearing and farming land required almost endless manual labor. While raising their food and making their clothing made them individualistic and self-reliant, pioneers were also cooperative because some tasks such as building a log cabin required the help of neighbors. Settlers had a fondness for the companionship of others and made the most of these cabin-raising occasions. When the work was over it was time for pitch-in suppers, conversation, relaxation, and recreation. Games and contests were rambunctious and often required as much physical prowess as building the log cabin.

Such respites were rare, however, and men, women, and children worked almost incessantly to establish civilization in the southern Indiana wilderness. The physical labor took its toll; quite often a parent, usually the mother, died at a young age, causing increased hardship for the family.

The enterprising Anthony Livers, Minton's maternal great-grandfather, was the first of his forebears on the new frontier. He arrived in 1814, the start of the period known as the Great Migration. Defeat of the Indians allayed the fears of prospective settlers, and Indiana's population swelled by more than one hundred thousand people in five years. This migration gave Indiana the people and wealth necessary to achieve statehood, which it did in December 1816. Livers, a native of Maryland, arrived in New Albany just a year after the river town's founding by the Scribner family of New York.[1]

New Albany at that time was forbidding territory characterized by dense timber stands, heavy undergrowth, uneven terrain, and yawning ravines. Shortly after arriving Livers acquired property near the river on what is now Main Street. He sold it at a sizable profit four years later and then acquired 171 acres deeper into the interior of Floyd County to begin farming. His efforts to carve out a living from the soil were made even more difficult by the financial panic of 1819 when the federal government tightened credit, farm exports dropped, prices fell, and unemployment rose.

Livers, however, soon had help in his struggle to make farming productive and profitable. In 1823 he married the widow Nancy Hanger who bore him two sons, one of whom was Lafayette, Minton's maternal grandfather. Lafayette possessed many of the physical features and the personality that his grandson would exhibit years later. Lafayette was tall—six feet, four inches—strong and athletic and was known for his rugged good looks, quick wit, mischievousness, and sense of humor.

Life became considerably harder for Lafayette when his father died in 1834, leaving the burden of coaxing a living from the land to him, his younger brother Anthony—both still young boys at the time—and their mother. In 1849 Lafayette married Martha Susan Desper. They settled in Greenville, a small Floyd County community eleven miles northwest of New Albany, to farm and raise a family of eight children. Their second child Emma, Sherman Minton's mother, was born in 1864.

Two years earlier Minton's father John Evan was born in a log cabin east of Greenville to Jonathan and Savannah Cline Minton. His life, too, would be darkened by the premature death of a parent. Jonathan Minton, who had moved to southern Indiana from Pulaski County, Kentucky, in the 1850s, was not present for John's birth, having joined the thousands of Hoosiers who flocked to enlist in the Union army when the Civil War broke out. He only saw his new son once, during a brief leave. Shortly after returning to his unit, Company E, 53rd Regiment,

Jonathan, only thirty-one years old, died of apoplexy, leaving Savannah to raise John and four other children.

The loss of his father marked John for a life of struggle and instability. His childhood and early teenage years were devoted to helping his mother and siblings work the family farm. John and a brother, Henry Clay Minton, then moved in with a sister, Mary C. Coffman, in Greenville. When her husband died John and Henry helped support her and her two young boys. Soon John would be trying to meet the needs of his own family. He married Emma Livers on 7 April 1883, and they became the parents of four children—a daughter Ivy followed by sons Herbert, Sherman, and Roscoe.

The family was always on the move, living in rented housing, as John searched for steady employment. Soon after Sherman's birth the Mintons moved west into Crawford County where John worked as a watchman for the New Albany and St. Louis Air Line Railroad, later the Southern Railway, while wooden bridges were being replaced with iron structures. When that project was completed John's work with the railroad took the family back to Georgetown. He soon left that job and returned to Crawford County, where he operated a small grocery and meat market. The stories vary on what happened to John Minton as entrepreneur—his store failed because he was a poor businessman or he sold the store to pay gambling losses after betting on William Jennings Bryan in the 1896 presidential election. In any case the family once again returned to Georgetown, and John resumed his employment with the railroad.[2]

Despite the family's meandering, it was Georgetown, his birthplace, that was always home to Sherman Minton. It was the place where he made lifetime friends, where he tested his physical abilities, where his spirited nature had free rein, and where his life took on a direction. It was the place to which he always returned.

To Minton, whose youth had been filled with adversity and disruption, Georgetown provided the one real constant in his formative years. As an adult he relished going back because of his abundant and vivid memories and because the town had retained the fundamental character and charm of small-town southern Indiana.

Although Georgetown is Floyd County's oldest town, settled in 1807, it never achieved the growth or development its founders envisioned. The Georgetown of Minton's youth at the turn of the twentieth century was not too different from the Georgetown at the beginning of the nineteenth century nor vastly different from the Georgetown at the dawn of the twenty-first century. What Minton observed about his birthplace during the town's sesquicentennial celebration in 1957 is a timeless description: "Georgetown remains as a quiet, decent, homey, friendly place to live. No one is real rich and no one is real poor. A man's worth is measured in the eyes of his neighbors and not by the figure in his bank book."

Georgetown's population at the time of Minton's birth was about three hundred, and one hundred years later it had reached only two thousand. Although not an ideal agricultural area because of hilly terrain and light clay soil, farming nonetheless has always been important to the community. Also vital to the town's early economy was whiskey making; twenty or so distilleries dotted the bank of Little Indian Creek—known to the pioneers as Whiskey Run—along the southern border of the community. This industry spawned other ventures: sawmills for cutting lumber to build the distilleries and gristmills for making mash. By the late nineteenth century the railroad, which provided jobs such as station agents, telegraph operators, bridge carpenters, and postal clerks, had replaced distilleries as a major source of employment for Georgetown residents. The town's strict puritanical code and the moral force of its three churches also may have hastened the decline of the liquor industry. Although making whiskey and consuming it did not entirely disappear, religion and liquor had an uneasy coexistence.

The influence of Georgetown's churches forced the only saloon to locate outside the town's limits and altered the drinking routines of some patrons. Minton recalled that when the pillars of the community visited the saloon each evening "to get their daily snort," they always walked along the railroad tracks instead of through downtown "out of deference to the dear old ladies of the church who lived along the main street."

The last of the distilleries was operated by Silas Beard, a memorable character to Minton. "I can still see him looking more like a preacher or a doctor as he rode his high-wheeled cart through the main street over the hills to the still house," Minton recalled in his 1957 speech. Minton remembered taking apples to Beard's still with his father and brothers. "Silas was a gracious host and gave us boys a cup of cider and our father a shot of apple jack," Minton said. "Though Silas was proud of his apple jack he never drank it himself."

Minton, full of energy, imagination, and curiosity, exploited fully what tiny Georgetown had to offer in the way of excitement, entertainment, and exploration. Besides taking apples to a still, there were other simple pleasures such as tramping through fields, swimming and fishing in creeks, and gathering at the depot on Sunday evenings to watch the trains come in. Young Minton even found going to church an adventure. He said he went along with his parents to the Christian Church "more for excitement than anything else." Minton described his fascination with the proceedings: "For what could be more exciting than to see some of the old sisters get religion and go down to the mourners' bench shouting and when the shouting was over and the congregation departed we stood outside to see who got sacked when he asked to see some girl home."[3]

If the town did not produce enough entertainment on its own for Minton and his companions, they were more than eager and able to fill the void themselves. Most often

Minton led the way, "looking for trouble and generating some of his own if he couldn't find it otherwise," according to Minton's childhood friend Grant Berg. Berg called Minton the "meanest damned boy in Georgetown."[4]

Minton acknowledged his reputation years later at a local celebration honoring his appointment to the Supreme Court: "They've never known me here as a lawyer, senator or jurist. They remember me as one of the meanest kids who ever roamed these parts. Whenever a chicken squawked at midnight, or a pane of glass shattered and the rock went scooting across the floor, they thought of me. They still do."[5]

According to Berg, Minton had a natural eye with a rock or snowball and threw at just about any available target, apparently favoring the hats of traveling salesmen. Minton also was known to hurl a rock or snowball at the sign outside a local business, showering glass on the vagrants sleeping beneath it. Family members were not immune from his antics. He loosened a wheel on the family buggy, causing it to fall off while his older brother Herbert was using it on a date.[6]

The devilish Minton also schemed to get revenge on a woman whose backyard bordered the playground where he and his friends played baseball. When errant balls went over a fence and landed in her yard she refused to return them. Minton created a special ball with an inner core of gunpowder and waited for an opportunity to use it. One day, seeing the woman in her yard heating a big copper kettle full of apple butter, Minton tossed the rigged ball over the fence. She grabbed it and threw it into the fire under her kettle. The ball exploded, the kettle overturned, and apple butter covered the ground.[7]

Minton's early years were not all play. He shared in the family's struggle to raise crops from the feeble soil of their steep, cutover hillside farm. When Shay was eight years old his father suffered sunstroke on his job with the railroad and was permanently impaired, so Shay began a string of odd jobs to help support his family. Minton first got a job with a traveling crew of hay balers for twenty-five cents a day, riding bareback on a horse that supplied the power for the baler. When that job ended Minton was hired to wash the buggies of hotel guests at John Wolfe's Tavern and Livery Stable for ten cents each.[8]

The hardship of the Minton family was compounded not long after John became disabled when it was discovered that his wife Emma had breast cancer. Hospital facilities were unavailable, and even if they were, the family would not have been able to afford them. A doctor came to the house to perform surgery on 12 April 1900. Emma Minton, just thirty-six years old, died during an operation that was performed on the family's kitchen table. Her death devastated young Sherman and shattered his belief in religion and the concept of a just and loving God. As a result he avoided organized religion until late in his life.

Besides causing emotional trauma for the family Emma Minton's death added to the difficulties of making ends meet. In order to survive John and his children began raising and selling chickens and livestock, eventually earning enough money to open a confectionery and meat market in Georgetown. As part of their work in the new venture Shay and Herb occasionally went to Crawford County, twenty-five miles away, to get cattle and hogs to slaughter for their meat market or to sell in New Albany. Herding the livestock back on foot usually took the boys two days.

Although the first ten years of Minton's life were mostly filled with struggle, pain, and sweat, the contours of promise were present. Rather than inhibiting him, Minton's boyhood environment and experiences provided the impetus for later achievements. As a wage earner, at an early age Minton learned responsibility and the value of hard work, gained confidence in his abilities, and became self-reliant.

His parents, although poor and with little education, nonetheless were important influences. From his father, who had survived against constant adversity, Minton learned perseverance and acquired a passion for the Democratic party, politics, and the cause of populism. Shay was smitten in 1896 at the age of five when he attended a rally for presidential candidate William Jennings Bryan in New Albany with his father and brother Herb. A crowd of fifteen thousand cheered wildly as "The Great Commoner" belted out his familiar oratory about lifting farmers out of hard times by using silver to increase the nation's money supply. The event proved irresistible to young Minton, who took it all in while perched on his father's shoulders.[9]

Minton's mother, meanwhile, impressed upon him the importance of an education. She taught him to read and "inspired Shay to aspire for a college education," according to Roscoe, Minton's younger brother.[10] Her encouragement paid off. Minton developed a superior reading ability, and he devoured routine class work at such a rate that one of his teachers in grammar school, Harry K. Engleman, had to design special assignments for him. "He was a bright lad, and I had to figure out a way to keep him occupied," Engleman said.[11] Engleman, who later became a country doctor, remembered that Minton's shoes were always muddy. When Minton dropped by to see his former teacher years later and inquired whether he could enter the doctor's inner office, Engleman replied, "Come in, if your shoes are clean."[12]

Minton's love of school was such that when he had no place else to go after completing the eighth grade he repeated the grade the following year. Although he excelled as a student Minton did not shed his boyish pranks and mischievousness at the schoolhouse door. As the instigator of many classroom disturbances and other capers, he frequently found himself in trouble. On one occasion, to avoid detention, he jumped out a second-story window at the two-room grammar school.

Another act of defiance actually may have been the turning point in his life. It happened when he disregarded

Georgetown's ban on bicycle riding on sidewalks while making a delivery on his newspaper route. Minton was apprehended by the town marshal and taken before the imposing justice of the peace, John Thomas, who also operated a general store. Thomas conducted the proceedings sitting behind a packing case of Arbuckle's coffee, on top of which rested a large book he called "The Law." Minton was found guilty and fined a dollar plus costs.

Years later, recalling the profound impression the incident made on him, Minton said: "The justice read out of a big book, and everything was very formal. Right then, I decided to study law. Maybe I thought it was an easy way to make $3."[13]

Although hardships would persist in the next decade of Minton's life, he now had a goal and realized he needed to be educated to reach it. How earnestly Minton pursued education was apparent in the way he—at the age of fourteen—assumed control of his destiny.

MARY ANNE CALLANAN COLLECTION

Sherman Minton (at left) at the 1904 graduation of the Georgetown grammar school.

After finishing the eighth grade for the second time, Minton left his family and Georgetown in the spring of 1905 to begin making his own way in the world. He joined his brother Herb in Fort Worth, Texas, and, like Herb, found a job at a Swift and Company meatpacking plant. Shay was hired to work on the production line at the Swift plant for twelve and a half cents an hour, later raised to fifteen cents an hour. The days were long and the work grueling, but the rigors of southern Indiana farm life had conditioned Minton for endurance and hard manual labor.[14]

Shay and Herb were reunited with the rest of their family later in 1905 when their father John, his second wife Sarah, and the two other children—Ivy and Roscoe—also moved to Fort Worth. After working a year and a half for Swift, Shay, however, was ready to go back north. He had saved enough money to resume his education and wanted to continue his schooling in Indiana. Minton explained his reasoning: "I was imbued with the propaganda of the time that the Hoosier educational system just couldn't be beat. I convinced my parents I should go to school there."[15]

Upon his return to Georgetown, Minton moved in with relatives. His school plans, however, were nearly derailed when a bout with typhoid exhausted his savings and a cousin lured him to take a job at a penny arcade in Louisville that paid fifteen dollars a week, big money at the time. Minton's job was to jerk the levers of a make-believe excursion boat to give customers the impression of sailing on the high seas. Despite the high pay Minton quit after two weeks to enroll in school.[16] He first attended Edwardsville High School near Georgetown. That school closed after his freshman year so for the next three years Minton went to New Albany High School. These years would prove to be pivotal for him.

At New Albany Minton blossomed scholastically, physically, and socially. He came to the attention of caring and gifted educators who nurtured his fertile mind;

he tested and honed his physical prowess in athletic competition; he found romance and courted the person he would later marry; and predictably he probed the limits of authority with new ways of making trouble. Notwithstanding his proclivity for the latter, by the time Minton graduated in 1910 he was a young man with purpose and direction.

The teacher who did the most to bring out the best in Minton at New Albany was Albert L. Kohlmeier, who taught history and civics. Minton, whose interest in politics had been kindled by the Bryan rally years earlier, was naturally drawn to these subjects. He reveled in learning about and discussing political philosophy, national politicians, governmental systems, and the burning public policy issues of the day.[17]

Although Minton had long carried a torch for Bryan, his studies introduced him to a new political hero. After reading Woodrow Wilson's book, *Constitutional Government in the United States*, for class, Minton was impressed by the wisdom and insight of its author and accurately predicted great things for Wilson. After Bryan was defeated a third time for president in 1908, a teacher good-naturedly teased the downcast Minton about the election. "Whom will your party find to run for President now?" he asked. "Woodrow Wilson. And he will be elected," the politically precocious student replied.[18]

Minton read widely about current events and issues and, given his background and devotion to Bryan, he was a tailor-made populist. He was especially concerned about the growth of monopolies and how the corresponding concentration of economic power affected the lives of common people.

Outside the classroom, Minton vented his views on trusts and other topics in a debating club he helped organize at New Albany High School called the Wranglers and as a member of the school's debating team. In these extracurricular activities he again came under the influence of his favorite teacher Kohlmeier, who, as the sponsor of both groups, was instrumental in molding Minton into a public speaker. Kohlmeier required Minton to write his speech carefully, making certain that "he understood what he was saying and that what he was saying was absolutely true."[19]

The climactic event for Minton as a high school debater came in 1910 during his senior year when he was selected as the captain of a three-member debate team that would oppose a team from a Louisville school. The New Albany team was to argue that the British parliamentary form of government was superior to the American system, and to prepare for the competition Minton studied Wilson's political philosophy. Kohlmeier, recalling the debate, said: "I had no difficulty in picking Minton. He had the height, a fine face, clear enunciation, a modulated voice, and terrific emotion. When he spoke from conviction, his emotion and voice would ring the changes from sarcasm and ridicule to pathos."[20]

New Albany won decisively, and Minton in particular had been persuasive. According to an account of the debate in the school's yearbook, the *Vista*: "Sherman Minton, our second speaker, displayed the best delivery of the evening. He showed that the American system of checks and balances might defeat the will of the people, that it was conducive to corruption and lack of interest in national affairs, that it was inefficient in its jurisdiction over such social evils as child labor and the great trusts. He also proved that it was the cause of a continual waste of the people's money."[21]

Despite his debating skills and the intellect he demonstrated in the classroom, Minton was best known in high school for his athletic abilities. His trim and muscular body had been ideally conditioned for sports through years of hard labor on the farm and in the factory and from all those hours spent throwing rocks. In football Minton first played tackle, then moved to fullback, where he was a threat to

MARY ANNE CALLANAN COLLECTION

Members of the New Albany High School football team, circa 1909; Sherman Minton is third from the right.

run or throw a pass. Because of his strong and powerful arm he played center field on the baseball team and was described as the "Best fielder and base runner ever in school."[22] He also ran relays on the track team.

As might be expected, Minton also exhibited his playful nature in high school. He and close friend Walter Heazlitt were fond of sliding down an air shaft into the school basement. On one such occasion Minton's joyride was dampened when he ripped his trousers. The venturesome twosome also played hooky one day to ride atop the monkey wagon in a circus and added to their merriment by imitating the flea-picking ritual of monkeys. Minton, of course, was quite capable of getting into trouble on his own. His most serious offense, at least in the eyes of school officials, was his outburst at the news that a girl he was dating had won a singing contest. Minton leaped from his chair in the auditorium and ran down the hall shouting, "Hurrah for our side." For this indiscretion he was suspended from school and readmitted only after signing an agreement to behave and making a public apology before the entire student body.[23]

Whether this episode led to the subsequent rift in his romance with the talented singer is not known. In any case Minton soon began a relationship with another classmate, Gertrude Gurtz, that would last a lifetime. Minton and Gurtz made a striking couple whose union seems to support the notion of opposites attracting. She was a classic beauty with dark, groomed hair, gentle features, natural grace, and a reserved, sensible disposition; he was ruggedly handsome with a shock of brown, curly hair, strapping physique, an engaging exuberance, and a gregarious personality.

Besides standing apart physically and intellectually from the crowd in high school, Minton also possessed other arresting attributes. He had a maturity and confidence that came from being self-sufficient since the age of fourteen. Each summer Minton returned to work at the Swift plant in Fort Worth to earn enough money for the next year. While attending school in New Albany he lived in boardinghouses but also spent much of his time at the home of his friend Walter Heazlitt. The Heazlitts, in fact, came to think of Minton as one of their own. Walter's father Howard encouraged Minton to set his sights high and even mentioned aspiring to the Supreme Court. Heazlitt told Minton, after attending a session of the Court during a business trip to Washington, that he expected one day to see him become a Supreme Court justice.[24] His classmates at New Albany were just as sanguine as Heazlitt about Minton's future and just as uncanny in their accuracy. The writer of the class prophecy for the 1910 yearbook saw in her crystal ball "A band wagon with 'Vote for Minton for Senator.'"[25]

MARY ANNE CALLANAN COLLECTION

Besides playing football and baseball at New Albany High School, Sherman Minton also ran relays for the track team; he is seated behind a table full of trophies.

Before Minton could begin trying to fulfill the promise others had forecast for him, however, he needed to accumulate the wherewithal to continue his education. For this purpose, it was back to Fort Worth and Swift where Minton worked as a traveling salesman, first selling meat and then the company's new brand of soap. He also earned five dollars a game playing semiprofessional baseball during the summer. Minton performed so well in sales and on the ball field that he might have had a career in either business or sports if it was not for his long-standing attraction to law. A company official told him that there was a future for him at Swift, and a major league scout tried to sign him to a contract. But Minton, firm in his desire to become a lawyer, declined both overtures.

By the fall of 1911 Minton, nearly twenty-one years old and with a nest egg of one hundred and fifty dollars, arrived on the campus of Indiana University to resume his education. As he had in high school, Minton worked his way through college while excelling academically and athletically. He also found time to pull an occasional stunt.

When Minton entered college, students needed to finish only two years of undergraduate work before going on to three years of law school. Minton made this five-year fast track even shorter by completing requirements for his law degree in just over two years. Despite carrying a heavy course load he graduated at the top of his class in 1915, earning As in ninety-two credit hours out of more than one hundred hours taken, with the rest of his grades being either B+ or B.[26]

Minton's academic record as an undergraduate, although good, was not as stellar, due to his involvement in campus life. He naturally gravitated toward activities and organizations that coincided with his interests in politics, socializing, and sports. He made the varsity debating team;

MARY ANNE CALLANAN COLLECTION

Sherman Minton, who played semiprofessional baseball, is tagged out at third base.

joined the Jackson Club, the campus organization for young Democrats; was a member and later president of the Indiana Union, which managed and organized activities in the Student Union Building; pledged Phi Delta Theta; and played varsity football and baseball.

The small-town boy had become a big man on campus. In his sophomore year in 1913 he won, fittingly, the annual William Jennings Bryan oratorical contest, speaking on the subject of "The Relationship of the Executive to the Legislative Department of the United States." Minton also was part of the clique of budding Hoosier politicians that included Paul V. McNutt and Wendell Willkie. Later both would play key roles in Minton's career: the former boosted it, while the latter helped derail it.

Just as in high school, Minton, strong and agile at six feet and 175 pounds, probably was best known in college as an athlete. He played end and fullback on the varsity football team in his sophomore year, earning a reputation as a fierce tackler and blocker. It was on the baseball field, though, that he starred. Known as a scrapper who would do whatever he could to win, Minton was aggressive on the field and at the plate and constantly yelled encouragement to teammates or razzed the opposition. From his center field position he had the range and quickness to make brilliant catches and the strong arm to cut down runners with direct throws to home plate. With his chin jutting out, Minton was a fearless hitter who stood his ground in the batter's box. His biggest thrill in baseball came when he hit a home run against Ohio State in the spring of 1915. Forty years later, recalling the details for *Indiana Alumni Magazine*, Minton wrote, "Babe Ruth or Mickey Mantle never got the wood on the ball better than I did." He noted that the center fielder was still chasing the ball when "I walked in from third base."[27]

As might be expected Minton displayed his daring and bravura off the field as well as on. At least two of his escapades in college could have ended in tragedy, but Minton was able to escape unscathed. One day when a

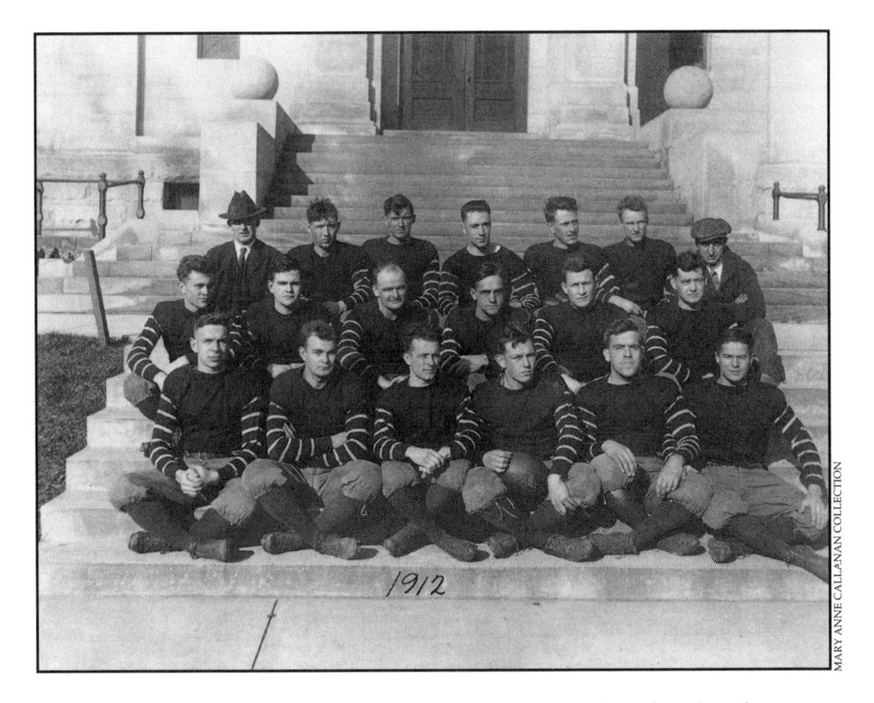

Sherman Minton (third from the right, second row) played end and fullback for the Indiana University football team.

flash flood swelled the normal trickle of the Jordan River, actually a creek that winds through the Bloomington campus, Minton plunged into the churning water and was swept away. With great effort he managed to pull himself to safety after grabbing hold of a bush. Another stunt left Minton hanging to a window ledge by his fingertips. He and his Phi Delta Theta brothers, determined to see an all-girl show at the old Assembly Hall, built a scaffold to a second-story window for a ringside view. The scaffold collapsed, and Minton lunged for the ledge and clung there as his cohorts scattered in all directions. Fortunately, he dropped to the ground without injury.[28]

To support himself during college Minton worked for room and board by waiting tables, firing the furnace, and operating a lunch and candy counter at his fraternity house. He held a series of summer jobs, including trying to sell washing machines in northern Indiana, working in a lumberyard, and doing office work at Swift in Texas. He was forced to live like a peasant the one summer he stayed in Bloomington to attend classes. Minton and a friend had only ten dollars between them to last the summer. They lived in the fraternity house and existed primarily on the wild berries they picked, the stale bread they bought at two loaves for a nickel, and the free milk they coaxed from a milkman.[29]

Minton's living conditions improved somewhat during law school. Because of his top scholastic record he was entitled to a job as a law librarian, which paid his tuition and a stipend of thirty dollars a month. Even more important, because of his hard work and superior performance as a law student at Indiana University, a promising career seemed practically assured. Minton's already bright prospects took on added luster when he won a five hundred dollar scholarship for a year of postgraduate study at the Yale University School of Law, where he continued to distinguish himself inside and outside the classroom. He graduated cum laude in 1916 with a master's degree in law, earning nine As and only one B. A classmate said of Minton, "He was the outstanding member of my class at Yale. No one in the class received higher honor or recognition from the University. The entire faculty and student body recognized his unusual legal ability and character."[30] One member of the eminent law school faculty who clearly saw Minton's potential was former United States president and future Supreme Court chief justice William Howard Taft. Taft reportedly remarked that Minton's examination paper in a constitutional law course was one of the best ever written at the university.[31] And in one class session, when Minton was arguing with this august professor over a Supreme Court ruling, Taft commented: "I'm afraid, Mr. Minton, that if you don't like the way this law has been interpreted, you will have to get on the Supreme Court and change it."[32]

While his time for extracurricular activities was limited, Minton pursued his interest in oratory and helped found the Yale Legal Aid Society for the Poor. He won the fifty dollar first prize in the Wayland Club extemporaneous speaking competition, open to all Yale graduate law students, with his presentation on the short ballot. In a case for the legal aid society Minton won a worker's compensation award for a wagon driver injured in a fall.[33]

Minton also maintained his interest in Hoosier Democratic politics. When United States senator Benjamin Shively died in early 1916, Minton wrote to Gov. Samuel M. Ralston to suggest that Ralston name then Attorney General Evan B. Stotsenburg of New Albany to the vacancy. In pleading his case Minton analyzed the situation like a seasoned political pro: "No one, I am sure, knows better than yourself his pre-eminent fitness to serve his party, state and nation in that capacity, especially in these trying times when calm, sound judgement, party fealty and genuine Americanism is [*sic*] so necessary. Furthermore since your appointee will probably be the candidate next fall, Mr. Stotsenburg with his strong public record would add great strength to the ticket when victory at the polls is the cherished hope of all good Democrats."[34]

During his year at Yale, Minton, who by this time was an expert at stretching a dollar, made the most of his five hundred dollar scholarship by eating all his meals at the university dining hall. He wrote to a friend that he had "grown an automatic appetite; it shut off after fifteen cents worth."[35]

The days of poverty and penny-pinching, however, were drawing to a close as Minton completed his studies at Yale and prepared to return to New Albany to fulfill his professional and personal dreams: to begin a law practice and to marry his high school sweetheart Gertrude Gurtz.

Before he could do either, though, Minton had to replenish his finances, which he did that summer as platform manager of a Chautauqua lecture circuit through the Midwest. The position paid the princely sum of forty-five dollars a week and brought Minton into contact with his idol

William Jennings Bryan, who frequently spoke on the circuit. Minton also began a lifelong friendship with a fellow worker, Bo McMillin, who was later the football coach at Indiana University.[36]

With his savings of three hundred dollars from the Chautauqua job, Minton returned to New Albany in the fall of 1916 to open his law office. He won a settlement for his first clients, a group of lowland farmers who complained that their farms were being ruined by silt dumped into a creek by the city waterworks. Another early case was not so successful. Years later Minton recalled what happened when he assisted the county prosecutor in a murder trial:

> It was Kirke's [the prosecutor] first murder case and he asked me if I wouldn't like to help him for the experience. I needed nothing so much as experience and I accepted with alacrity. A good woman had killed a bad man. It was cold-blooded first degree murder as a matter of fact and law. But Judge Paris knew it was not murder in the eyes of men—the jury. While Kirke and I gave the State a bang-up prosecution calling for the vengeance of the law, the jury knew better and acquitted, and I think they would have given the defendant a medal if they had the power to do so.[37]

Minton's fledgling law practice, however, was interrupted when the United States declared war on Germany in the spring of 1917. Like his grandfather, Minton rushed to enlist in the army. Upon being commissioned an infantry captain after officers' training at Fort Benjamin Harrison near Indianapolis, Minton returned to New Albany on a brief leave to marry Gertrude on 11 August 1917. He continued his training in the states until being sent overseas in July 1918. Minton served on the Soissons, Belgian, and Verdun fronts, and following the armistice he remained with the Army of Occupation until his discharge in August 1919.[38] When hostilities ended Minton took advantage of the opportunity of obtaining additional legal education. In spring 1919 he studied international law, Roman law, civil law, and jurisprudence in the Faculte de Droit at the Sorbonne in Paris.[39]

Minton also capitalized on an opportunity to display his cavalier nature at the palace in Versailles on the day the peace treaty was signed. Minton recalled how his actions that day got him close to another of his political idols, Woodrow Wilson: "A sergeant drove up with President Wilson's car. Being a captain, I just got on the running board, ordered the sergeant to proceed and I waved the crowds away while we went back into the palace courtyard and parked the car, ready to transport the President back to Paris."[40]

When the big four—Wilson, Georges Clemenceau of France, David Lloyd George of Great Britain, and Vittorio Orlando of Italy—emerged and posed for pictures on the palace steps, Minton, with his camera, "barged right in with the official photographers and shot a whole roll of film."[41] Unfortunately Minton lost the film because he put the roll in a pocket that had a hole in it.

Minton had more important matters on his mind than a roll of film. A few months earlier Gertrude had given birth to their first child, Sherman, Jr., making Minton even more eager to return home. Also, he had decided that when he was discharged he would enter the Democratic primary race for Congress in spring 1920.

CHAPTER THREE

Minton, McNutt, and the Machine

Launching a political career proved to be far more difficult than Sherman Minton imagined. He failed in his first two attempts at elective office, but he had learned perseverance at an early age. In the fourteen years between his first defeat and eventual success he learned how to play in the rough-and-tumble, highly partisan, patronage-based game of Indiana politics. It was a system perfectly matched to Minton's skills and instincts, and it remained in his blood, even as a Supreme Court justice. As a true Hoosier politician Minton was dead serious about his politics, and he was especially serious about loyalty to his party and to his political benefactors.

Minton had decided that once home from the war he would put his law practice on hold to run for Congress in 1920. He believed that with his war record he could win the Democratic primary in the Third District and then defeat the Republican incumbent, James Dunbar, in the fall.[1] Campaign posters featured Minton in his army uniform, and the newspapers that supported him usually referred to him as Captain Minton to emphasize his war service.

While Minton had the backing of some Democratic leaders in the district, another New Albany attorney, John Ewing, was the choice of the party organization. Minton conducted

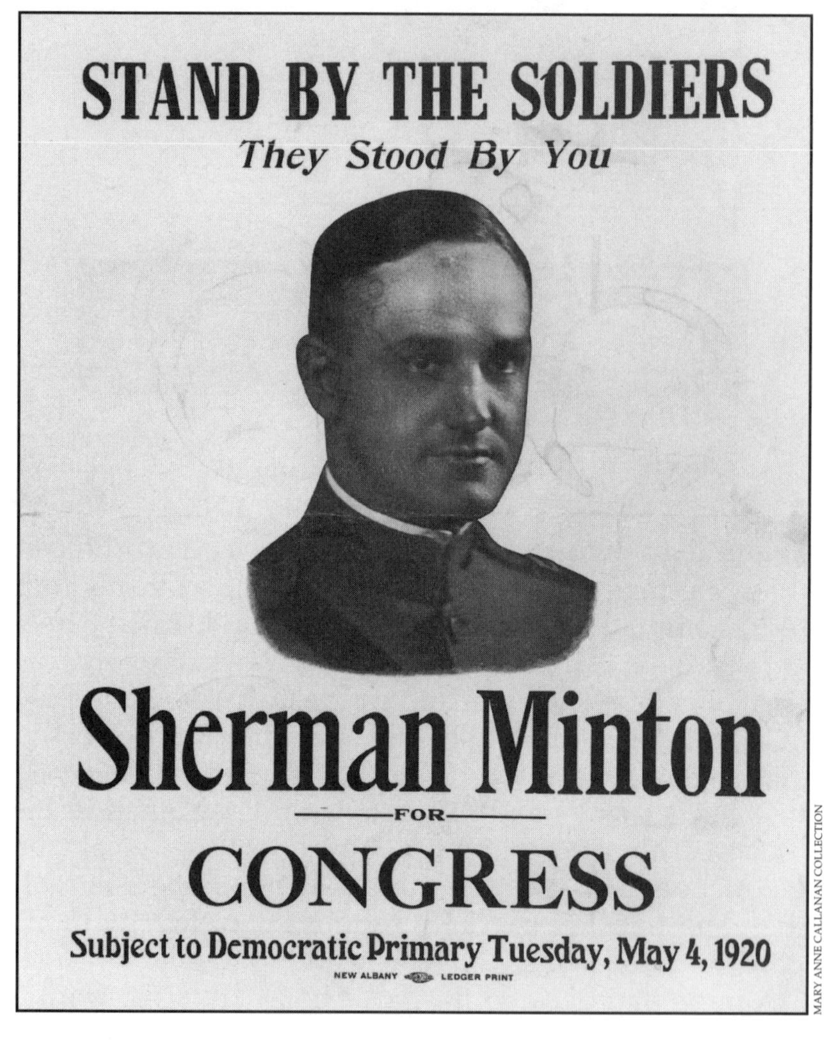

MARY ANNE CALLANAN COLLECTION

Campaign poster for Sherman Minton's first race for Congress in 1920.

a vigorous campaign, touring the district in a used Model T, but he finished a distant second to Ewing, 6,502 to 3,170. Minton impressed many with his strong effort and, displaying his strong sense of party loyalty, campaigned in the fall for Ewing, who was narrowly defeated.

Besides the lack of the party's endorsement, Minton's campaign was underfunded and his status as a veteran hurt rather than helped because of the district's large German-American population. Minton also admitted that his "knowledge of practical politics was sadly deficient."[2] It was a problem he worked diligently to correct.

Between his first and second bids for the Democratic nomination for Congress Minton began practicing law in earnest. By joining the New Albany firm of Stotsenburg and Weathers in 1922 (which became Stotsenburg, Weathers and Minton) he also came under the political tutelage of partner Evan B. Stotsenburg. The politically astute Stotsenburg had served one term as a state representative and four terms as a state senator and had been Democratic floor leader, president pro tempore of the senate, and state attorney general.

The law, however, began to assume a larger role in Minton's life, and for a brief period in the mid-1920s he appeared to have abandoned his political aspirations. In 1925 Republicans were in the ascendancy in Indiana politics, so Minton looked around for greener pastures in the legal profession. He left New Albany to join the law firm of Shutts and Bowen, the largest firm in Miami, Florida. Frank B. Shutts and Crate D. Bowen were former Indiana lawyers who knew Minton and persuaded him to join their firm. Minton decided if he "could not achieve political fame he could at least attain wealth and legal prominence."[3]

While he was with the Miami firm Minton had an opportunity to work with his political hero William Jennings Bryan. Through an arrangement made with the firm, Bryan used its law library to do research for the prosecution's case in the famous Scopes trial in Tennessee. The firm assigned Minton to assist Bryan in finding what he needed in the library.

Minton became the fourth senior partner in the firm, but by 1928 he decided to return to New Albany, in part because his wife and children were not happy in Miami. Also, he felt the primal call of politics, and the most logical place for him to pursue his political dream, he concluded, was Indiana. Fortunately for him changes in partisan strength that favored the Democratic party were beginning to occur both in Indiana and the nation.

When Minton ran for Congress in 1920 the political patterns of party support in Indiana were basically what they had been since the Civil War. The state was divided along sectional lines, north against south. The southern part of the state had been settled by frontiersmen who came from southern and border states. The northern part of the state was populated by migrants from the Middle Atlantic and New England states. These ethnic differences were reinforced by the Civil War. The southern part of the state, which had been sympathetic to the Confederacy, became primarily Democratic. The north, where pro-Union sentiments were strong, was predominantly Republican.[4]

However, the main differences between the Republican and Democratic parties concerned finance and liquor. The Democratic party stood for "soft money and hard liquor." Republicans opposed both. As Indiana became increasingly industrialized it sided with the hard money policies of the East, and the Democratic party was left behind, especially in the urban areas. The Democratic party's primary support came from those who were foreign born and those who were opposed to prohibition. By 1928 the percentage of those who were foreign born had decreased significantly, but a shift to the Democratic party did occur that year in those urban areas with large Catholic populations.

In Indiana the Catholic vote tended to be Democratic, in part because of the anti-Catholic bias of the Ku Klux Klan, which was closely aligned with the Republican party in the state. The Klan's strong influence in Indiana was demonstrated in the 1928 presidential election when the Democratic party's nominee Al Smith, an Irish-born Catholic, was beaten badly in the state. Still, Democratic candidates for state offices lost by only narrow margins, indicating the party was gaining ground. More significant and permanent shifts in partisan loyalty were to follow in 1932 and 1936 due to the Great Depression, giving the Democrats an advantage in state and national politics. In addition, the Democrats benefited from the scandals involving Republican governor Edward L. Jackson and Klan leader D. C. Stephenson.[5]

Minton returned home in the midst of these shifting political fortunes. He rejoined his old law firm, and in less than two years his hat was back in the ring. Clark County Democrats, meeting in Jeffersonville on New Year's Day, 1930, urged him to become a candidate for Dunbar's congressional seat. Minton's primary opponent was Democratic district chairman Eugene B. Crowe of Bedford, an area that had given Minton his strongest support in the 1920 race. As district chairman Crowe had obvious advantages, plus he had superior financial and organizational resources. Minton, relying primarily on the voluntary efforts of his personal friends, was overmatched. He lost to Crowe by four thousand votes, winning only three counties in the ten-county district.

Crowe beat Dunbar in the fall election and continued to hold the seat until 1940 when Republicans, with Indiana native Wendell Willkie as the party's presidential candidate, returned to dominance in virtually every aspect of state politics except the governor's office. As he did in 1920 Minton campaigned vigorously in 1930 for his primary opponent, and he and Crowe formed a long-standing friendship. Years later the two reminisced about their race at a bar association party hosted by Crowe at which Minton was the guest of honor. Reminded of the fact that Crowe was born in Clark County, raised in Washington County, and had moved to Lawrence County, Minton said, "You can't beat a man who is from almost every county in the district."[6]

Though he could joke about it later, at the time Minton's second electoral defeat was hard for him to accept. Although he was almost forty years old and a two-time loser, he did not abandon politics. Minton continued to be active in the Democratic party as well as the American Legion, which he had joined when he returned from the war. The American Legion, a major force in Indiana politics in the 1930s, 1940s, and 1950s, served many purposes for aspiring politicians. The Legion offered young men the opportunity to develop organizational skills and through Legion elections to gain invaluable experience in conducting campaigns. The most important political benefit, however, was making personal contacts that were invaluable to someone with political ambitions.[7]

Minton was typical of the young men whose careers were boosted by American Legion activities. He served as temporary chairman at the first meeting of New Albany's Bonnie Sloan Post. He spoke on the purposes of the Legion and was named publicity chairman. Minton held the position of post service officer, in which he was responsible for assisting disabled veterans, and later served as post commander for one term. He was judge advocate at the state level, as well as chairman of the state legislative committee. He also held positions at district and state conventions.[8] Minton was often a speaker at Legion conventions and later said he was sure it was his convention speaking that brought him to the attention of the two men who would be responsible for his political ascension—Paul V. McNutt and Pleas E. Greenlee.

McNutt, who knew Minton from their student days at Indiana University, was the most politically prominent member of the Indiana Legion, having been elected state commander in 1927 and national commander in 1928. Closely allied with McNutt in the Legion was Frank McHale, an Indianapolis attorney who had engineered McNutt's election as national commander. In fact, McHale is credited with making the Legion the political force that it became in producing candidates for political office.[9] Another important Legion ally for Minton was Greenlee, state adjutant of the organization and a newsman from Shelbyville. Using the power of the Legion, McNutt and his lieutenants challenged and deposed the old guard of the state Democratic party.

These Young Turks first made their mark on party affairs at the 1930 Democratic state convention when they succeeded in having McNutt named keynote speaker. McNutt's speech, "a rousing piece of oratory, blaming Republicans for the economic crisis," was well received in the press and by Democratic partisans and it helped launch his bid for governor. The younger Democrats, mostly American Legion men, demonstrated "that they held the future of the Indiana Democracy in their hands."[10]

They intended to flex their power in the 1932 gubernatorial race with McNutt as the standard-bearer and with McHale and Greenlee as top strategists. Minton, a member of the campaign executive committee headed by McHale, was in charge of the McNutt campaign activities in southern Indiana and chairman of the statewide Veterans Committee for McNutt. Rank-and-file members got on board for McNutt as well, showing up as vocal supporters at his speeches, where Legion bands turned out to play.

Not surprisingly the McNutt juggernaut alarmed other elements of the party. Two groups in particular watched the phenomenon with suspicion. One source of opposition came from South Bend Democrats, including Frank Mayr, himself an aspiring gubernatorial candidate, who had been elected secretary of state in 1930. In this position, Mayr controlled the automobile license bureaus throughout the state and used them to build up his support.

The other group wary of McNutt consisted of the older members of the party leadership who had stuck with the party through the lean years of patronage under Republican control and who expected to be rewarded when the party regained control. The leader of these forces had been Thomas Taggart, an Irish immigrant with a long political career: former three-term mayor of Indianapolis, former United States senator, and former chairman of the Democratic National Committee. Taggart functioned as the acknowledged leader of the party until the late 1920s. He was also owner of the French Lick Springs Hotel, which was the site of numerous state and national Democratic party gatherings until well into the 1950s. Taggart died in 1929 and was replaced by his son Thomas D. Taggart, who was never the political force that his father had been.[11]

The absence of a strong party leader in 1930 created a vacuum that McNutt and his forces intended to fill. The state party chairman was R. Earl Peters of Fort Wayne, who had held that office since 1926. Peters's power was so tenuous that he threw his support to McNutt in 1931 to secure his own position, an act that obviously did not endear him to the Mayr or Taggart forces. The Mayr and Taggart groups saw the McNutt forces as outsiders who were building a strong organization independent of the traditional party machinery, and they began to lay plans to stop McNutt.

In 1931 Minton heard that some of the old party stalwarts, led by Taggart, were unhappy because they were not being treated properly and also because they blamed McNutt for Peters's election as state chairman. Minton wrote to McNutt that these arguments were "damn weak, but is the old story of Hans and the dike." Although Minton felt it was too soon to begin an open movement for McNutt, he thought it was "time to 'dig in' so their barrage gets no casualties." His advice to McNutt was not to "let them bill you for so many speeches—you can talk yourself out."[12] To counter this move McNutt called a meeting at the Athletic Club in Indianapolis to plan his strategy. McNutt wrote to Minton that "each one of the new Congressional districts will be represented by one or two who can be trusted absolutely." He added that he was eager to have Minton present.[13]

The stop-McNutt campaign went nowhere. Minton was named permanent secretary of the 1932 state Democratic convention, and McNutt easily won the nomination with what was described as "a machine organization whose rule is absolute."[14] McNutt's organization also was responsible for selecting Frederick Van Nuys as the United States senatorial nominee. A native of Falmouth and graduate of Earlham College and Indiana University Law School, Van Nuys was an old-line Taggart Democrat.

Things did not go so well for McNutt and his comrades, however, at the 1932 National Democratic Convention that followed the state gathering by a few days. Before the convention began James A. Farley, Franklin Roosevelt's chief political operative, sought Indiana's support for Roosevelt's nomination. McNutt remained noncommittal. When Farley offered him the nomination for vice president, McNutt told him he would not consider it.[15] The Indiana delegation, led by McNutt, McHale, and Greenlee, opposed the Roosevelt forces on many issues at the convention, and, most important, they withheld the votes that they controlled until the fourth ballot. By then it was too late; Roosevelt had enough votes to win without their support. Farley never forgot or forgave McNutt for his refusal to support Roosevelt. Thereafter he would refer publicly to McNutt as that "platinum blond S.O.B. from Indiana."[16] Farley never missed an opportunity to remind Roosevelt, whenever the president was contemplating appointing McNutt to a high position, about McNutt's failure to support him at the 1932 convention.[17]

Although the motives for withholding the votes are often attributed to McNutt's desire to become president himself, in 1932 that was not a realistic possibility. A more plausible explanation is that Boyd Gurley, publisher of the *Indianapolis Times,* a Scripps-Howard newspaper, and McNutt worked out a deal: Gurley agreed to support McNutt's campaign for governor in exchange for McNutt's support of Newton Baker, general counsel for the newspaper chain, as the presidential nominee.[18] Also, Farley claimed that Roy Howard, national manager of Scripps-Howard newspapers, promised editorial support for the Democratic state ticket if Baker got a minimum of eight votes from the Indiana delegation. Baker got the eight votes on the first ballot.[19]

While McNutt and McHale denied Roosevelt their support, state chairman Earl Peters did not. He controlled fourteen votes, and Roosevelt received all of those on the first ballot. Farley rewarded Peters for his support by intervening in the selection of the party's candidate for United States Senate in 1934, a race that included Minton.

McNutt's stumble at the national convention did not affect his gubernatorial election, and he overwhelmed Republican Raymond S. Springer, a circuit judge, by a record margin, becoming the state's first Democratic governor in twenty years. Indeed, a new Democratic era of dominance was dawning: Democrats now held margins of forty-three to seven in the State Senate and ninety-one to nine in the House; Van Nuys beat incumbent United States senator James E. Watson; Democrats won all twelve congressional races; and Hoosiers gave a Democratic presidential candidate a majority for the first time since Woodrow Wilson's election in 1912.

The election also propelled Minton's political fortunes. Noting his effectiveness as a campaigner, the *Indianapolis Star* reported: "His oratorical service in behalf of the national ticket headed by Roosevelt and [John Nance] Garner and the state ticket headed by Paul V. McNutt was termed masterful by party members."[20] McNutt rewarded Minton with his first public office. The governor, who had stressed the need for public utility reform in the campaign, named Minton as public counselor to the Public Service Commission, a newly created position, to represent consumers in rate cases. Initially Minton was reluctant to accept because his law partner Evan Stotsenburg had been named state highway commissioner, and Minton was concerned that the law firm could not spare both of them. At a meeting called by McNutt, Minton succumbed to the pressures of the governor, Greenlee, and others. In accepting he said, "It's a poor fellow who won't go along with his friends."[21]

Minton became public counselor on 8 March 1933. He lived in Indianapolis at the Athletic Club with Stotsenburg and two other state officials—Moie Cook of Logansport, who was a member of the Public Service Commission, and Harry E. McCain of Shelbyville. Minton commuted to his home in New Albany on the weekends, establishing a pattern that repeated itself many times in his political career, since his wife Gertrude preferred living in New Albany.

Given his populist bent and the skills he had developed as a trial lawyer, Minton was ideally suited for his new role of representing the public before the Public Service Commission, and "he sailed into the water and electric companies with religious fervor."[22] The country was in the depths of the depression, and despite the fact that prices and wages had plummeted the utilities, protected from competition, refused to reduce their rates. Attacking this kind of arrogance was just the sort of fight that Minton liked. Rather than waiting for utility customers to come to him with their complaints, Minton went on the offensive, ordering utility companies to appear before the commission to explain why rates should not be reduced. On several occasions he got voluntary reductions, thus avoiding the long and expensive process of a public hearing.[23] His first skirmish was over rates of the Indianapolis Water Company, a case already scheduled for hearing in federal court. Minton assisted in the preparation of evidence and sought to prove that the utility company's earnings were too high and excessive. After months of legal maneuvering, the master in chancery in the water company case ruled that rates should be lowered by $205,000.[24] Minton then initiated an investigation into the earnings of the Public Service Company, now PSI Energy. His work produced $800,000 in savings for utility customers in 199 cities and 50 counties.[25] In the fall of 1933 Minton started proceedings against telephone companies for their exorbitant charges for cradle-type telephones. This effort brought all telephone companies in the state under the commissioner's orders, saving customers a reported $60,000. Action against Indianapolis Power and Light produced a compromise in which rates were reduced by $525,000 a year.[26] In a matter of months utilities made settlements that resulted in annual rate reductions of $3 million. Many of these agreements were reached through the governor's office, but McNutt made it a practice to clear them with Minton and gave him public credit for the savings.

While still serving as public counselor Minton decided to run for the party's senatorial nomination in 1934. His position in state government clearly had provided an excellent springboard for such a race. His successes in reducing utility rates were front-page news, and he was invited to give speeches throughout the state to both political and nonpolitical meetings. Minton relied on his oratorical skills to lambaste the general failure of utility rate regulation in the United States. In his standard speech Minton called the rate-setting system "a Frankenstein, which unless modified, will destroy all regulation." He told his audiences to take good care of municipally owned and operated utility plants because they might need them "as a shotgun to prevent total subservience to the utility interests."[27]

To be successful in his quest for the Senate nomination Minton obviously needed the support of McNutt's formidable political organization, which was fueled above all else by McNutt's ambition to become president. As far back as 1928 Frank McHale, who was called McNutt's Jim Farley, was motivated by one overriding goal—to put Paul McNutt in the White House. Engineering his election as both state and national commander of the American Legion was part of that grand design. Once McNutt was elected governor, McHale laid the groundwork for a political machine that was once described as being so efficient it would have put General Motors to shame.[28]

Four programs formed the foundation of the "McNutt Machine." These consisted of passing the Reorganization Act of 1933, expanding the use of patronage, creating the Hoosier Democratic Club, popularly known as the Two Percent Club, and establishing a new system for controlling the importation and sale of alcoholic beverages.

The Reorganization Act, which brought 169 separate agencies of the state under eight departments, allowed state government to operate more efficiently. More important, however, it resulted in an unprecedented centralization of power in the hands of the governor, which McNutt freely used, especially when it came to patronage. Patronage always had been a vital aspect of Indiana politics; McNutt raised it to an art form. Pleas Greenlee, who had become one of Minton's staunchest political allies, was in charge of dispensing spoils.

Of all the measures devised by the machine to ensure party loyalty none was more effective or received more notoriety than the infamous Two Percent Club. It collected from all state employees 2 percent of their wages or salaries for the party coffers to pay for political campaigns. In theory the funds were contributed voluntarily, but it was generally understood that those who refused to contribute lost their jobs. Although McHale has been described as "the brains behind the 'Two Percent Club' law,"[29] the idea actually originated with Greenlee. He adopted it from a practice in Pennsylvania politics that he learned about from a former World War I buddy.[30]

The Two Percent Club did provide the party with substantial money to fund the campaigns of its candidates. Approximately $10,000 a month flowed into the party treasury and, according to one estimate, the annual income of the club reached $225,000 before the end of McNutt's term of office.[31]

The final cog in the McNutt machine was engineered by legislation in 1933 that brought the importation, manufacture, and sale of alcoholic beverages under strict state control. It has been described as "perhaps the boldest effort of the McNutt administration to reward loyal Democrats."[32] Although all kinds of alcoholic beverages were controlled, the most extensive provision of the legislation concerned beer. To import, manufacture, or sell beer required a license granted by the state. Those receiving licenses had to pay fees and post bonds, a small sum for such a lucrative plum, especially licenses for importers and wholesalers. These licenses were restricted in number and amounted to monopolies. As a result, "a man with nothing but a dusty desk for an office could make a large income in a year without lifting a hand."[33]

Alcoholic beverage licenses were valuable political favors to be handed out only to deserving Democrats, a fact that was openly admitted. For example, in April 1933 the Wilson Democratic Club in Lake County sent a telegram to Governor McNutt that read: "Democrats of Lake County oppose and strenuously object to the giving of wholesale beer permits and licenses in Lake County to bootleggers racketeers or Republicans."[34] For McHale, one of the major justifications for the liquor control law was that "it kept some 'deserving Democrats' from starving."[35] Receiving licenses, of course, entailed a quid pro quo for the party. Kickbacks and campaign contributions were a documented part of the system.[36]

A very powerful political organization was built up as a result of these measures, an organization that was loyal to McNutt rather than to the state Democratic party. Through this machine McNutt and McHale wielded almost absolute control over party nominations and government appointments throughout the 1930s. Trusted friends and supporters who could be useful to McNutt's presidential ambitions were given machine support. Others were given the machine's blessing because they were a means of defeating McNutt's rivals for power within the party. McNutt's eventual support for Minton in the 1934 race for the Senate nomination appeared to fall into the latter category more so than the former.

If McNutt was grooming Minton specifically for the Senate seat it was very much a muted effort. Actually, Greenlee was Minton's patron, although McNutt doubtlessly approved of Minton making the race since he permitted Greenlee to conduct a vigorous campaign in Minton's behalf. The governor sought to remain neutral because all the candidates except Earl Peters were friends and supporters.

McNutt, constantly calculating how events in state politics would affect the future, viewed the 1934 Senate nomination in terms of his presidential ambitions. Any political contest was an opportunity to demonstrate his control over the party machinery and to undermine opponents who could harm his political reputation. In fact, McNutt himself had been urged to run for the Senate nomination, but he refused to become a candidate.

While he refused to be a candidate, McNutt had not yet anointed anyone else. He knew only that he did not want Peters, who had resigned after seven years as state party chairman following his feuding with McNutt over control of funds of the Two Percent Club. Shortly after his resignation in late 1933 Peters signaled his intention to be a candidate for the United States Senate nomination. Because of his early support of Roosevelt, Peters had the behind-the-scenes support of the Roosevelt administration, mainly through the efforts of Jim Farley, Democratic national chairman. Farley's support was as much the result of long-standing hatred for McNutt as it was repayment of a debt to Peters.

McNutt had several obvious advantages in the confrontation. He was governor after all, and by tradition in Indiana governors have always had a major influence on state party conventions. And with the power of his carefully constructed organization behind him McNutt could wield more power than previous governors. This was especially true because of the repeal of the state's direct primary law in 1929, which restored power to the party and especially to the governor.[37] McNutt's dominance was apparent at the convention. He was chosen temporary chairman, introduced the permanent chair, Senator Van Nuys, and delivered the keynote speech, in which he touted the successes of his administration.

On the eve of the 1934 convention the Democratic *New Albany Weekly Ledger* said Minton's victory "can be predicted with a great deal of certainty," adding that Minton "was confident of victory in the convention, and satisfied himself and his friends that he will win in November."[38] The paper also reported that Minton had established his campaign headquarters in the same rooms in the Claypool Hotel occupied by McNutt at the state convention in 1932. Minton said he "selected these official quarters for good luck and the sake of pleasant memories."[39]

Peters was equally confident of victory. He declared after the 8 May primary, when convention delegates were selected, that he had enough strength to win on the first ballot. Greenlee, Minton's campaign adviser, claimed that his candidate would win on the third ballot. Greenlee's prediction came closer to the mark.

As it turned out Minton won the nomination on the fourth ballot. There were nine candidates altogether. In addition to Peters the other principal candidates were Reginald Sullivan, mayor of Indianapolis, Clarence E. Manion from South Bend, and Albert H. Cole from Logansport, a relative of songwriter Cole Porter. The last candidate to enter the race was Louis Ludlow, a congressman from Indianapolis. An interesting set of alliances developed over the nomination and revealed a lack of unanimity in McNutt's forces. Greenlee supported Minton while McHale favored Cole, and Van Nuys favored Sullivan. Although McNutt had sought to remain neutral, by balloting time he concluded that Minton was his best hope of stopping Peters and thus gave him his support. McNutt's support probably came too late to really help Minton since by then all the delegates were pledged.[40] Had McNutt supported Minton from the beginning, it "undoubtedly would have suppressed Frank McHale's campaign for Albert Cole."[41]

Greenlee expected Minton to run behind Peters on the first ballot, move ahead of him on the second ballot, and win on the third ballot. Manion had agreed to switch his votes to Minton on the third ballot if Manion lost ground in the second.[42] Although it took one more ballot than Greenlee predicted, the balloting went pretty much according to his plan. On the first ballot Peters had 620½ votes to Minton's 598. Manion and Sullivan had 282½ and 279 votes respectively. Cole, McHale's candidate, had only 145, and the remaining candidates had about 200 votes among them.

Both Minton and Peters increased their votes on the second ballot, with Minton pulling ahead of Peters. Minton had 682½ votes, Peters had 639½, Sullivan was a distant third with 284 votes, followed closely by Manion with 265, and Cole with 119. When it became apparent that Minton was the only candidate who could defeat Peters, McNutt asked McHale to switch Cole's support to Minton. The manager of Cole's campaign, Mike Fansler, an Indiana Supreme Court justice, refused to switch. Sullivan, Manion, and Cole were hoping for a deadlock between the two leaders, but Minton's lead on the third ballot increased to 827, while Peters decreased to 526. Sullivan had 281 votes, Manion had 262½, and Cole dropped to 85.

At various stages of the voting on the fourth ballot Minton strategists tried to create the impression of a bandwagon, but it was not until St. Joseph County switched its votes from Manion, its own candidate, to Minton that "the stampede was on."[43] Before the balloting was over Peters realized that his cause was hopeless and moved to make Minton's nomination unanimous. Fourteen years after his first try, Minton had finally reached the first plateau of elective office. To complete the dream he would have to defeat incumbent Republican senator Arthur Robinson in the fall.

Greenlee obviously was the mastermind behind the Senate nomination, but Minton also owed something to McNutt. After he had been nominated to the Supreme Court in 1949, Minton replied to a congratulatory letter from McNutt, acknowledging his debt to the former governor: "I appreciate very much your warm message of congratulations, and your friendship throughout the years which has meant so much to me. I never forget that you were in the position to have checked my career, but you didn't and you gave me your blessing—without which I could not have succeeded."[44]

For his part Minton had been willing to do whatever was necessary for the good of the party. He commented on McNutt's late show of support in a letter to his close friend Val Nolan, United States district attorney in Indianapolis: "No one knows better than you that no 'go' sign was given anyone in my race until daybreak on the morning of the Convention. However, Pleas had the word from me at all times during the pre-convention campaign, that if he thought it advisable to pull me out of the race, it was all right with me and I stood ready to do whatever in his judgment seemed best for the Party. Fortunately it did not seem necessary to take me out, but had it been necessary, I would have accepted it, although I would have been disappointed."[45]

This statement sums up Minton's view of politics and how the game is played. If personal ambition had to be sacrificed for the sake of the Democratic party, then the loyal soldier Minton was prepared to make it. He felt a person must do what is best for the party, and throughout his political career he was true to that brand of loyalty, sometimes to his detriment.

Shortly after his defeat at the convention Peters was appointed head of the Federal Housing Administration in

Indiana. The position gave Peters control of federal funds and jobs and the opportunity to remain a thorn in McNutt's side.

Minton, meanwhile, was welcomed home to New Albany with a big public celebration. Republican mayor C. B. McLinn, putting aside partisan differences, spoke with pride to the crowd about Minton and his southern Indiana roots: "These hills do something to a man that makes him plant his feet firmly on the earth, stiffen his backbone, and turn his face to the stars. Sherman Minton has that stability of the Hills; the relentless urge of the River. He is a man among men."[46]

Despite the hyperbole of the mayor's words, they were an appropriate tribute to the Floyd County native. In acknowledging Minton's origins the mayor focused on one of the major influences in Minton's life. Throughout his career Minton often paid tribute to his roots in the hills of southern Indiana and the values that he learned growing up there. Speaking to the crowd that gathered to celebrate his victory, Minton said he was proud "of the lessons and values taught in this rugged country."[47]

About a month after capturing the nomination Minton left his post as public counselor to the Public Service Commission to campaign for the Senate. Although the campaign did not begin officially until Labor Day, for all practical purposes it began shortly after the convention. Minton toured the state in the summer, and from the start he made his support for the New Deal and President Roosevelt the keystones of his campaign. It was a popular message, since in 1934 Hoosiers were strongly behind Roosevelt and his New Deal programs. Minton's opponent, Senator Robinson, initially responded by attacking the New Deal for its fiscal irresponsibility and reckless spending. The New Deal was criticized by the Republican press for trying to play Santa Claus. Minton took the sting out of that criticism with his own message. "I believe that the spirit of the New Deal truly is the spirit of Santa Claus," he said. "After all, who is Santa Claus but the spirit of one who, in infinite pity, reaches down and helps his neighbor; who restores him to hope and health and a place of respect among his fellow-men?"[48]

One of Minton's favorite responses to the charges of excessive spending by the New Deal was to acknowledge that although government expenditures had increased significantly under the New Deal, the increases were for a just cause. He said if the country could afford to spend $23 billion to fight World War I, then "in the name of heaven why can't we spend a few million that men, women and children might live in this country?" He then asked: "Is it wasteful to help the farmer to a profit, to put industry on its feet, to take millions of unemployed men and women out of the breadline, to restore prosperity and happiness in this land of the free and home of the brave? I say 'No.'"[49]

It was Minton, the son of poverty, the high school orator, and the William Jennings Bryan devotee at his best. He saw no reason why the power and financial resources of government should not be used to meet the needs of the people. He was firm in this belief and made no apology for it in his campaign.

When Robinson's strategy of attacking the ever-popular Roosevelt proved ineffective, he assaulted the New Deal's programs on the grounds that they were unconstitutional. Robinson's battle cry became "Back to the Constitution." The issue of constitutionality was one of the most prominent and hotly debated issues throughout the campaign. Speaking at the annual meeting of the Indiana Democratic Editorial Association in mid-August, Minton charged that Robinson and the Republicans stood idle while constitutional rights and human liberties were perverted under successive Republican administrations. Calling them "self-appointed defenders of the Constitution," he challenged them to "tell the people of Indiana where you were when the banks all closed and the credit structure of the nation collapsed, wiping out the earnings and savings of the frugal people who had trusted you." Minton intoned that "the Constitution is the people's creation, designed and intended to bring the greatest good to the greatest number," and he said the New Deal programs of the president were doing just that.[50]

Minton officially opened his campaign in Terre Haute on 11 September. McNutt was present to introduce him to the crowd of ten thousand. Minton cited the accomplishments of the Roosevelt administration, but again he turned to the issue of constitutionality, making what became his famous "You Can't Eat the Constitution" speech. Actually, he said, "You can't walk up to a hungry man today and say, 'Here, have a Constitution.'" Minton was roundly criticized for the speech, even by some of his supporters, but he hardly intended his remarks as demeaning to the Constitution. Indeed, in his speech he called it "one of the noblest documents ever conceived by the mind of man." Minton, however, maintained that "government under its provisions was never intended to operate the way three Republican national administrations have permitted it to operate—to drift and to bring the country to the very brink of ruin."

Ridiculing his opponent for making the Constitution an issue, Minton said, "For ten years the senior Senator [Robinson] and Hoover had the Constitution and all the agencies of government in their charge and keeping. It was during this time that people lost their right to earn a living and wound up in the bread line and in the army of the unemployed." He added, "You can't frighten people by talking to them about the loss of their liberty as if liberty was something apart from human happiness. You can't frighten people today about the loss of their constitutional rights when they are struggling to live."[51]

Within a week of Minton's speech launching his campaign, Republican newspapers across the state lambasted him for his position on the Constitution. The *Indianapolis News,* in a front-page editorial, accused Minton of undermining the Constitution, and questioned: "With what solemnity could he swear to support the Constitution after making a campaign in which he derided it?"[52] The controversy over his remarks endured, coming back to haunt him even in 1949 when he was nominated to the Supreme Court.

In defending the Roosevelt administration's handling of the economy Minton said Republican newspapers tell about the failures of the New Deal on the editorial page, but people "learn the truth by turning to the market page where they are compelled to tell the truth about actual business conditions." To support their candidate's stand Democratic newspapers throughout the state carried a party-line story analyzing the business page of "the rabid Republican metropolitan dailies" and quoted headlines that referred to improved conditions in retail trade, oil futures, loans to farmers' cooperatives, employment, jobs in various industries, such as housing and steel, and the like. The story ended with the rhetorical question, "How does that compare with Senator Robinson's statements about the failure of Roosevelt recovery?"[53]

Sensing that their strategy of challenging the failure of the New Deal, as well as its constitutionality, was not working, the Republicans shifted the focus of their attacks to Governor McNutt. In the final phase of the 1934 senatorial campaign the GOP inveighed against the programs of the McNutt administration, criticizing the governor's political machine, his Two Percent Club, and the Reorganization Act.

As McNutt became the main issue in the waning days of the campaign some Democratic leaders, who considered the governor to be a liability, actually advised Minton to avoid mentioning McNutt. By 1934 McNutt was regularly condemned by three-fourths of the state's newspapers, and "Stop McNutt" signs began appearing throughout the state.[54] One loyal Democrat, M. G. French, wrote a tongue-in-cheek poem about the Republican strategy, which he sent to McNutt:

> We've got to have an issue,
> Which the G.O.P. can strut,
> So pedal soft on Roosevelt,
> Raise hell with PAUL MCNUTT.
>
> Shay Minton is a Dumb-bell,
> He's dead as old King Tut,
> The only way to head him off,
> Is, castigate MCNUTT.[55]

Minton responded to the "Stop McNutt" campaign by turning the tables on the sloganeers. He asked what should McNutt be stopped from doing: "Saving the taxpayers of this state $6,000,000 a year in the cost of their state government? Stop him from securing reductions of three and a quarter million dollars a year in utility charges? Stop him from making Indiana one of three states in which all the schools were open and all the teachers paid during the past year?" According to Minton, the Republicans had plenty of experience in stopping things: "They stopped several million people from working. They stopped the whistles from blowing on your factories, the business man from seeing anything but red on his books, the farmer from making a profit on the farm and they stopped the working man from drinking a bottle of beer."[56]

The attacks against him stirred McNutt into action, and he went on the offensive using a tactic that he called the "open forum." When appearing before a public gathering he extended the following invitation to his audience. "When I get through with my talk if there is any question in your mind about the Democratic state administration I want you to ask it. If there is any criticism I want to hear it and be given a chance to answer. If I can't answer we are licked."[57] This strategy proved to be particularly effective in stanching the vocal criticism from his opponents who showed up to heckle the governor.

Although Minton spent a great deal of his time answering charges by Robinson he also attacked Robinson and the Republican party as the defenders of wealth and privilege. Speaking in Fort Wayne late in the campaign, he said the senator and his party "have been taking care of wealth and the millionaire for years and today 97 per cent of the wealth of the country is in the hands of 3 per cent of the people."[58]

One of the specific issues over which Minton and Robinson sparred was agricultural policy. The policy was of particular importance in Indiana where farming was still a vital part of the economy, and it was especially important in Minton's home area of southern Indiana. Minton reminded Hoosier farmers of the $20 million they had reaped from the Agricultural Adjustment Act, and he criticized Robinson for abandoning the program, which at one time he had supported.

Robinson was criticized in the Democratic press for his "crooked cousin" story, an example Robinson had used about his cousin who had never been a very productive farmer but who had made money from a New Deal farm policy through fraud. The *Greenfield Hancock Democrat* urged that Robinson, "as a servant of the taxpayers, as a good citizen and as a patriot, might consider turning over this information to the department of justice so that his crooked cousin could be forced to disgorge his ill-gotten gain and not permit the money to taint the coffers of the Robinson family."[59]

Another major issue in which Minton differed with Robinson was over assistance to veterans. On this issue Minton benefited from his background in the American Legion. In the New Albany Legion he had been post service officer, which meant he was responsible for the welfare of veterans and their families, especially those who were disabled and in dire circumstances. He declared that "if I am elected United States senator from Indiana no act will ever be passed by the congress with my vote which will work an injustice to the veteran, the veteran's widow or to his family."[60] Minton went on to decry policies that, in the name of economy, had discriminated against worthy veterans and kicked disabled veterans out of hospitals because of a shortage of beds.

Of all the issues in the campaign relating to veterans, the most prominent concerned the early payment of veterans' bonuses. The topic had generated substantial controversy since 1932 when thousands of jobless veterans had marched on Washington demanding immediate payment of their bonuses. Rioting occurred when the veterans' demands were rejected, and they were turned back by troops led by Gen. Douglas MacArthur. The veterans had vowed to fight for their bonuses at the polls. They had been buoyed by Roosevelt's election, but they soon discovered that their cause was not a top priority of the administration. Roosevelt vetoed a veterans' bonus bill in 1933, and the veterans' lobby was making its strength felt in 1934.

Robinson favored the early bonus, and Minton was only partially in support. Speaking before a Knox County crowd in early October Minton advocated payment of the bonus at the earliest possible date, but he maintained that the government's first obligation was to the completion of the recovery. While Minton's sympathy was with the veterans, he maintained, even after his election, that healthy men should not be given these bonuses. He deplored a system that "permits pension chiselers, able bodied men like myself . . . to take money which should be going to the disabled veterans, to the widow and the orphan."[61]

At the outset of the campaign both Minton and Robinson enjoyed the support of organized labor, but through some questionable tactics at the convention of the Indiana State Federation of Labor in early September in South Bend, Minton and his strategists worked to discredit Robinson with union members. The *Indianapolis Times,* a Democratic paper, reported that Minton's name was warmly greeted by the conventioneers and that Robinson had snubbed the convention by not sending a telegram of greeting as Minton had done.[62] Actually, Robinson did send a telegram, but it disappeared in a classic case of "dirty tricks."

The principal actors in carrying out the deed were Rolland E. Friedman, a delegate to the convention, and Thomas Taylor, president of the labor organization. They not only managed to conceal the telegram that Robinson had sent to the convention, but they also killed a statement of support for the Republican candidate. Friedman, writing McNutt on 13 September about the missing telegram, said, "You know it was funny where that Robinson wire went. Well the seal is on. You say I can't put things over if you like—Hell man, I can have them doing that all over the State."[63] One delegate informed Greenlee that "President Taylor killed the resolution that was supposed to support Arthur Robinson. He accomplished it in a very clever way and [it] was never introduced."[64] A telegram from Taylor to McNutt read: "Robinson movement killed. Minton's wire made part of record. Friedman has complete record."[65]

Just how important these events were to Minton's success in the campaign is not known. There is no analysis showing how labor voted in the 1934 campaign, and even if such information did exist it could not prove that these shenanigans were responsible. Although there is no evidence linking Minton to these episodes, given his closeness to McNutt and Greenlee it is difficult to believe that he was not aware of the plans.

Minton's campaign received assistance in more conventional ways as several of the state's congressmen as well as several prominent Democrats from other states crisscrossed Indiana making speeches in his behalf. United States senators Robert F. Wagner of New York, Hugo L. Black of Alabama, Joseph Robinson of Arkansas, Alben Barkley of Kentucky, and Millard Tydings of Maryland, and Representative Gordon Browning of Tennessee campaigned for Minton as did assistant United States attorneys general Joseph B. Kennan and Harry B. Flaherty. Indiana congressmen Louis Ludlow, William H. Larrabee, and

James I. Farley also stumped for him. Also in the Indiana tradition, Albert H. Cole and Clarence Manion, two of his opponents for the Senate nomination, supported Minton.

One of Minton's former opponents noticeably absent from the campaign trail was Earl Peters. Peters had repeatedly told his friend Jim Farley and presidential adviser Louis Howe that Minton could not win. Apparently, as a result, they diverted a five thousand dollar contribution from Bernard Baruch intended for Minton's campaign to races in Michigan.[66]

Some prominent state Republicans broke ranks to support Minton. One was Will H. Craig of Noblesville, a member of the Republican party for forty years and a one-time delegate to the Republican National Convention. Craig made a strong indictment of Robinson, claiming that Ku Klux Klan leader D. C. Stephenson had dictated Robinson's appointment by Governor Jackson in 1925 after the death of Sen. Samuel M. Ralston.[67] In 1926 Klansmen and former Klansmen testified during a congressional investigation of Klan activities in Indiana on behalf of the candidacies of Senators Watson and Robinson. Both men denied any Klan connections or sympathies.[68]

Another Republican who endorsed Minton was John W. Scott, former Republican district chairman in Lake County, who had been a member of the state legislature and a candidate for Congress. Scott declared that he was "putting my love for my country above my partisan affiliations." He called Robinson "the greatest bogus statesman Indiana ever sent to Washington."[69]

Naturally the state's Democratic press went all out to help Minton in his campaign against Robinson. An item from the *Monticello White County Democrat* on 14 September is a good example. Under the headline, "Artie voted for NRA, AAA," the paper reported that Robinson supported a host of New Deal bills, including the Emergency Banking Bill, the Federal Emergency Relief Act, the

National Recovery Act, and the Agricultural Adjustment Act, and then "did all he could to block the Roosevelt program." The article said Robinson harangued the administration at every point, but added that his "attacks served as recess periods for the Senate. Tolerantly the Solons would sit through his tirades and when the Republican Senator would end his remarks, the august group would resume its interrupted business."[70]

The *White County Democrat* also doubted Robinson was a true representative of the people of Indiana because he "was born in Ohio, educated outside the state, and first became senator through appointment by Governor Ed Jackson, without an expression of a choice by voters." The paper was quick to point out that Minton "is a native Hoosier who knows the problems of Indiana people in all walks of life."[71]

Democratic newspapers carried cartoons, usually with a sports motif, in which Robinson was invariably called Artie or Li'l Arthur. One cartoon, with the caption "Li'l Artie Can't Take It; Can't Make It," shows Robinson on the ground, felled by a hurdle, labeled "Qualifications," at a track meet, while "Shay" Minton glides easily over a more distant hurdle.[72] A cartoon with the caption, "Backward-Always Backward," shows the football player "Li'l Arthur" running in the opposite direction of the goal of "Recovery." On the sideline the public is represented as the coach, with an arm around "Shay" Minton, saying, "You go in for Li'l Arthur, Shay—Every time he gets the ball he runs the wrong way."[73] A third example shows a series of signposts all pointing backwards with Senator Robinson tugging on Uncle Sam to get him to turn back. The caption reads, "The Only Direction He Knows."[74]

Minton ended his campaign on the eve of election in New Albany promoting the New Deal, whose purpose, he said, "was to put men back to work and to improve their condition as working people, and to recognize their right to collective bargaining and to abolish child labor." He said

Roosevelt's programs also were intended to restore profits to farmers, business, and industry. "The New Deal is just the square deal as President Theodore Roosevelt conceived it," Minton said.[75]

On 6 November 1934 Hoosiers as well as voters throughout the country, turning out in unusually high numbers for an off-year election, gave their ringing endorsement to Democrats. Minton was elected to the United States Senate with 52 percent of the vote. Democrats won eleven of the twelve congressional seats, and the party, while slipping some in the state legislature, retained firm control with a sixty-five to thirty-five majority in the House and a thirty-eight to twelve margin in the Senate. Just as the Indiana results gave McNutt a strong vote of confidence, voting nationwide demonstrated faith in Roosevelt and his New Deal. Democrats gained ten seats in the Senate, giving them a sixty-nine to twenty-seven advantage, the biggest majority ever held by either party, and they increased their strength in the House to 319 seats compared with 103 for the Republicans.

Savoring his victory from his home in New Albany, Minton declared, "The New Deal lives, and I am proud to be a part of it."[76] Minton obviously benefited from the support enjoyed by the McNutt and Roosevelt administrations. Acknowledging his personal debt to the governor after arriving in Washington, Minton wrote: "I want to make good over here as much on your account as any other. I know without your loyalty to my cause, I could never have had this opportunity."[77]

Minton himself deserved a big share of the credit for his election. In fact, the *Christian Science Monitor,* calling Minton's victory an upset, concluded that the chief reasons for the outcome were the New Deal and the candidate himself. The paper said, "Mr. Minton conducted a heads up campaign, [and he] was an attractive man on the platform and over the radio."[78]

GARY YOHLER/FREDERICK VOLLRATH, TIFFANY STUDIO, *INDIANAPOLIS TIMES* COLLECTION

Senator-elect Sherman Minton and his wife Gertrude on vacation in Miami Beach, 17 December 1934.

At long last his political apprenticeship was over. Now Minton was in a position to apply the first lesson of Indiana politics: reward your friends and punish your enemies, both of which he would do with fervor and flair.

CHAPTER FOUR

Fulfilling His New Deal Promise

When the first session of the 74th Congress convened in January 1935 Sherman Minton took his seat in desk number 92 in the back row of the United States Senate chamber. His freshman status and backbench position notwithstanding, Minton made certain that over the course of the next six years he would be at the center of the action and attention. He was firmly in the president's camp during his Senate term because he had campaigned and won on a New Deal platform, and he intended to live up to his promise. Furthermore, his populism, which sprang from his firsthand experience with poverty, committed him to helping the less fortunate and pricking the wealthy and powerful.

Minton and others in the freshman class of senators, who became known as the Young Turks, were eager to transform campaign words into legislative action. Accordingly, they ignored the time-honored custom of the staid Senate that new members should be seen and not heard. Not only were they heard, but they also often led the charge in pushing the second round of Roosevelt's New Deal, a troublesome task since the administration had ditched the "concert of all interests" approach used in the New Deal's first phase for an assault on entrenched interests and big

MARY ANNE CALLANAN COLLECTION

Sherman Minton on his first day in the U. S. Senate with members of his staff and well-wishers.

business. Moreover, the president was under attack from those on the left who wanted the recovery process accelerated and from those on the right who warned that the New Deal imperiled liberty.

In the Senate, which prides itself on being the world's most deliberative legislative body, Minton's competitive nature and his considerable skills as a spirited debater could be exercised to their limits. The Senate was also the ideal place for the combative and assertive Minton to demonstrate his knowledge of the law, grasp of the issues, homespun wisdom, dramatic flair, quick wit, and biting humor. He relished a good fight even when his opponents were the powerful press and the lofty Supreme Court. Minton's voice and views also reached across the country on radio, then a relatively new medium of communication that he frequently used.

Minton and other freshmen Democrats, including Harry Truman of Missouri, Lewis Schwellenbach of Washington, Francis Maloney of Connecticut, Joseph Guffey of

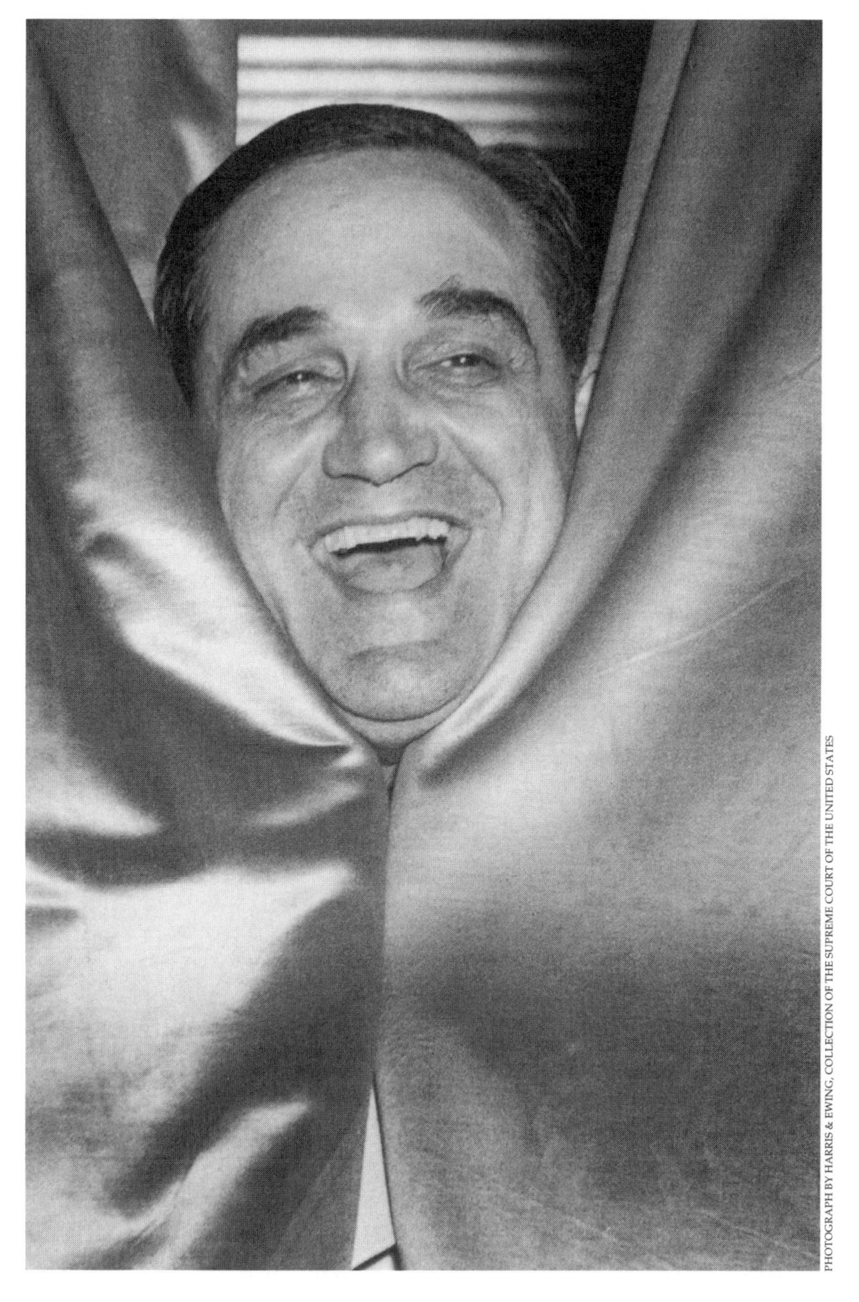

PHOTOGRAPH BY HARRIS & EWING, COLLECTION OF THE SUPREME COURT OF THE UNITED STATES

Sen. Sherman Minton was the subject of a series of photographs called "shooting the famous in funny poses."

Pennsylvania, George Radcliffe of Maryland, and A. Harry Moore of New Jersey, wasted little time in making their presence felt. In June 1935 they went after and caught the Kingfish himself—Sen. Huey P. Long of Louisiana. The first-termers, who had tired quickly of Long's obstructive tactics and the leadership's unwillingness to curb him, denied Long the customary senatorial courtesies during his filibuster against extending the National Recovery Act (NRA). Whenever Long tried a maneuver that would give him a little rest, a cry of "we object" rang from the freshmen in the back row. Finally, after filibustering for fifteen hours and thirty-five minutes, Long relented, clearing the way for passage of the NRA measure. Minton said, "As far as I'm concerned, I'm going to battle him as long as I'm here. Senatorial courtesy? That fellow hasn't any courtesy about him."[1]

Minton's first chance for real action came when Roosevelt, in his annual address to Congress in January 1935, urged the breakup of powerful public utility holding companies. The development of pyramided holding companies had put control of most of the nation's electric and gas utilities into the hands of a few empires, which often consisted of six or seven subsidiary companies. Through intermediate subsidiaries, holding companies monopolized the utility business and exploited the operating electric and gas companies through excessive fees for supplies and services. These costs were passed along to consumers in higher utility bills. Also, at each level of the pyramid a new issue of securities—often risky—were offered to the investing public.

This issue was ideal for Minton, who, as public counselor of the Indiana Public Service Commission, had taken on the utilities and won millions in rate reductions for Hoosiers. After his election to the Senate Minton vowed to make affordable energy his main concern. He got the opportunity to fulfill his pledge by gaining membership on the Senate Interstate Commerce Committee.

Shortly after Roosevelt's call for the end of utility holding companies Burton K. Wheeler and Samuel T. Rayburn, chairmen of the Senate and House Interstate Commerce Committees, introduced legislation to regulate and eventually abolish those conglomerates that could not justify their existence as sound economic entities; this was the so-called death sentence provision. Proponents of the Wheeler-Rayburn legislation claimed that these pyramid-like organizations needed to be dismantled because they put too much control into the hands of a few industry moguls, were inefficient, bilked investors, drained the resources of subsidiaries, and added to the costs consumers paid for gas and electricity.

The proposed legislation set off a storm of opposition. Congressmen were buried under a blizzard of letters and telegrams, ostensibly from ordinary citizens outraged over the breakup of utility holding companies. The apparent interest by so many in an issue as complex as the labyrinthine corporate structure of utilities struck many legislators as odd. Both houses decided to investigate this lobbying blitz.

The Senate created a special Lobby Investigating Committee chaired by Hugo Black of Alabama. Black asked that Minton, because of his experience in dealing with utilities, be named to the five-member committee. Another freshman senator, Schwellenbach, who had led the confrontation with Huey Long, also was appointed to the panel. Republican members of the committee were Lynn J. Frazier of North Dakota and Ernest Gibson of Vermont.

Black's committee dominated the headlines during the summer of 1935 as the fiery chairman relentlessly pushed the investigation, uncovering in the process a trail left by big utilities that included forged telegrams, intimidation, and lavish spending to fight the Wheeler-Rayburn bill. The committee, inquiring into 816 telegrams sent to a Pennsylvania congressman from people whose names began with "B," discovered that they were sent by a representative of a large utility holding company who had simply picked the names from a city directory. In fact, Black said, the committee found that holding companies had paid for about 250,000 protest telegrams. Furthermore, a Western Union messenger told the committee that he was paid three cents apiece to get signatures on telegrams opposing the legislation.[2] Howard C. Hopson, president of Associated Gas and Electric Company, who testified before Black's committee only after being cited for contempt of the Senate, admitted that his company, then one of the nation's largest public holding companies, used the power of its advertising dollars in an attempt to influence newspaper coverage of the Wheeler-Rayburn proposal. The company withdrew its advertising in the *New York Times* because of what it considered unfavorable coverage of the holding company issue.[3] Hopson also disclosed that his company had spent almost a million dollars to campaign against the Wheeler-Rayburn measure.

In the end Roosevelt got the substance of what he wanted in Wheeler-Rayburn, although the death sentence provision was eliminated. The final version of the bill abolished all utility holding companies more than twice removed from their operating companies and increased the power of the Securities and Exchange Commission over holding companies. Within three years most of the big utility empires were dissolved.[4]

Just as important for Roosevelt as this legislative triumph were the continued investigations of the Black committee into what it considered lobbying irregularities. The Democratic-controlled panel, emboldened by its success in exposing fraud by the utilities, pursued its mission with zeal, partisanship, and occasional disregard for constitutional guarantees. Under Black, and later Minton, the highly visible committee generally interpreted a lobbying abuse as any opposition to the New Deal, and it sought to discredit opponents by whatever means necessary.

The committee's importance to the administration increased in 1936 when Roosevelt abandoned his "unity" strategy for a concerted attack on the rich and powerful, promising to rid the country of those he called "economic royalists." In response, conservatives, business groups, and the anti-Roosevelt press stepped up their criticism of the New Deal.

As the war of words escalated, the Senate Lobby Investigating Committee used its power, often imperiously, in an attempt to sway public opinion to the president's side. In early 1936 it was revealed that the committee had issued blanket subpoenas to Western Union and postal telegraph companies for copies of telegrams relating not only to the utility holding company bill, but also for thousands of messages sent by corporations, organizations, and individuals in behalf of various causes. The subpoenas covered correspondence to and from leading administration adversaries, including newspaper publishers William Randolph Hearst and Col. Robert McCormick, the Liberty League, the Crusaders, the National Economy League, and Sentinels of the Republic.

The panel's actions were widely condemned by the press and lawyers as a violation of the Fourth Amendment's protection against unreasonable search and seizure. The Chicago law firm of Winston, Strawn & Shaw, which received a subpoena because it had served as counsel for several large utility interests, challenged the committee in a District of Columbia court and won. The ruling enjoined the Senate lobbying committee from seizing Strawn telegrams on the grounds that its blanket subpoena was too broad and violated the Constitution.

Just as the Black committee was losing this round in court, another legal fight surfaced, but the litigant in this case, William Randolph Hearst, actually proved to be a blessing to the committee. Hearst, claiming that the constitutional guarantee of freedom of the press was being infringed, sought an injunction to block the committee's

Sherman Minton (second from the right) on a hunting trip to Pennsylvania in 1937; Vice President John Nance Garner (third from the right) and Harry S. Truman (far left) were part of the group.

access to telegrams exchanged between Hearst and his editorial employees. A lower court judge dismissed the suit, ruling that the First Amendment was not involved and that he lacked jurisdiction over a Senate committee. The decision was later upheld by a federal appeals court.

The skirmish with Hearst was a godsend, according to Arthur Krock, the noted *New York Times* columnist. He wrote that Black and his committee supporters could "cover their blunders and illegalities" by launching a furious personal assault on Hearst, who was generally unpopular. The campaign "was to be as ruthless with Mr. Hearst as he, in his time, has been with others," Krock said.[5]

Minton gleefully responded to Hearst's lawsuit in a speech to the Senate. He denied that the Black committee was violating anyone's fundamental rights and lashed out at the powerful newspaper magnate. Noting that Hearst raised constitutional questions in his suit, Minton drew laughter with his comment that Hearst "would not know the Goddess of Liberty if she came down off her pedestal in New York Harbor and bowed to him. He would probably try to get her telephone number." Minton called Hearst "the greatest menace to the freedom of the press" in the country because he used his vast media holdings as propaganda outlets for his beliefs rather than "to disseminate the truth to the people."[6]

A few days after this speech Minton resumed his assault on Hearst in the Senate. This time Minton was upset over an editorial titled "A subservient Congress invites dictatorship in America," which had just been published in the Hearst-owned *New York American*. The country was not in danger of a dictatorship by the president, Congress, or the courts, Minton said, but rather the danger was from "a purse-proud, insolent, arrogant, bulldozing newspaper publisher by the name of William Randolph Hearst. That is the kind of dictatorship we need fear in this country today."[7]

Minton, who had an intrinsic need to bash people of wealth and power, particularly relished his fights with the anti–New Deal press lords, believing them to be nothing more than propagandists for the Republican party. By taking on Hearst and other publishers Minton also enhanced his standing with the president. In fact, when Black left the Senate for the Supreme Court in the summer of 1937 the administration worked behind the scenes to install Minton as chairman of the special lobby committee.

One of Minton's first missions as chairman was to pursue opponents of the president's proposal to reorganize the executive branch. The plan, coming in the wake of Roosevelt's attempt to enlarge the Supreme Court and in the rise of European totalitarianism, convinced conservatives in Congress and throughout the country that the president was scheming to erect a Hitler-style dictatorship.

Minton trained his sights on newspaper publisher Frank E. Gannett, who had mobilized his group, the National Committee to Uphold Constitutional Government (NCUCG), to oppose reorganization. The ensuing battle between Minton and Gannett was a bruising one that raged for weeks in the Senate, in the headlines, and over radio airwaves. In the end Roosevelt failed to get his plan through Congress in 1938, although a milder version of reorganization passed the next year.

When Minton's committee attempted to subpoena contributor lists, correspondence, and other documents from Gannett's organization it encountered strong resistance. Dr. Edward A. Rumely, a former New York City newspaper publisher who was a leading figure of NCUCG though he held no official position, was defiant and uncooperative in his appearance before the committee. He refused to produce material on the grounds that the subpoena was merely "the gear for a fishing expedition."[8] Minton then turned the focus to Rumely's past career and associations, hoping to darken the public image of the NCUCG. Rumely had been convicted after World War I for failing to report that the purchase of his newspaper, the *New York Evening Mail*, had been financed by the German government. Rumely noted that he was later granted a pardon by President Calvin Coolidge.[9] After the session Minton said the committee would attempt further action, but would not seek a contempt citation. The subsequent action was mainly a war of words between the principal pugilists—Minton and Gannett—that settled little.

In a radio debate of the reorganization bill Minton departed from his prepared text to warn listeners not to be "mislead by Mr. Gannett as he directs his propaganda machine from his villa in sunny Florida." Minton further stated that Gannett "hasn't any more idea of saving you and your Constitution than the Liberty League had."[10] Gannett, who demanded and received radio airtime to

GARY YOHLER/FREDERICK VOLLRATH, TIFFANY STUDIO, *INDIANAPOLIS TIMES* COLLECTION

Sherman Minton (left) rejoices with James F. Byrnes (center) and Lewis B. Schwellenbach (right) over the passage of the reorganization bill on 28 March 1939.

respond, denounced the lobby committee for "its vicious and unlawful activities." He said the Senate should abolish the committee and its members should be prosecuted because their blanket subpoenas violated constitutional protection against unwarranted search and seizure.[11]

Minton parried with another radio address. He defended the committee's methods as the same type used by other Senate committees to expose such scandals as Teapot Dome, and he shrugged off as intimidation Gannett's call for prosecution of committee members. Minton said Gannett and his organization had a right to "propagandize," but the public and Congress had a right "to know how this propaganda machine is set up, who pays the bill . . . and the kind of misleading propaganda they are using." He said if the opposition succeeds in thwarting Roosevelt, the country "will have a return to the good old days of Harding, Coolidge and Hoover" and a system of government "run on special privilege for the few."[12]

As raucous as his encounters with Hearst and Gannett were, the fiercest period in Minton's relationship with the press was yet to come. Minton was upset because the American Newspaper Publishers Association had just issued a report that warned against the misuse of radio for propaganda purposes, citing Roosevelt's "fireside chats" as a precedent that in future years might encourage dictatorship.[13] Minton, calling the report an exhibition of "unmitigated gall," said, "Of course it is all right to use the newspapers in any way you please, for any purpose you please, especially political purposes. We found that out in the last election. But you dare not use the radio in that manner. That is wrong."[14] Minton claimed that newspapers wanted to curb radio because it "gives the lie to the propaganda that appears in the sheets of this country," and he added that the administration used radio because it "cannot get a story into the 'free press' of this country."[15] On 28 April 1938 Minton introduced a bill that would make it a felony for the press "to publish as fact anything known to be false." Minton's Senate bill ignited like an incendiary throughout the newspaper industry.

The reaction to the Minton proposal was swift and predictable. His old nemesis Gannett commented: "Senator Minton's desire to curb newspapers reveals his intolerance for anything that does not coincide with his own views." Paul Patterson, publisher of the *Baltimore Sun,* retorted: "Senator Minton's statements are indefensible. Fortunately they will mislead only the stupid."[16] The *New York Times,* commenting editorially, wrote that Minton's proposal may seem innocent enough at first glance, but "the intent of his bill is to set up a censorship of the press: a censorship to be imposed by publishers themselves under the threat of heavy Federal penalty."[17] The *Times*, noting that each state in the country already had libel laws that held the press accountable for publishing false statements, declared that there was no justification for the Minton bill.

Minton, who withdrew his proposal shortly after it was introduced, said later he was just trying to "get after" the newspaper publishers association. "I knew a speech wouldn't be enough," Minton said. "I knew I'd have to goad them, knife them a bit, so I just dashed off that little bill. I didn't think it was going to backfire on me the way it did."[18] In a letter to William Allen White, the influential editor and owner of the *Emporia Gazette* in Kansas, Minton wrote that he had no intention of pressing the bill, "but I know enough about newspapers to know that my criticism of them would never have gotten a line if I hadn't hit them where it hurts."[19]

White responded that he was glad to have Minton's explanation. Still, White was concerned that the public was more trusting of radio and thus could be manipulated more readily by its "charming voice." He said people have "built up newspaper resistance" and are able to discount its exaggerations and overstatements, but with radio the public "simply shall have to set up a new defense." He added, "The people themselves will have to teach themselves out of the wisdom of their hearts and after their fingers are burnt."[20]

While he was scorched for the ill-fated libel proposal, Minton was hardly chastened by the experience. He even went before a meeting of the American Press Society, an organization of journalists, in August 1938, to defend the bill. Concerning his motive for introducing the bill, Minton said he "assumed that if the press had set for itself the task of cleaning up the house of radio, it wouldn't mind putting its own house in order." It was an industry in need of reform, Minton asserted, because newspapers had passed from great editors of honesty, principle, and independence such as Horace Greeley, Charles Anderson Dana, Joseph Pulitzer, and the Scripps family into "the hands of men trained in foreign fields of finance and big business." According to Minton, the rise of newspaper chains and monopolistic wire services had ushered in "control and censorship as dangerous and repugnant as those found under dictatorial governments."[21]

Minton also kept the heat on the press through another investigation by his lobby committee. In this instance he turned his attention to *Rural Progress*, a Chicago-based magazine that was distributed free to farmers in seven Midwest states. The publication, which was started in 1934, did not arouse Minton's interest because of any lobbying it had done in opposition to a specific Roosevelt proposal; rather he felt "the general tone of some articles was unjustly critical of the administration" and contained "subtle propaganda."[22] For this reason the magazine's publisher, Maurice V. Reynolds, was subpoenaed to appear before the lobby committee.

At a subsequent hearing Reynolds was pressed about the magazine's financial condition, investors, and the claim that it was distributed free because expenses were covered by advertising. Based on information that *Rural Progress* had lost nearly a million dollars since its founding and its investors included executives of big corporations, Minton and his Democratic colleagues tried to demonstrate that the publication was not a legitimate business venture but instead a propaganda medium subsidized by wealthy businessmen. Sen. Theodore Green of Rhode Island said to Reynolds: "You gave your readers the impression that the advertisers are paying for the magazine, not that these great capitalists were paying for it." Reynolds conceded that advertising revenue had not yet covered all expenses, but he felt the venture eventually would be profitable. He noted that he and his wife and family had put up a sizable sum to meet losses, and the rest had been obtained from others who felt the publication was a sound investment.[23]

What Reynolds revealed in the hearing was less notable than the committee's treatment of Dr. Glenn Frank, editor of *Rural Progress*. When Reynolds was unable to answer questions about editorial policies, Frank, who was chairman of the Republican program committee and a former president of the University of Wisconsin, volunteered to respond, but was shouted down each time he tried to speak. "This committee doesn't intend to permit you to use this as a forum to air your Republican views," Schwellenbach of Washington said. In a statement after the hearing adjourned Frank charged that Minton's committee was part of a "carefully laid campaign of terror and intimidation against the newspapers and magazines of this country which dare to criticize or even to discuss objectively the policies and activities of the New Deal."[24] In a later nationwide radio address over NBC, Frank further lambasted Minton and the committee, saying the Indiana senator "seems incredibly hazy on the American Bill of Rights." He said Minton apparently was determined "to browbeat the press and citizens of the nation into as near universal submission to his philosophy as he can."[25]

Despite such criticism Minton again was unrepentant and even tried one more maneuver in his war with the press. He sought a supplemental appropriation from the Senate for an investigation by the lobby committee to determine the accuracy of news in the nation's press. He proposed employing a journalist to analyze stories in both anti–New Deal and pro–New Deal papers, looking for bias and inaccuracies. The Senate, however, was unwilling to open such a Pandora's box, and Minton was forced to withdraw the measure when Nebraska Democrat Edward R. Burke threatened a filibuster. After this defeat Minton relinquished the chair's position to his close friend Schwellenbach and left the lobby committee.

For four years Minton used his position on the committee to bludgeon New Deal critics. This helped him immeasurably in his relationship with the administration, gaining him access to the White House inner circle and propelling him to a leadership position in the Senate. In the process, though, he had made powerful enemies in the press and the public who understandably questioned his fidelity to constitutional guarantees of privacy and of the freedom of speech and of the press.

Minton's fidelity to the New Deal, however, was absolute, and a recalcitrant United States Supreme Court gave him another opportunity to demonstrate it. In his first major speech in the Senate Minton lashed out at the six to three vote of the Court that declared the Agricultural Adjustment Act (AAA) unconstitutional, saying there is "nothing sacrosanct about the opinions of the Court."[26] Minton called the Court's action, which invalidated the government's attempt to raise farm prices by limiting production, "the most strained, forced construction of the Constitution, and the most highly flavored political opinion to come from that Court since the Dred Scott decision." Minton said the majority broke a fundamental rule in declaring AAA unconstitutional. He explained, "I have always understood that when the Supreme Court was considering the constitutionality of statutes, even a State statute, that the A B C's of such construction were that if an act is subject to two constructions, one of which renders the act unconstitutional and the other constitutional, the latter must be adopted."[27]

Minton said the Court could have ruled AAA constitutional if it had viewed the law as an exercise of congressional power granted in the Constitution to tax and spend for the general welfare of the country. Instead, he said, the majority took the position that Congress used its taxing power to compel regulation in an area reserved to the states, wrongly basing its decision on the *Second Child Labor* case. The tax in *Second Child Labor* differed because it was designed to enforce regulation, but the levy in AAA did not coerce the taxpayer into complying with any regulation. In a letter to Indiana University law professor Hugh E. Willis that discussed this point, Minton wrote: "If one of your Freshman Law students couldn't distinguish between that case [*Second Child Labor*] and the present case, I am sure you would flunk him. Just as Judge [Harlan Fiske] Stone pointed it out in his dissenting opinion, it seems to me that even a Supreme Court Justice could see it."[28]

In his reply Willis agreed with Minton's position "on what was the real holding in this decision, and also as to your criticism of the majority opinion." In words that must have warmed every populist fiber of Minton's being, Willis wrote that the result of recent decisions by the Supreme Court "will be to protect the capitalistic system against social control either by the states or by the federal government," adding that when economic matters are national in scope, such social control should be by the federal government. However, Willis said, the Court has refused "to stretch the Constitution to meet the present emergency as Justice Marshall and other Justices have done in the past."[29]

Minton, expressing a similar concern in his Senate speech, graphically called attention to the danger posed by the aging members of the Court: "The blight of the cold, dead hand of the Court must not be permitted to contaminate the blood stream of the Nation and destroy the right of the people to live and prosper."[30]

The next ruling of the Supreme Court on New Deal legislation was more to Minton's liking. In February the Court, by an eight to one vote, upheld the right of the Tennessee Valley Authority (TVA) to sell surplus power from its Wilson Dam at Muscle Shoals, Alabama, to a private utility, the Alabama Power Company. Minton was asked to explain the Court's decision on a NBC radio program, a recognition of both the senator's knowledge of the Court and his speaking ability. He delivered a fact-filled account of the development of TVA, a chronology of the lawsuit, and the particulars of the decision. Minton, naturally, could not resist tweaking the Court's lone dissenter in the case, Justice James C. McReynolds, or Roosevelt's critics who had labeled the TVA as socialistic or communistic. Of McReynolds's concern that Congress, "under the pretense of exercising granted power," may have had a broader goal in mind when it created TVA, Minton said, "He [McReynolds] finds fault with the honesty of Congress' purposes. This is hardly the function of a judge."[31] To those listeners concerned that the TVA was un-American, Minton said: "Let me assure you that if you have been reading Liberty League propaganda and have been looking in the closet and under the bed every night, expecting to find a Socialist or Communist with a red flag in one hand and a cheese knife in the other, to be lurking there, you may now rest your weary head upon your pillow in peace, for the Supreme Court assures you the T.V.A. is constitutional and American."[32]

In a letter complimenting Minton on the speech David E. Lilienthal, a director of TVA, said he thought it "will have a wide influence in giving the public the facts about a project which is the subject of much misrepresentation."[33]

Despite the favorable verdict in the TVA case Roosevelt's record for New Deal initiatives brought before the Supreme Court in early 1935 was anemic. In rapid succession the Court demonstrated its narrow interpretation of the national government's power over the economy by striking down, in addition to AAA, the National Industrial Recovery Act, the Frazier-Lemke Farm Relief Act, and the Railroad Pension Act. The Court also limited the president's authority to remove members of independent regulatory commissions. Besides TVA the administration had prevailed in only the "Gold Cases," which upheld the New Deal's monetary policies. Later in 1936, however, the Court overturned the Guffey-Snyder Bituminous Coal Act, which brought the coal industry under federal regulation, and the New York Women's Minimum Wage Law. Adding to the administration's worries was the fact that both the National Labor Relations and Social Security Acts were coming up for review by the Court in 1937.

Minton, in assessing what the Court had already wrought, proposed a measure that would require a majority of seven justices, instead of five, to declare an act of Congress unconstitutional. Unveiling his plan in a speech before the Federal Bar Association, an organization of attorneys employed by the federal government, Minton said, "Such regulation by Congress is logical and consistent with the mechanics of checks and balances and the philosophy upon which our form of Government is constructed."[34] He asked, "Is it wise to place in the hands of five of nine men that constitute the Court, the absolute power to veto an act of Congress?" Saying he did not question the Court's power to rule on the constitutionality of legislation, Minton nevertheless questioned the wisdom of it being done by a simple majority. Minton noted, "It is quite evident that we are not a Government by majority," and that "more than a majority of Congress" is required for such actions as the override of a presidential veto, impeachment, and treaty ratification. Minton said it was also evident that Congress had the power to change this "mere rule of practice" of the Supreme Court. "Granting the power of the Court to hold Acts of Congress unconstitutional, there seems to be no doubt but what Congress may prescribe the practice in such cases by proper regulation," he said.[35]

Before Minton had the opportunity to introduce his bill he was preempted on 5 February 1937 by Roosevelt's infamous Court-packing plan. On that day Minton was prepared to offer his proposal in the Senate, but after the president's bombshell he threw the bill and its accompanying speech in the wastebasket and, ever faithful, stated his unqualified support for the administration's plan.[36]

Roosevelt's proposal was startling, not just because of the content, but because it came with almost no warning. The president had played his cards close to the vest, not even mentioning the Court during his reelection campaign in 1936. Furthermore, when Minton, after a meeting with Roosevelt at the White House in mid-January, announced that the president would convene a conference to discuss ways of limiting the power of the Supreme Court, he was quickly repudiated. Stephen Early, assistant secretary to the president, denied that Roosevelt was planning such a conference. In Early's version Minton had called on Roosevelt to seek endorsement of his own Court proposal, but none was given. Early also said that the president told Minton that the attorney general's office was studying the relationship of Congress and the Supreme Court and Minton would be invited back when the studies were finished to discuss the findings with the president and Attorney General Homer Cummings.[37]

Actually, Roosevelt, in the afterglow of his resounding 1936 reelection, immediately gave Cummings his marching orders to come up with a plan to deal with the obstructionist Supreme Court. The centerpiece of Cummings's proposal was laden with sweet irony. In searching for an inclusive principle that would shroud Roosevelt's scheme to subjugate the Court, Cummings hit upon the notion of a judge's age. In 1913 Attorney General McReynolds, now the leader of the Court's conservatives who had a perfect score of ruling against every New Deal measure, proposed that when any federal judge, except Supreme Court justices, stayed on the bench past retirement age, the president could appoint another judge. Cummings, extending this plan to the Supreme Court, calculated that by putting the retirement age at seventy, Roosevelt could appoint six additional justices. Thus was born the Court-packing plan, which Roosevelt tried to conceal by making it part of an omnibus measure to reform the federal judiciary. He fooled very few. Opponents in Congress had little trouble in revealing that what the president really wanted was a Court more amenable to the New Deal.[38]

That the proposal would lead to disaster was hardly evident when Roosevelt announced it in early 1937. Smooth sailing should have been possible in Congress because the 1936 election had reduced the number of Republicans to 89 in the House compared with 331 Democrats and to 16 in the Senate compared with 76 Democrats. Furthermore, initial congressional reaction was mostly positive, but there were strains of discord, most significantly from Hatton Sumners, chairman of the House Judiciary Committee. Upon learning of the proposal he said, "Boys, here's where I cash in my chips."[39] Because of his opposition, the White House decided that the Senate should take up the plan before the House. There were critics in the upper chamber as well, including usually reliable Roosevelt men who were upset by his method and duplicity.

Nonetheless, the president did have his so-called New Deal bitterenders in the Senate who included, naturally, Sherman Minton. As debate over the president's Court plan got under way Minton was more committed than ever to the administration, having been named to the newly created position of assistant whip by Senate Majority Leader Joseph T. Robinson at the beginning of the new Congress in 1937. Such an appointment after only two years in the Senate indicated Minton's effectiveness as a New Deal advocate. At age forty-seven he also brought youth and vitality to the aging leadership of Robinson, sixty-four, and Senate Whip J. Hamilton Lewis, seventy-four. Moreover, Lewis was a maverick, occasionally voting against administration proposals.

There would be no worries of Minton defecting, especially on an issue so important to Roosevelt as packing the Court. Indeed, Minton became a key player in pushing the president's plan by making a number of spirited speeches in the Senate—liberally sprinkled with partisan and personal attacks. He later served on a "new council of war" to forge a compromise when the original Court proposal ran into trouble.

Minton's first assignment was to deliver a radio address, explaining the judiciary proposals and seeking public support. Roosevelt considered Minton's speech on the evening of 15 February so vital to the campaign for the bill that he delayed the time for his own speech at the James A. Farley testimonial dinner to clear the air for it.[40]

In his address Minton argued that the nation's economic recovery was being stymied by "five men on the Supreme Court" who have "absolute veto power over the legislative policy of the people's elected Representatives." These five men, he charged, "exercise more power than 435 Congressmen, 96 Senators, and the President, and that in a field where they have no restraint except that imposed by their own conscience." The veto power of the Supreme Court was absolute, Minton claimed, adding that the president's plan to expand its membership was an attempt to restore the balance of government.

Turning to questions raised about the bill, Minton noted that on several occasions Congress "has used its power to increase the size of the Supreme Court to meet the prob-

GARY YOHLER/FREDERICK VOLLRATH, TIFFANY STUDIO, *INDIANAPOLIS TIMES* COLLECTION

Senate leaders elected at the caucus of Senate Democrats on 31 December 1938. Sherman Minton (right) was elected assistant party whip along with Alben W. Barkley (center) as majority leader and J. Hamilton Lewis (left) as party whip.

lems of the day." Concerning the charges that the bill encouraged dictatorship, Minton outlined four checks against this: the president nominated the new justices, but the Senate confirmed them; both the president and senators would have to face the electorate sooner or later; appointed justices had lifetime tenure; and the fourth check "is the honor and integrity of President Roosevelt in whom you and I have confidence." Ridiculing the contention that Roosevelt was trying to "pack the Court," Minton said it was "packed now by appointees of administrations gone and repudiated."

Minton informed his listeners that the problem of powerful and obstinate justices also confronted Jefferson, Jackson, Lincoln, and Theodore Roosevelt "as they sought to serve the masses of the common people and found their purpose thwarted by the opinions of the court." He added that Franklin Roosevelt "today meets with constitutional power the same challenge, in a courageous effort, not to destroy your Government, but to make it work for the masses of the people."[41]

Minton's highly visible role during the Court bill debate meant he received a heavy volume of correspondence from his constituents back home. Ten boxes of letters, telegrams, proclamations, petitions, and form letters concerning the Court-packing proposal make it clear that the issue unleashed a torrent of reaction from those on both sides.

Reaction, in one case, went to the extreme. Minton received a note wrapped around a shotgun shell that read: "Dont mistake. I am educated. If you support Roosevelt's Court Bill we will get you—you dirty rubber stamp."[42] Minton dismissed the threat as he did opposition to the Court plan in general. At one point he facetiously remarked that he had adverse correspondence analyzed and found that "99.9 percent of them came from rock-ribbed, hard-working Republicans."[43] Conversely, his Democratic colleague from Indiana, Frederick Van Nuys, a member of the Senate Judiciary Committee, reported that his opposition to the president's plan received solid support from rank-and-file Democrats.[44]

That same contention was echoed by Fort Wayne businessman F. E. Hoffman who wrote Minton that "a very considerable number of the people who voted Democratic last fall are not only opposed to this proposition but are horrified by the very idea of it." Hoffman added, "My own personal allegiance has been until recently entirely with the Democratic party, but you can't expect support in an effort to subject our Courts to the same kind of control that Congress has pretty well yielded to."[45]

Minton responded that the bill "doesn't destroy or weaken in the least the power of the Court," claiming that the only effect "will be to bring about a change in the present personnel of the Court, or the power now wielded by the four extremely conservative members." Minton added: "I realize that this is a controversial matter and that thoughtful people may well disagree. I have given an unusual amount of thought and study to this problem and I am thoroughly convinced that the President was right in his suggestion, and that whether it passes or not, he has rendered a genuine service to the country in focusing our attention upon the Court."[46]

Dorothea Garber of Indianapolis wrote Minton that the Court bill had aroused "unprecedented interest . . . even among people not much concerned with politics," adding that "this interest is largely expressed in the form of concern, consternation, hostility and bitter opposition to the President's plan." She said that Roosevelt's reelection "was not a blanket approval of dictatorial methods such as he now proposes."[47]

In his letter of opposition Nathan M. Ely of Terre Haute said the problem in Washington was in Congress, not the Court. "I doubt if any less intelligence can be found in any group of citizens anywhere in these United States, than is to be found in the present Congress."[48] Minton responded that from the tone of Ely's letter it was unlikely that he was open to a rational discussion of the Supreme Court issue. Minton did make a point, however, about the three cents in postage due: "By the way, when you have occasion to write me a long letter, please put enough postage on it to pay its freight, as I am not enamored with paying the excess baggage on such letters."[49]

From letters of support Minton must have been especially heartened by the one from such a credible source as legal scholar Thomas F. Konop, dean of the law school at the University of Notre Dame, who wrote, "I am for the President's proposal, 100%." Konop enclosed a copy of his response to Frank E. Gannett, the newspaper publisher and head of the National Committee to Uphold Constitutional Government, who was seeking signers for a petition opposed to Roosevelt's plan. In his five-page letter Konop said he supported the Court bill because he thought that the "present Supreme Court has been an anchor that has stayed the progress of our Ship of State" by declaring unconstitutional those acts of Congress passed "during a serious economic and industrial depression." He said the Constitution "was not written for a decade or a century"; reasonably and liberally construed it "will adapt itself to our progress."[50]

Another letter of support came from Abram Simmons of Bluffton. Simmons wrote to congratulate Minton on his February radio address, saying, "it has the true ring and the President should be upheld." He added, "You may command me at any time and if I can be of any use to you while the battle is on I will be a willing soldier."[51]

In his first major speech in the Senate on the issue, Minton seized upon the Court's decision in a second minimum wage case as an illustration of the need to enlarge the Court. In late March 1937 the Court upheld by a five to four vote Washington State's minimum wage act, which was substantially similar to the New York legislation that had been ruled unconstitutional the previous June by a five to four margin. In his address Minton said, "Those who have accused President Roosevelt of seeking to amend the Constitution must now admit that the Supreme Court itself has in effect amended the Constitution." He added that "the Constitution on Monday, March 29, 1937, does not mean the same thing that it meant on Monday, June 1, 1936."

He said that unless the Court is enlarged, every new and debatable constitutional issue would come before a Court composed of four justices hostile to adapting the Constitution, four justices favorable to construing it in light of changing conditions, and one justice moving "around we know not where." Minton was referring to Justice Owen J. Roberts, who had switched his position in the Washington State case. Minton, continuing his assault on Roberts, said it was intolerable that the "adaptability of the Constitution and the continuity of legal growth should rest upon the vacillating judgment and human frailty of a single Justice." He added, "I am unwilling that the policy of this country shall be committed to the instability of Mr. Justice Roberts' mind."[52]

Minton resumed his attack in the Senate on Roberts after the Supreme Court upheld the Labor Relations and Social Security Acts with Roberts voting with the majority in both cases. He said that Roberts, in upholding the validity of the Labor Relations Act, reversed his decision in finding the Guffey-Snyder Bituminous Coal Act unconstitutional. Likewise, Roberts did an about-face from his ruling in the AAA case by voting with the majority in the Social Security case. Minton asked, "Why did he do it? You will search the reports in vain; you will find not a word from Mr. Justice Roberts as to why he did it." However, Minton said he knew the reason: "there is no other explanation for this about-face except politics." He said Roberts had been "just listening to the wee small voice of the Chief Justice (Charles Evans Hughes) that was talking politics to him. There is no other explanation for such an unprecedented, unknown about-face on the part of a Justice of the Supreme Court."[53]

Politics or not, the dramatic change in Court opinions, which became known as the "switch in time [that] saved nine," demolished the rationale for Roosevelt's proposition. An additional blow to his plan came in mid-May when Justice Willis Van Devanter, one of the four conservatives on the Court, announced his intention to retire. Still, Roosevelt wanted something passed so he turned to Majority Leader Robinson to fashion a compromise proposal. Robinson, working with his small group of Senate lieutenants that included Minton, devised a modified version that authorized the president to name one justice a year for each member of the Court who was seventy-five years old. Shortly after the Senate began deliberating the compromise, Robinson died of a heart attack and all hopes for the proposal vanished. On 22 July the bill was recommitted to the Judiciary Committee and died.

Two days before this vote Minton wrote to his former law partner Evan Stotsenburg that "I fear the jig is up. It has been a great fight & one I hate to lose." The defeat of the Court proposal was more than just a political setback to Minton. It was a blow to populist ideology. "The forces that we beat at the polls in November mastered us in July," he wrote. "It is the old story of liberalism being unable to sustain itself in power & vigor for long."[54]

While Minton was on the losing side in the Court battle, his stock in Washington rose as a result of his intimate involvement with the issue. He had impressed Joseph Alsop and Turner Catledge, who chronicled the Court-packing saga in their book *The 168 Days*. They wrote that while Minton's political thinking seldom transcended the partisan, it was "honestly liberal and deeply felt. He was one of those rare politicians who really mean most of what they say about the 'common man.'" Alsop and Catledge saw Minton as someone with "agreeable, straightforward manners, an excellent ability to deal with his fellows and a good, shrewd head" who had "commanded the respect of those with whom he worked."[55]

Other journalists who had observed Minton during this legislative tussle likewise were impressed. Thomas L. Stokes, a feature writer with the Scripps-Howard Newspapers Alliance, wrote that Minton "orated and wise-cracked his way to a place among the select few in the Senate who can do a piece of speaking which will hold their colleagues tight to their seats."[56] Minton, according to Mark Thistlethwaite of the *Indianapolis News,* became known as "Minute Man Minton" during deliberations of the Court bill because he was "on constant guard for instant action whenever and wherever needed. He is regarded as a rough-and-tumble, catch-as-catch-can debater well able to tackle any opponent and to take good care of himself under any or all circumstances."[57]

Drew Pearson and Robert S. Allen, in their syndicated newspaper column "Washington Merry-Go-Round," wrote that Minton and Lewis Schwellenbach "emerged as strong men" out of the confusion that struck the Senate with the sudden death of Majority Leader Robinson. "A great deal is going to be heard of them in the future," they wrote. "Their unyielding attitude made a tremendous impression on the President, and in his councils of war he brushed aside other party chieftains and turned to the two freshmen."[58]

As further evidence of Minton's rising stature, he was Roosevelt's guest during a weekend cruise on Chesapeake Bay shortly after the defeat of the Court plan. "The weekend trip with Roosevelt stamps the junior Indiana Senator as an outstanding liberal in the Roosevelt tradition," wrote Daniel M. Kidney of the *Indianapolis Times*.[59]

Despite his inescapable image as a Roosevelt man, Minton did oppose the administration on occasion. In 1936 he voted to override the president's veto of the $2.5 billion bonus payment to World War I veterans, and he demonstrated his independence on other issues as well, most notably in his vigorous support of a federal antilynching bill and his opposition to extending the Hatch Act to state government employees.

While Roosevelt denounced lynching and was willing to permit a vote on an antilynching bill, he refused to make it "must legislation" out of concern that southern committee chairmen might impede his economic proposals. Without Roosevelt's backing supporters of antilynching legislation were unable to break a filibuster by southern Democrats.[60] Minton, addressing the Senate on 15 February 1938, responded to claims by opponents that since the number of lynchings was decreasing yearly there was no need for the legislation. Conceding that the numbers were lower, Minton added, "while there were eight lynchings in the United States last year, there was not a single prosecution. In other words, there was 100 percent failure to prosecute for the most heinous crime." In defending the bill against attacks on its constitutionality, Minton argued that when the Fourteenth Amendment "throws its cloak around all persons against a denial by the State of due process of law, and affords equal protection of the laws, it throws it around all persons," adding, "I am interested in State rights; but I am much more interested in human rights."[61]

Minton was indeed interested in defending states' rights in early 1940 when the Senate began debating an extension of the Hatch Act to state workers paid in whole or in part with federal money. The first Hatch Act, passed the year before, not only prohibited federal employees from active involvement in elections, but it also protected them from pressures to support certain candidates or to make campaign contributions. Minton, who had unsuccessfully battled the original legislation, likewise opposed the second Hatch bill. His concern was both pragmatic and philosophical. The practical impact of the proposed legislation was clear. The Democratic party in Indiana was still in control of the machinery of state government and had the most to lose if the bill passed. It was estimated that

PHOTOGRAPH BY HARRIS & EWING, COLLECTION OF THE SUPREME COURT OF THE UNITED STATES

Sherman Minton (right) with good friend Sen. Carl A. Hatch, Democrat of New Mexico, on 7 March 1940 after passage of the Hatch Act, which Minton opposed.

state employees contributed about ten thousand dollars monthly to the Hoosier Democratic Club, or Two Percent Club. The second Hatch Act would reduce the total by about three to four thousand dollars.[62]

In deliberations of both Hatch bills Minton favored those provisions that shielded workers from any forced participation, but he objected to provisions prohibiting people from voluntarily participating in politics. "The curse of democracy is that you cannot get citizens interested enough in politics to get out to the polls and vote," Minton said in a Senate debate. "And here we are outlawing all vigorous political activity."[63]

The prohibition against political activity by state workers also invaded states' rights through indirect federal regulation of state elections, curtailed the freedom of speech of affected employees, and generally punished the "little fellow" while letting the "fat cats" off scot-free, Minton felt. He charged that the second Hatch Act might be effective in destroying patronage organizations, such as Indiana's Two Percent Club, "but that doesn't mean purity, or the end of organizations in politics. It only means another kind of organization will grow up in its place." The new organizations will be "of paid workers, paid by the Party that's got the money to pay, and that Party will have the money that is controlled by the 'money-bags' of this country." Minton's remarks left little doubt that he was singling out the Republican party. Minton believed the bill's enactment, rather than cleansing politics, would stain the system with the power of money. "There is the menace," he claimed. "Money is the most pernicious, corrupting influence in politics, and the Hatch Bill fosters the building of political organizations with money."[64]

Patronage organizations, such as the one operated by Hoosier Democrats, were just as pure as the alternatives, according to Minton. In a Senate speech he said that Hatch "is shooting at the two-bit fellows out on the highway with a sickle in their hands cutting the weeds, and letting Joe Pew and the Du Ponts and the Annenbergs and the Ernest Weirs and all of the big-boodle boys get away."[65]

In opposing the bill Minton, the loyal Democrat, was aligned against two men to whom he would normally defer: Roosevelt and Majority Leader Alben W. Barkley of Kentucky. For practical political reasons Roosevelt and Barkley supported the second Hatch Act. Roosevelt, keeping his options open for a possible run at an unprecedented third term in 1940, did not want to be branded as a foe of election reform. By his support Barkley was seeking redemption, after being sullied with the charge that he misused the WPA in Kentucky during his reelection campaign in 1938. Minton's opposition to the legislation also put him at odds with Carl A. Hatch of New Mexico, the bill's sponsor and one of Minton's closest friends.

Minton, however, was not one to stray for long from the Roosevelt fold or to let ideological disputes interfere with personal relationships. After passage of the second Hatch Act, Minton proclaimed that he and Barkley would again be shoulder-to-shoulder fighting for the New Deal, adding, "There will not be any split in the Democratic ranks simply because we happen to disagree a little about this particular bill."[66] Similarly, Minton and Hatch, though tenacious opponents in debate over the legislation, continued to be the best of friends. A few weeks after the dust had settled, Minton directed a good-natured dig at his former adversary. When Minton was leaving the Senate chamber to greet United States Attorney Val Nolan of Indianapolis, who was visiting Washington, he said to Robert LaFollette: "You hold Senator Carl Hatch here, because I am going out and talk to my District Attorney and he might think that I am violating his law."[67]

Although not normally one for circumspection, Minton did tread carefully when confronted with the highly charged issue of war and peace. He understood that as a representative of isolationist Indiana he had to walk softly and carry a small stick. Minton supported Roosevelt's cautious steps, believing, as did the president, that it was possible for America to remain out of harm's way while Hitler gobbled up Europe and Japan warred in Asia. When it became apparent that the flames of aggression might spread across the Atlantic and Pacific, Minton advocated preparedness at home, but not intervention abroad.

As the situation in Europe grew grimmer almost daily in the fall of 1939, Roosevelt wanted to aid the Allies without making it appear that the United States was edging closer to direct involvement in the war. He sought changes in the Neutrality Act that extended the "cash and carry" principle to arms and munitions. The measure, which Congress eventually passed, was obviously intended to benefit the Allies since Britain still controlled the seas. Minton, in a radio debate with Sen. Gerald P. Nye of North Dakota, a leading isolationist, on 30 September 1939 argued that the proposal's enactment would neither plunge the country into war nor help one side over the other. "I venture to say the sale of munitions never got any nation into war," Minton claimed, adding, "We are at peace and we intend to stay out of war unless we are directly attacked." Furthermore, he said the bill did not alter the country's neutral position because any nation that "wants to buy munitions or supplies from us . . . can buy if it comes and gets them, pays for them, and takes them away in its own ships." He noted, "We don't want to help Hitler, or Stalin, or Britain or France, neither do we want to prevent either of them from helping themselves."[68]

Minton also hewed to the neutrality line when Congress refused to consider a $60 million loan package for Finland after it had been invaded by the Soviet Union. "I don't want to make such a loan either directly or indirectly," he said. "Our whole efforts should be directed to keeping out of Europe's wars."[69]

Throughout 1940, while continuing to maintain that Americans had no business fighting "over there," Minton pleaded for preparedness at home. In a speech to the Young Democrats of Indiana he said, "Prudence dictates but one course—prepare, and do it now. We must face the facts, and the facts are that from henceforth we must be an armed camp. We have no other alternative."[70] In a Labor Day address Minton warned his audience that the country had "to be strong enough to defend America's shores, even against the hordes of Hitler, the most brutal, evil genius in human history." If Hitler turned his war machine toward the United States, Minton said, "We want to be so strong in our defense preparation that he dare not attack us."

To Minton, preparedness meant having modern weapons and trained soldiers to use them, as well as guarding against internal subversion. There "must be no Fifth

Column in America," declared Minton. "The greatest weapon Hitler has used in the destruction of the countries he has conquered is the weapon of the Fifth Column, made up of unpatriotic, treasonable men and women who betrayed their country." Earlier in the year Minton had voted for the Smith Act, which made it unlawful to teach or advocate the violent overthrow of the government.

In his Labor Day speech Minton also advocated compulsory military service because a volunteer system would be inadequate. He acknowledged that the "military life is repugnant to the American sense of freedom and independence," but he added that "in a world whose life is ruled and dominated by war, and threats of war, we have to accept the ways of war."[71]

To Minton the issue of a draft was cut and dried. He frequently invoked personal references to underscore his strongly held belief that those able to serve in the defense of their country should do so. In his speech to the Young Democrats Minton assured his audience that "the last thing in the world I'd want to do would be to vote to send your boy, or mine, to war." But if it came to that, "I would be ashamed of my sons if they turned their back upon the flag my grandfather died for, and I offered my life for in 1917."[72]

Perhaps Minton's most heated exchange with a fellow senator came during debate over the Burke-Wadsworth Compulsory Selective Service bill, which ushered in America's first peacetime draft after it was passed in September 1940. When Rush D. Holt of West Virginia spoke out against compulsory military service Minton launched a vituperative personal attack on Holt, charging that he was from a "slacker family." "When I was over in France in 1917 and 1918 the father of the Senator from West Virginia was preaching that people should not raise any food to send to me and my comrades who were fighting for this country," Minton charged. "The father of the Senator from West Virginia sent his son, who was eligible for service, to hide away in South America to avoid the draft."

Holt acknowledged that although his father opposed America's entry into World War I, he enlisted in the Civil War when he was thirteen. He added that his brother did not evade the draft but served as a noncombatant, building military camps. "If ever the Administration wants filth thrown, they get the Senator from Indiana to throw it," Holt charged.

"And when Hitler wants it thrown you throw it," Minton shot back.[73]

The two men continued their dispute the next day with equal furor, leading the chairman of the Senate Rules Committee, Matthew M. Neely, to remark that the dignity of the Senate had been reduced "to the level of a barroom."

Holt was asked by Sen. Josh Lee of Oklahoma to withdraw the statement he made the previous day that "Senator Minton is not in fit shape to be on the floor," implying he was intoxicated. Lee said, "I went over and had the Senator from Indiana blow in my face. There was not one scintilla of liquor on the Senator's breath. I never saw the Senator intoxicated and never saw him take a drink." Holt responded that he was "glad the Senator from Oklahoma has become an expert on halitosis."

Minton repeated his charge that Holt came from a "slacker family," but later softened his remarks, saying, "I have no doubt the Senator's father was a great man. My sole purpose yesterday was to point out his doctrine and teachings. It takes a brave man to stand up and express a minority viewpoint."[74]

Minton's relationship with Holt, best characterized as mutual animosity, was an aberration. Minton's no-holds-barred approach to legislative battles almost never left permanent scars on his relationships with his Senate colleagues. A survey conducted by Fort Wayne publisher, and Minton loyalist, William A. Kunkel, Jr., demonstrated that Minton had the ability to maintain cordiality with both his Democratic and Republican opponents. After reading a statement in a newspaper column of 24 April

1939 by Joseph Alsop and Robert Kintner that Minton "is actively disliked by most of his other colleagues," Kunkel wrote to the senators for their reaction to the claim.

Of the sixty-six senators who responded, nearly all rejected the columnists' observation about Minton. Even after discounting the rule of the Club that no senator should speak ill of a colleague, the letters to Kunkel are persuasive evidence that Minton was highly regarded. Many senators noted that Minton had just been unanimously elected majority whip in the Senate. According to Robert F. Wagner of New York, it "was an exceptional tribute to Sen. Minton because as a rule that office goes only to a senator having many more years of service in the senate." Others responding to Kunkel took the opportunity to impugn the columnists. Lynn J. Frazier, Republican of North Dakota, labeling the comment about Minton "a slurring statement," said, "some of these so-called columnists do not seem to be particular about the truth of the statements they make." Several senators noted that Minton's hard-hitting debating style might be misinterpreted. Anti-New Deal Democrat Guy M. Gillette of Iowa said that Minton's statements do not always contain the "suavity or tactful choice of words that many of his colleagues use in debate." Nevertheless, he wrote that Minton "has the affection of a large majority of his colleagues."[75]

While Minton was gratified by this impressive display of respect from fellow senators he realized that the endorsement of Hoosier voters in the fall of 1940 was the only test that really mattered, and he was prepared for the worst. Writing a letter of condolence to William G. McAdoo, an incumbent Democrat senator from California who had been defeated for renomination in 1938, Minton prophesied: "When the citizens of Indiana get around to it, I have a feeling that I'll be looking for work in 1941."[76]

CHAPTER FIVE

The Tide Is Running Out

It was somewhat surprising that Sherman Minton worried about losing the job he had worked so long and so hard to attain. As a freshman senator he had achieved an unusual degree of prominence and power, but that achievement was a double-edged blessing. His aggressive and dogged advocacy of the New Deal and most other items on Franklin D. Roosevelt's agenda brought him to the attention of the president, who helped advance his career. Roosevelt tapped Minton as a key strategist, often inviting him to the White House for policy discussions and using him to make radio speeches for the administration. Minton's standing with the White House and his popularity with Democratic colleagues in the Senate, in turn, helped him win election in the spring of 1939 as majority whip, the second-in-command position that normally went to a senior legislator. His increased clout in Washington often translated to benefits for his constituents. In January 1937, for example, when Hoosier communities along the Ohio River, including Minton's hometown of New Albany, were devastated by flooding, he used his access to the White House to expedite the release of federal money for disaster relief and for flood control projects in southern Indiana.

What gained him influence and notoriety, however, also contributed to his downfall. His close—some said blind—allegiance to Roosevelt branded him a "rubber stamp." Even more damaging was his caustic and volatile way of reacting to any threat to the New Deal. His assaults on critical news coverage were interpreted as attempts to hammer the press into subservience. Likewise, he left the impression that he desired the same obedience from the Supreme Court when he assumed a leading role in pushing the president's attempt to pack the Court with sympathetic justices.

In addition to the problems Minton created for himself by being identified as someone who was opposed to a free press and an independent judiciary, his precarious prospects in 1940 also stemmed from developments and conditions over which he had little or no control. Certainly, he could not manage the vicissitudes of international events, and the difficulties on the home front were just as intractable. The twin pillars of Minton's political potency—the New Deal and the "McNutt Machine"—were teetering.

The onset of the New Deal had improved conditions in Indiana, but there were still the lingering problems of low farm prices, high local taxes to pay for relief programs, and increased business regulations, arousing in Hoosiers their inherent conservatism. Discontent with the national government grew when the economy convulsed during the so-called Roosevelt Recession that began in the fall of 1937 and continued well into 1938.

The well-oiled Indiana Democratic political apparatus was sputtering. Enmity grew between the state party's disparate factions, and the Two Percent Club and Paul V. McNutt came under investigation for federal income tax evasion. Minton's reelection bid also came at a time when McNutt and Roosevelt, his two chief political patrons, vied for the 1940 Democratic presidential nomination.

Although he knew he was in trouble, there was little Minton could do. After such steadfast support of the New

Deal it was not possible for him to do an about-face even if he wanted to. It was a matter of staying the course and damn the consequences. Minton, summarizing his predicament in a letter to Fort Wayne newspaper publisher William A. Kunkel, Jr., wrote, "We go with the New Deal tide and cannot go against it. If the tide is running out, we go out—if the tide is running in, we go in."[1]

The tide *had* turned on Indiana's Democratic party, but Minton was no more likely to repudiate it than he would the New Deal. The years of infighting, largely over patronage matters, had weakened the party, and in early 1940 it was revealed that the Bureau of Internal Revenue, the forerunner of the Internal Revenue Service, was investigating the Two Percent Club and several prominent Hoosier Democrats for possible income tax evasion. The prolonged inquiry, which received considerable press coverage throughout much of the year, hampered McNutt's presidential campaign and caused his supporters to charge that he was the victim of dirty politics. The tax issue was resolved in early May 1940, although details of the settlement were not released publicly. The Treasury Department received a payment of $84,000 from Bowman Elder, who for several years had been treasurer of the Two Percent Club, that settled the organization's tax delinquencies.[2]

Minton was not a target of the federal investigation, but the scandal involving the Two Percent Club could not have come at a worse time for him since it coincided with congressional action on the Hatch Act, commonly referred to as a clean politics bill. In opposing the Hatch Act, Minton made spirited defenses of the state party's patronage system, proudly calling himself a product of the Two Percent Club. While that might not have been the most politically prudent thing to say, it was right on the mark.

During his term in the Senate Minton was a wheelhorse for the McNutt machine, devoting considerable time and energy to insuring that his political benefactor maintained primacy in battles over patronage. It was patronage, rather than any ideological differences, that splintered Democrats into factions: the McNutt wing, composed of younger members who had used the American Legion as a springboard to power; the Taggart Democrats, to which Sen. Frederick Van Nuys belonged; and those Democrats loyal to former state chairman R. Earl Peters.

Minton's close association with McNutt, whose wishes generally prevailed, gave Minton the upper hand when he challenged the other factions over federal patronage. It was an advantage he promptly pressed. In mid-1935, for example, a Senate committee rejected George W. Carrier, who had been selected by Van Nuys and Tenth District congressman Finly H. Gray, for postmaster of New Castle after Minton objected. Carrier's transgression was his opposition to Minton's senatorial nomination at the state convention in 1934. A new candidate was found and confirmed. Commenting on the episode, an observer remarked that the triumph of Minton and the McNutt organization "has aroused Indiana Congressmen, who heretofore have had full say in the selection of postmasters in their district."[3]

Later, Minton sought the blessings of national party chairman James A. Farley, who was also postmaster general, on a plan that would insure dominance for the McNutt organization in divvying up jobs. Minton suggested that all federal appointments be coordinated with the Democratic State Central Committee, which was controlled by McNutt. Minton complained that "the Home Owners Loan Corporation, dominated by Senator Van Nuys patronage exclusively, and Federal Housing Administration set-up by Earl Peters, are not friendly to the State organization. It is very unfortunate that we should have these rifts due to Federal set-ups."[4] Van Nuys and most of the Indiana congressional delegation understandably were opposed to this arrangement, and Farley, who distrusted and detested McNutt anyway, did not push the issue. As a result, the competition over patronage continued.

In his efforts to insure that McNutt Democrats received jobs and other governmental bounties, Minton worked closely with two of the most energetic power brokers in Indiana: Pleas E. Greenlee, the governor's patronage chief and the person who had played a major role in advancing Minton's political career, and Hugh A. Barnhart, the state excise administrator and chairman of the Alcoholic Beverage Commission (ABC).

Minton and Greenlee wasted little time in forming their patronage team. Less than a month after Minton became senator, his assistant, James C. Penman, wrote Greenlee to recommend how the system should work between Washington and Indianapolis. Penman suggested that job seekers "fill out their applications and have them properly indorsed and clear[ed] thru State Hqs., and you furnish us with a preferred list."[5] Greenlee, who had no trouble in compiling such a list, responded to Minton: "We can furnish anything from a hack driver to a federal judge."[6]

In a letter asking Minton to help settle a dispute over a post office appointment, Greenlee provided another glimpse into the workings of patronage. Greenlee argued that the selection of his candidate, a Democratic county vice-chairwoman, would be "in keeping with our policy," which meant that "the county chairman should have first say and then the vice-chairwoman when any jobs were to be given out and so on down thru the precinct."[7] A contested postal job at the Indiana State Soldiers' Home in Lafayette prompted another letter to Minton. Noting that one candidate was the mother of a Republican county chairman, Greenlee said, "there would be one hell of a blow-up if there were a slip-up and she were appointed."[8]

Having Republicans in jobs that Democrats could just as easily fill outraged Minton and Greenlee. In writing Minton about one such situation, Greenlee complained: "It seems a damn shame for a good fellow like that to be working for $1800.00 a year when you have four Republican

Deputy Internal Revenue Collectors on the job and the assistant, . . . another Republican, still hanging on and drawing $4600.00. Let's do some business with these fellows and put some Democrats in there."[9]

The jobs the two men tried to fill with deserving Democrats varied widely in importance and pay. Minton wrote Greenlee seeking help for a candidate who had lost his race for judge. "I am writing you with the hope that you can find something in the State's set-up where he wants to be, that will please him."[10] Greenlee wanted Minton to find "any kind of job" for the son of a party official who was planning to attend college in Washington. Greenlee also asked Minton "to find a job or two for some of our good Democratic colored voters." He added that "some of the states are getting some appointments for the colored people and I think if you could get us a job or two that it would put you ace high with these folks."[11]

Likewise, Minton and ABC Chairman Barnhart concerned themselves with jobs of varying stature. Barnhart wrote Minton in behalf of a substitute mail carrier in the Valparaiso post office who wanted to fill one of the vacancies of rural route carrier.[12] On another occasion Barnhart wrote Minton about an attorney with the Reconstruction Finance Corporation (RFC) in Chicago who was being laid off. Barnhart, noting that the man "comes from an old Democratic family," complained that the RFC legal department "is still well filled up with Herbert Hoover men and that these men remain while the Democrats are being turned out and dropped by the wayside. Investigation will prove this, and it is something that should be given immediate attention."[13]

Another Minton-Barnhart exchange concerned a disgruntled ABC employee who wrote Minton to gripe about not getting a pay raise. Barnhart explained that the employee, although capable, "seems to be of such disposition that she cannot get along with her fellow workers in a congenial manner." When the woman discovered that others had been given an increase and she had not, "she created quite a scene and the disturbance was general for some time," Barnhart reported. He told Minton that he had talked to the worker to assure her that her job was not in jeopardy and he put her under his supervision "in hopes that this may help a troublesome situation." Barnhart added, "I have gone at length to explain this to you, Shay, because I know you are concerned and also because you may hear from Marie again due to these salary changes."[14]

When the ABC was considering revoking the license of a salesman for a New Albany distributor, Minton interceded on the man's behalf. In a letter to Barnhart he said, "If this is a case of minor infraction, as it is represented to me, I hope you'll be good enough to give this case careful consideration, with a view to reinstating him."[15]

The Minton-Barnhart correspondence also was concerned with the need to keep loyal Democrats in control of the alcohol trade in Indiana. Barnhart frequently sought Minton's advice on matters before the ABC, especially if they concerned southern Indiana. On one occasion Barnhart sent Minton a telegram asking for his opinion of an applicant for a wholesaler's permit. Responding to the inquiry Minton said, "The party you inquired about would not do at all." He explained that the applicant's relatives were professional gamblers and one had even served prison time for murder. "They are racketeers at heart and would operate the business with that kind of an approach," Minton wrote. "It would be a sad mistake to license them and I sincerely hope you will not do so."[16]

Although Minton and Van Nuys represented different political factions and, thus, were never close, Minton received help from his senior colleague shortly after taking office. Van Nuys acceded to Minton's wishes by supporting Clarence E. Manion, a Notre Dame law professor whose withdrawal from the senatorial race at the 1934 convention cleared the way for Minton, as Indiana's representative to the National Emergency Council. Further agreement between the two on appointments, patronage, and other issues was rare. Writing to Greenlee to report on progress in job placements, Minton noted that one of their candidates had lost out to Van Nuys's choice for the job. "There was nothing for me to do but go along and keep peace in the family," Minton said.[17]

If the acquiescence by Minton in this instance brought peace to the Hoosier Democratic family, it was only temporary. A lasting peace eluded the party throughout the 1930s, although there were truces from time to time. One was arranged after Minton and Van Nuys differed over the appointment of a United States marshal for the state's southern district. Wayne Coy, head of the Indiana Works Progress Administration (WPA), wrote to Roosevelt suggesting he "could make a contribution to party harmony in Indiana" by asking the senators to withdraw their candidates in favor of a compromise candidate.[18] Not only was the White House able to strike such a deal over this particular appointment, but it also forged a long-term arrangement that gave each senator control over patronage along geographical divisions. Essentially, Minton ruled the southern half of the state and Van Nuys the northern.

But just as one battle was resolved, fighting broke out on another front. This time the fracture came within the McNutt ranks when Greenlee, who long had harbored ambitions to be governor, "impertinently informed McNutt" at a meeting in late 1935 that he would seek the office and that he expected McNutt's support.[19] A few days after this encounter McNutt ousted Greenlee from his position as head of state patronage; McNutt's candidate for governor would be his lieutenant governor, M. Clifford Townsend. Van Nuys, not to be outmaneuvered, weighed in with his own gubernatorial entry, E. Kirk McKinney, head of the Home Owners Loan Corporation in Indiana, a major source of patronage for Van Nuys.

Faced with the difficult choice of opposing McNutt, Minton, nevertheless, supported Greenlee, although apparently he had some doubts that his candidate, who had not completed grade school, was qualified to be governor. Expressing his concerns in a letter to retired Indiana University history professor, Dr. James A. Woodburn, Minton conceded that Greenlee "hasn't as much background as I would like to see in my candidate for Governor." Nevertheless, Minton added that "he has an uncommon amount of common sense, and is thoroughly honest and forthright in all he thinks and does."[20]

Minton campaigned for Greenlee, albeit not as vigorously as he might have. For example, when he delivered a speech in Greenlee's hometown of Shelbyville on 14 February 1936 Minton used the occasion to praise McNutt and Roosevelt and never even mentioned Greenlee's name. In fact, in a remark that must have made Greenlee uneasy, Minton said that "no man can have or deserve to have the Democratic nomination for governor of Indiana who does not wholeheartedly endorse the splendid administration of Governor McNutt."[21]

At the state convention that summer Minton placed Greenlee's name in nomination, but he must have known it was a futile gesture. With the McNutt organization strongly behind him, Townsend was easily nominated. Townsend and the Democratic candidate for lieutenant governor, Henry F. Schricker, were elected in November.

With Minton's backing Greenlee was appointed a member of the Bituminous Coal Commission, the federal regulatory agency, in the spring of 1937. Two years later Minton tried to have Greenlee appointed Internal Revenue collector for Indiana. This entreaty was quickly squashed by Treasury Secretary Henry Morgenthau, who learned that Greenlee had failed to report income from a beer business on his federal tax returns. This matter led Morgenthau to launch his investigation not only of Greenlee's tax returns but also those of other Hoosier politicians, including McNutt.

Writing to his friend, United States District Attorney Val Nolan in Indianapolis, about the opposition to Greenlee for the Internal Revenue position, Minton said, "I am so distressed about the Collector's job. This patronage racket is hell." Minton wanted Greenlee back in the state mainly for the sake of party harmony. "I thought if Pleas came back to Indiana he would be the contact with the organization for his many friends who feel that they are outside," he wrote Nolan. "They don't feel they have a friend in Court & do not feel free to contact anyone. If Pleas were in there they might be satisfied."[22]

However, the prospect of Democratic unity became more remote as the 1930s drew to a close. In 1937, when his term as governor ended and he became high commissioner of the Philippines, McNutt was still in full control of the party; however, it was a party greatly weakened by internal strife as the friction between McNutt and Van Nuys intensified. Van Nuys charged that employees of Indiana's WPA had been pressured to support Townsend's nomination, a charge refuted by Harry L. Hopkins, national head of the WPA. Hopkins said an investigation revealed that while a number of WPA administrators in Indiana had been "indiscreet" in expressing their political preferences, "there is no evidence from any source to show that any of them exercised, or attempted to exercise, coercion or to improperly influence those working under their direction to vote for or against any candidate."[23]

Not only did the WPA incident exacerbate the McNutt-Van Nuys chasm, it also angered Roosevelt who felt Van Nuys had "unjustly embarrassed the New Deal in order to score points in a state dispute."[24] Van Nuys, who was up for reelection in 1938, irritated the president even further in 1937 when he opposed the Court-packing plan. As a result of his factious behavior, Van Nuys was slated for political extinction when it came time for renomination.

The movement to dump Van Nuys went public on 14 July 1937 when Governor Townsend, after meeting with the president, claimed from the steps of the White House that no "power in the state could nominate him [Van Nuys] and our organization is unaccustomed to trying the impossible. I don't think our organization could nominate him even if it wanted to."[25]

Van Nuys was not without the means to fight back and on 12 July 1938, almost a year to the day after the governor's declaration, he accepted his party's renomination by acclamation at its state convention in Indianapolis. From the beginning the wily Van Nuys had vowed to fight the ouster attempt and even threatened to run as an independent if he was denied his party's nomination. His David-like campaign against the Goliaths Roosevelt and McNutt generated considerable support in and out of Indiana. Van Nuys Clubs, whose members included anti–New Deal Democrats and business people drawn to the senator's conservative economic views, were formed throughout the state. A group of at least twenty Democratic United States senators, all opponents of the Court-packing proposal, announced they would help Van Nuys in his reelection battle. Although Minton, who presided over the convention, Townsend, and others tried to put the best face on the proceedings, clearly the party had been damaged by the Van Nuys fiasco.

Van Nuys had skillfully turned the tables and no one was more aware of the potential dangers than McNutt, who saw his presidential aspirations jeopardized by these developments. To mount a credible campaign for the White House in 1940 McNutt had to hold his own state in 1938. If Van Nuys ran as an independent, as he threatened, he could draw enough votes away from the Democrats to swing the election to the Republicans. In the face of this possibility, McNutt decided to compromise. He called Townsend from Manila and ordered him to offer Van Nuys the nomination. On 4 July 1938 Townsend sent a telegram to Van Nuys which read: "I am inviting you to become a candidate for United States Senator at the convention July 12, and, so far as I'm concerned, you will find it a wide-open convention."[26]

Even though the wayward senator was welcomed back to the fold at the convention, Hoosier Democrats still faced formidable obstacles in the fall election because of Roosevelt's declining popularity and a resurgent state Republican party. Indiana Republicans, after a decade of internal strife, approached the 1938 election with a newfound unity and optimism. The party's resurrection was boosted by Homer E. Capehart, a prosperous businessman who organized the famous Cornfield Conference in the summer of 1938. The gathering, held on Capehart's sprawling Daviess County farm, was attended by twenty thousand party leaders throughout the state and the Midwest and is generally considered the turning point in the fortunes of the Republican party in Indiana.[27] Van Nuys also had to battle against charges that he himself had played a prominent role in raising corruption in the Democratically controlled state WPA, the Two Percent Club, and the alcoholic beverage trade.

Minton, who had worked behind the scenes to deny his Senate colleague renomination, characteristically became the loyal team player once the deal was struck that put Van Nuys on the party's ticket. In the fall Minton delivered more than thirty-five speeches throughout Indiana; his typical stump speech, however, was more a defense of the Roosevelt record than an endorsement of Van Nuys. In fact, Minton barely mentioned the candidate, focusing instead on a comparison between the Hoover and Roosevelt administrations. Minton made a special appeal to Hoosier farmers, who had become increasingly unhappy because they felt that the New Deal tilted toward industrial recovery and urban relief at their expense. Minton asked, "What did the Republican Party do for the farmer? It led him into bankruptcy and ruin when it was in power. What is it doing for him now? Trying to frighten him and make him dissatisfied."

Under Roosevelt, Minton said, farm income in Indiana had increased from $134 million in 1932 to $292 million in 1937 or "more than twice what it was under Hoover's last year." Then, in a phrase reminiscent of modern presidential campaign rhetoric, Minton said to farmers, "as you are driving home tonight, ask yourself if you are not better off than you were under Hoover."[28]

In a radio speech two days before the election Minton also singled out for special attention two other important Democratic constituencies—labor and the elderly. Again, he contrasted how both groups fared under Hoover and Roosevelt. With Hoover in office labor faced "endless days of unemployment and the cruel suppression of their right to organize and protect their rights to work and to live by their work." On the other hand, Minton said, Roosevelt was the best friend labor ever had. "He looked around him and saw millions of men and women out of a job, and faced with starvation for themselves and their families. He gave them work." Under Roosevelt, Minton said, labor also got organizing and bargaining rights, unemployment insurance, and fair wages and hours. He noted that Van Nuys supported these pro-labor measures while his opponent Raymond E. Willis, an Angola newspaper publisher, "has a hundred percent record against labor."

In addressing the elderly, Minton said, "There were old people under the Republican Administration, but there never was any Old Age Pension law passed under a Republican Administration. It took the Democratic Party to put the Old Age Pension on the books." Again, he noted that Van Nuys supported this measure while Willis opposed it and "said so in the editorial columns of his newspaper."[29]

Van Nuys won despite the obstacles, but his margin was only 5,179 votes, 788,368 to 783,189. The renewed vigor of the Indiana Republicans was evident as they captured the office of secretary of state, their first statewide office in ten years, and took six congressional seats from the Democrats, giving them control of seven of the twelve districts. The GOP also won a majority in the state House of Representatives while the Democrats clung to a narrow majority in the state Senate.

This outcome certainly did not bode well for Hoosier Democrats in 1940, the year Minton was up for reelection. Following the 1938 election, national chairman James A. Farley asked Indiana party leaders for an assessment of the results. The responses listed several factors, but the main reason for the poor showing was the unpopularity of the New Deal because of the "Roosevelt Recession."

The economy, however, had lessened as an issue by the time Minton faced voters two years later because of an economic recovery that occurred after Roosevelt abandoned his tight-money policy in favor of deficit spending and monetary expansion. Still, there were plenty of other problems to concern Minton. Although he was not directly implicated, his reelection chances were hampered by persistent reports throughout 1940 that a major scandal would result from a federal investigation of possible tax evasion by the Two Percent Club and McNutt.

From its inception under McNutt in 1933 the Two Percent Club was controversial and regarded by many as a shadowy, tainted political practice. The actions of club officials and McNutt only encouraged such invectives. When it appeared that the club might violate state statutes, laws were either circumvented or changed. One change in the state Corrupt Practices Act engineered by McNutt's minions in 1937 permitted the club to establish a special-purposes fund from which it could make expenditures that were exempt from official accounting.

The federal government had scrutinized the Two Percent Club and other political fund-raising activities in Indiana several times before the Internal Revenue investigation. In

1934, for example, the Civilian Conservation Corps (CCC) investigated the club and cleared it of charges that it was soliciting contributions from federally paid CCC workers. The allegations were "thoroughly investigated and found that they were unfounded," an official of the agency said.[30] The Interior Department probed the Two Percent Club in 1935. Minton, in a letter to Val Nolan about this investigation, said he was "certain that [the] Club was very careful in everything it did, and at no time was there ever any intention on the part of anybody to violate any Federal statute." He claimed the investigation was started "in quarters that are now, and always have been inimical to the best interest of the Democratic Party, and bitter and resentful to that element of it which has been identified with the 'Two Percent Club.'"[31]

Another Interior Department investigation in the summer of 1940 concerned allegations that employees of the Indianapolis office of the Federal Coal Commission were being required to contribute 2 percent of their salaries to a Minton campaign fund. Minton said he neither approved of nor benefited from such a scheme, claiming that when he found out about it he told the office manager at the commission that he "wanted no part of such funds which obviously were collected in violation of the Hatch Law." He added, "I am not at all sure that it ever was established on my behalf. Surely I never received a penny of such funds."[32]

While he did not condone illegal campaign practices, Minton, as the Hatch Act debates amply demonstrated, saw nothing wrong in principle with the brand of patronage politics practiced by Hoosier Democrats. To Minton the Two Percent Club was a way common people could balance the scales against the power and influence of the wealthy. In a letter to Professor Woodburn, Minton defended the club as preferable to going "hat in hand to the big fat boys, with the tacit understanding that special privileges will be given them in return." He claimed that was the method of the Republican party, adding that "a glance at the roster of the large contributors in 1928, and the refund of taxes allowed them after Hoover was elected, shows conclusively that there was a 'quid pro quo.'"[33]

Minton also was compelled to defend the Two Percent Club in 1939 when it became an issue in McNutt's confirmation hearings to be head of the newly formed Federal Security Agency, roughly equivalent to the present-day Department of Health and Human Services. The fireworks started when Sen. Styles Bridges, a Republican from New Hampshire, introduced a resolution to prevent McNutt from establishing a Two Percent Club in the Federal Security Agency. Although the proposal was tabled, Bridges launched an attack on Indiana-style patronage. Bridges said he had known McNutt for years and "have nothing personally against him," but he considered the Two Percent Club "one of the most brazen samples of political racketeering I know of in the entire Nation." Bridges said the club "not only smells but its odor could be described by even a stronger term."[34]

Minton, always eager to pick up the gauntlet, responded that every political party must have money, or the "sinews of war," and the Two Percent system established by Hoosier Democrats was "an honest, honorable, straightforward way of getting money to finance a campaign." Minton, letting his rhetoric overrule reality, claimed that McNutt was not responsible for the club, but rather Democratic employees of state government "placed upon themselves a voluntary obligation to contribute 2 percent of their earnings . . . to help defray the expenses" of the party. He added that employees were "proud" and "glad" to pay the assessment and that "no one has been fired because he did not pay . . . two percent of his salary."[35]

Despite Minton's hyperbole, Hoosier-style patronage evidently had broad support in the state, even among Republicans. A committee that analyzed Indiana government reported in 1934 "that a formal merit system was highly desirable," but concluded there was little support by the public for such a change.[36] Democrats as well as Republicans believed that patronage preserved the two-party system because it gave incentive to the party faithful to work hard during elections.[37]

While not endorsing the Two Percent Club, political commentator Richard L. Strout of the *Christian Science Monitor,* in an article prompted by the McNutt hearings and passage of the Hatch Act, cautioned that "there is a danger of being smug about it; after all the McNutt scheme was brutally frank, it was relatively open and aboveboard, it dragged the forbidden subject into the air." In much the same vein as Minton, Strout asked whether it is worse to have a party financed by that method or "by secret political contributions of special interests in return for favors made after the election?" Strout, agreeing that money has to be raised, maintained that "The question is, Shall it be by '2 percent clubs,' by contributions from the wealthy, by patronage, or by some other means as yet unexplored in America?"[38]

The flap over the Two Percent Club did not prevent McNutt's confirmation as Federal Security Administrator; however, both the club and McNutt, because of the Internal Revenue probe, continued to be in the headlines throughout 1940. McNutt was news for another reason during this period, and once again the reelection prospects of his ally Minton were affected.

For years McNutt had made no secret of his burning desire to be president, and 1940 appeared to be the best year for him to make his move, depending, of course, on the incumbent. Roosevelt was calculatedly vague right up to the convention that summer when his campaign managers orchestrated Roosevelt's nomination for a third term by what appeared to be spontaneous acclamation. Until the matter was finally decided, Minton had been in the middle of the two men most responsible for his political career.

Without knowing the president's intentions, but believing he would retire at the end of his second term, Minton had aggressively supported McNutt's candidacy.

At the 1936 National Democratic Convention, for example, Minton lobbied, without success, to get McNutt named as keynote speaker as a way of enhancing his position for the 1940 presidential nomination. McNutt's old nemesis, party chairman Farley, stood in the way, declaring that McNutt "won't be the keynoter if I can help it."[39] Kentucky senator Alben Barkley gave the keynote, and McNutt gave a seconding speech for Roosevelt.

When his term as governor ended, McNutt officially launched his bid for the presidency in December 1936 at a banquet in Indianapolis attended by two thousand supporters. Minton, one of the main speakers at the event, said, "as we bid you goodbye at the Statehouse, we bid you Godspeed toward the White House."[40] In February 1938 Minton hosted a big celebration in Washington as an unofficial kickoff for McNutt's presidential campaign. The gala, which cost over six thousand dollars and was attended by an estimated four thousand people, was described as "one of the most sumptuous, not to say elaborate, fetes ever staged in Washington." Minton claimed the affair was purely social. "We just wanted him to meet the folks here in Washington."[41]

By being so prominent and public in pushing McNutt for president, Minton was risking the wrath of Roosevelt and those around him, national party chairman Farley in particular. Farley had never forgiven McNutt for failing to support Roosevelt at the 1932 convention, and he was constantly telling the president that McNutt could not be trusted. Nonetheless, Roosevelt favored McNutt with important appointments, although he doubted that the former Indiana governor was a suitable successor. As 1940 neared and Roosevelt appeared to be leaning toward a third term, the president became leery and even contemptuous of McNutt. In one meeting he and Farley joked about the difficulties McNutt was having in launching his presidential campaign. "I am satisfied in my own mind that he [Roosevelt] is not at all that displeased with the razzing McNutt is getting around the country," Farley wrote in his diary.[42]

Minton began hedging his bets in the presidential sweepstakes in mid-1939, stating that McNutt would step aside if Roosevelt ran. However, by then Minton's work on behalf of McNutt's candidacy already had lowered Minton's standing with the president. In fact, this one indiscretion, although minor compared with Minton's solid record of support for Roosevelt and the New Deal, most likely affected Roosevelt's decision to forgo a campaign appearance in Indiana in Minton's behalf. The president informed Minton by telegram in late October 1940 that he could not "come to your state as I had hoped to. But, as you know, it has been imperative that I stay close to Washington, and Indiana is a little too far away."[43]

A presidential visit undoubtedly would have helped Minton, who faced an uphill battle for reasons already discussed and because Republicans had nominated Hoosier native Wendell Willkie as their candidate for president. With the popular and charismatic Willkie at the head of the ticket and with the Republican resurgence in the state well under way, the chances of Roosevelt carrying the state for a third straight time were problematic, and this meant difficulty for the entire Democratic ticket in Indiana.

At their convention in late June 1940 Hoosier Democrats renominated Minton by acclamation and selected Lt. Gov. Henry F. Schricker as the party's gubernatorial candidate. Minton's Republican opponent was Raymond E. Willis, the newspaper publisher who came close to defeating Van Nuys two years earlier. Schricker, who wore a white hat and had the reputation to match, opposed Glenn Hillis, a former mayor of Kokomo.

Rather than running against each other, Minton and Willis focused their campaign oratory, with few exceptions, on the presidential contenders. Minton, who was elected in 1934 on a strict New Deal platform, sought to highlight the successes of the president's first two terms and vowed his continued unwavering support of Roosevelt if returned to the Senate. In his opening campaign speech in Sullivan, Minton said, "I have been charged with personifying and upholding the New Deal. I plead guilty. I also plead guilty to upholding the President."[44] In another speech Minton retorted, "My pledge in this campaign is the same that I made in 1934. I have been rubber-stamping the labor, farm, social security and humanitarian legislation which the Roosevelt administration asked you folks back home to help write."[45]

Willis said the election was a contest between two political philosophies: big government Democrats versus private enterprise Republicans. He warned that the opposition's approach had created a bureaucratic colossus that threatened individual freedom. Willis saw Roosevelt's unprecedented run for a third term as further proof that the nation's liberty was imperiled. "If there is no other issue involved in this campaign, it should be decided in Mr. Willkie's favor on the third-term issue alone," he said. "If we do not uphold the no-third-term tradition in this election, we may find ourselves with a permanent ruler. We are following the same path that was followed by monarchs of Europe in seeking perpetual power."[46]

Minton confronted the controversy in the beginning of his standard stump speech by saying, "There can be no third term issue in this campaign." Minton declared "that matter was taken care of by the constitution of the United States," and he recalled that "the first president had declared that an emergency might alter the number of times a president was a candidate to succeed himself." He added, "The people of this country should be without fear about the third term of President Roosevelt. What they should fear would be the first term of Wendell Willkie."[47]

Minton's campaign was, in fact, almost completely devoted to defending Roosevelt and attacking Willkie, a strategy born of the belief that if the president did not carry Indiana none of the Democrats would win. Minton paid scant attention to Willis, referring to him as "my opponent" on rare occasions. In his opening campaign speech in Sullivan on 3 October Minton said, "While I have been in Washington fighting for the New Deal, my opponent has been sitting at a desk in Angola trying to tear these things down." He described Willis's one term in the state legislature as "most reactionary."[48]

Willkie and the Republican administrations of Harding, Coolidge, and Hoover got the brunt of Minton's campaign barrage. Willkie in particular made the perfect foil for the populist Minton, who undoubtedly derived a great deal of pleasure from zinging the candidate who had been a corporate lawyer in New York and president of Commonwealth and Southern, a large utility holding company. Indeed, Minton said the 1940 presidential race was "between Wall street and Main street," and he sought to brand Willkie as the representative of wealth and privilege.[49] Speaking in Terre Haute, Minton called Willkie's candidacy "one of the most audacious hoaxes ever perpetrated on the people of a republic." Minton claimed that privileged interests, public utilities, and Wall Street speculators had seized control of the Republican party and were trying to "palm off one of their hired men upon the electorate as a suitable candidate for president."[50]

Besides labeling Willkie a sycophant for the rich and powerful, Minton suggested the GOP candidate lacked the necessary experience to be in the White House at a time when the nation faced ominous world conditions. "America's vital arms of national defense and mobilization for defense can not be left to one who has never mobilized anything but high electric rates and watered utility stock," Minton said, adding that no leader is better qualified than "Franklin D. Roosevelt, who organized and builded [*sic*] a section of naval defense. Here's a man who knows America's defense by heart and will not take four years to learn it."[51] Minton also assailed Willkie as a man who could not be trusted because of his vacillation on the issues. At a campaign stop in Clinton, Minton asked, "Why hasn't Mr. Willkie stuck to his original intentions of debating the accomplishments of the New Deal? Has he found that the manufactured third-term question is the only issue he has?"[52] In a speech in Princeton, Minton charged Willkie with trying to have it both ways on farm policy. "Mr. Willkie espouses a doctrine of unlimited production and says the way to prosperity is to glut the markets with products of the farms, yet vows that he admires the AAA and is in favor of continuing subsidy payments to the farmers. Could any such statement be more squarely on both sides of the fence?"[53]

In making the case for the president's reelection, Minton compared Roosevelt's eight years in office with the twelve years of his three Republican predecessors. "We had hard times under Harding, kept cool under Coolidge, were hungry under Hoover, rose under Roosevelt, and for goodness sake, don't let us wilt under Willkie," Minton said.[54] Answering Willkie's charge that business was in the doghouse and Roosevelt had not found a job for one man, Minton said, "The 1932 reports show that business was in the doghouse then, but the 1939 reports show that the democrats have let it out and destroyed the doghouse." As for employment, Minton said, "President Roosevelt has found jobs in private industry for 9,000,000 men, or more than half those who were unemployed when he took office."[55]

At an appearance in Hammond, Minton claimed that the Republican presidents had engaged in "traditional appeasement policies" that weakened the country's national defense program. "President Roosevelt has had the obstacle of too many G.O.P. umbrella toters to have been able to reach his objective in the building of strong national defenses, but he has nevertheless made remarkable progress," Minton said.[56] Specifically, Minton charged the Harding administration with disabling America's military might by agreeing to limitations on fleet strength at the 1921 Washington Naval Conference.

Minton returned home to New Albany on election eve to close out his reelection campaign, which had been especially exhausting since it was conducted in about a month's time. He struggled to make up for lost ground after being forced to cancel appearances in six Indiana cities in early October when his job as assistant majority leader of the Senate required him to be in Washington. Once on the campaign trail Minton concentrated on Democratic strongholds in the northern and western sections of the state. He often attracted large and enthusiastic crowds: six thousand in Sullivan, three thousand in Gary, three thousand in Vincennes, twenty-five hundred in Terre Haute, and a packed house at Tomlinson Hall in Indianapolis. Minton's speech before a "wildly cheering audience" at the Muncie armory was interrupted when someone outside the building threw a rock that shattered the glass of a large window behind the speaker's platform. Several men dashed outside looking for the vandal, but none was found. Minton resumed his talk, which was mainly an attack on Willkie, whom he termed a "bundle of strange contradictions."[57]

At the campaign windup in New Albany, Minton made what turned out to be his last speech as a candidate for elective office. Speaking in the Catholic Community Center gym before a spirited crowd of two thousand, Minton praised the New Deal and pledged his continued support of Roosevelt's program if he were returned to the Senate. He also said, "there isn't another leader in the world working more for peace than Roosevelt." Minton repeated his charges against Willkie as the product of private utility interests and Wall Street and past Republican administrations as inept and insensitive.[58]

Minton's apprehension about his reelection prospects were well founded as Hoosiers, captivated by having native son Willkie at the top of the GOP ticket, returned to their normal pattern of voting Republican, except in the governor's race. Schricker overcame the Republican tide, though just barely, winning by fewer than 4,000 votes, 889,620 to Hillis's 885,657. Minton, who had won his 1934 race by nearly 60,000 votes, lost by more than 23,000, 864,803 to Willis's 888,070. Roosevelt, who had won the state by margins of 185,000 in 1932 and 245,000 in 1936, finished behind Willkie by over 25,000 votes, 874,063 to 899,466.[59]

Minton assessed the reasons for his defeat in replying to the scores of letters he received from family and friends after the election. The loss of Indianapolis cost him reelection, Minton said in a letter to Nebraska senator George W. Norris. He had expected to carry the city by twelve to thirteen thousand votes, but lost it by three thousand. "If the President could have found it possible to speak at Indianapolis, we would have won, but he couldn't go everywhere," Minton wrote. Minton noted that other factors, including the war issue that was important to isolationist Catholics and nationalistic German Americans, hurt him in the state's capital. "We had organization difficulties. Our Catholic friends turned us down, and there is a large German vote in Indianapolis and the well-to-do voted in unprecedented numbers." Outside of Indianapolis, Minton added that "all of the German communities went heavily against us. The best evidence of this was that the only man on our ticket elected was our candidate for Governor, Mr. Schricker, who was a German Lutheran."[60]

Naturally, Willkie's candidacy had a big impact on the results. Minton, in a letter to Josephus Daniels, United States ambassador to Mexico, said, "We . . . were in the most difficult position in the country because Mr. Willkie was a native son and they put forth tremendous effort to carry the state for him." Noting that the GOP state committee spent $562,000 on Willkie's campaign, Minton added, "This takes no account of what the National Organization spent, the County Organizations or the numerous Willkie Clubs."[61]

In other letters Minton cited additional factors: the factional disputes in the state Democratic party; the loss of coal counties because of a ruling by the coal commission that made Indiana coal less competitive in the Chicago market; and the defection of farmers who were unhappy because they felt the New Deal tilted toward urban concerns. Losing the farm vote was especially upsetting. "The farmers are never grateful and are always envious of everybody else, and they gave us a good thumping," Minton complained to his brother Roscoe. "I think we were double-crossed by the Farm Bureau, which is headed by Republicans, who profess their love for you and then stuck a knife in our back."[62]

MARY ANNE CALLANAN COLLECTION

Sherman Minton with his brother Roscoe.

While his defeat was painful, Minton wrote in numerous letters that what mattered most was Roosevelt's reelection. "The fact that I fell by the wayside is of no consequence when we remember we won the war & kept FDR in the White House," Minton wrote to William G. McAdoo, former senator from California.[63]

Still, the fifty-year-old Minton, who would be out of office in a few weeks, was concerned with the practical question of his future. Although he had been one of the president's most ardent supporters in Congress, amazingly there was no immediate indication that the White House had a position for him. "I have had no intimation from the President that he has anything in mind for me, although I haven't had a chance to see him and probably won't get to see him until he gets back from his little vacation trip," Minton noted in a letter to a friend about a week after the election.[64] If no offers came, Minton was prepared to return to Indiana to practice law. Regardless of the uncertainty, Minton, at least in his letters, appeared undaunted. In a letter to another former Senate colleague, F. Ryan Duffy, he wrote: "I do not know what the future holds for me, but whatever it is, I can take it. All my life I have been getting up and dusting myself off, so it is no new experience to me to be whipped. My head's bloody, but unbowed."[65] In a letter to his brother Roscoe, Minton wrote that he had "no regrets, except that I failed. But sometimes dark defeat momentarily obscures the vision of a bright victory, and I am not discouraged."[66]

CHAPTER SIX

Far from Washington but not from Politics

The brief period between Minton's Senate defeat in 1940 and his appointment to the Seventh Circuit Court of Appeals in May 1941 was perhaps the most difficult of his public career. In addition to living with the verdict of the voters, which must have been extremely painful, he was confronted, at the age of fifty, with the prospect of embarking on a career outside of politics. After six years of being in the thick of partisan politics, battling for causes and issues about which he felt passionately, enjoying the taste of party leadership, and feeling the glow of national attention, Minton was cut off from his life's blood of politics.

Although it may not have been apparent to Minton at the time, this 1940 defeat did not mark the end of his public career, but rather ushered in a period of transition. With the exception of a four-month assignment as assistant to President Franklin D. Roosevelt, Minton spent the 1940s as a judge on the Seventh Circuit Court of Appeals in Chicago. Although it was far from the excitement of Washington politics, Chicago and the Seventh Circuit had much to offer Minton. When the door to electoral politics closed, the door to the Supreme Court edged open. As a federal appeals court judge Minton had the opportunity to tone down his partisan image, to highlight his legal expertise, and to demonstrate a proper judicial temperament.

Minton's public record during this time concerns his role as a judge and the decisions that he made. Behind his public record and appearance of judicial neutrality, however, Minton was still an avid partisan, maintaining a strong interest in and an active involvement with politics. Although physically removed from Washington, letters from Presidents Roosevelt and Harry S. Truman, sitting Supreme Court justices, and former Senate colleagues kept him in contact with the nation's politics. He maintained especially close ties with Truman, which enabled him to continue to exert an influence on patronage appointments at both the federal and state levels.

The most difficult time for Minton in the period of transition came immediately following his defeat, when his future was most uncertain. As a politician who had always believed in taking care of friends, he turned to people he thought could help him, but their responses were not promising. He was unable to mask his pessimism about his future when he wrote to Alabama senator Lister Hill in early December: "I just drift along with the tide and nothing is happening that I know anything about," he said. "I have no doubt that there may be some developments later on, but just when they will materialize, no one seems to know and I suppose when I get back to Indiana my interests may be forgotten."[1]

Hill and others lobbied the White House to find a place for Minton in the administration. They felt that it was the least Roosevelt could do in view of Minton's unyielding loyalty to the president and Roosevelt's lack of active support for Minton's reelection bid. Hill wrote to the president: "I know it is not necessary for me to tell you of the exceptional ability of Sherman Minton and his great loyalty to you and to the Roosevelt cause. I am most anxious to see him continue in the service of your Administration." Hill listed several possible positions for Minton, including governor of Puerto Rico, the Federal Reserve Board, and the Maritime Commission. Hill and others expected the president to offer Minton some kind of interim position "until perhaps some place on the Bench became available."[2]

On 3 January James Rowe, Roosevelt's longtime assistant, sent a memorandum to the president advising him that "Sherman Minton went off the public pay roll today." Rowe noted that "several senators have already called to point out the debt this administration owes to Minton, and also his really good legal ability." Rowe's memorandum makes it clear that he and Roosevelt had already discussed several possible appointments for Minton, and Rowe lists other possibilities. Rowe told the president that "Minton really wants to be a judge but there is no present vacancy in his Circuit. You want to find something for him temporarily until there is such a vacancy."[3]

On 7 January the president personally announced Minton's appointment as an administrative assistant. Roosevelt emphasized that Minton would not serve just as a liaison between the White House and Congress but rather in a general capacity. Although he stressed that Minton's service on the Senate Military Affairs Committee had given him experience in military affairs, the president was emphatic that Minton would devote his energies to more than national rearmament. Roosevelt said that Minton would "act as the President's eyes, ears and legs."[4] "Shay will have a passion for anonymity in the job as administrative assistant," the president said.[5] This description of Minton's new role seemed to reflect an effort to deemphasize his partisan image. As the president organized himself for war and for his role as a bipartisan president, perhaps he saw the need to distance himself from the too-partisan Minton. As administrative assistant to the president Minton's salary was ten thousand dollars, the same salary he earned as a senator.

If Minton ever felt that Roosevelt had failed him in his reelection bid, Roosevelt's actions on 7 January made up

PHOTOGRAPH BY HARRIS & EWING, COLLECTION OF THE SUPREME COURT OF THE UNITED STATES

After his defeat for reelection for the U.S. Senate, Sherman Minton served for several months as a special assistant to President Franklin D. Roosevelt.

for the disappointment. Minton was reported to be "all smiles when he left the White House [and that] his smile broadened after the President personally made the public announcement."[6]

Minton's appointment was met with a chorus of approval from his friends in the Senate, from back home in Indiana, and from across the nation. Both Roosevelt and Minton received numerous letters and telegrams about the appointment. Among those expressing their approval or congratulations were New York financier Bernard Baruch, Secretary of Agriculture Claude Wickard, and Sen. Raymond E. Willis, Minton's 1940 opponent. Fort Wayne newspaper publisher William A. Kunkel, Jr., wrote a poem in honor of the occasion:

> Shay takes charge at the White House
> Goes rumbling and tumbling through my head
> When Shay takes charge at the White House
> The opposition better roll over and play dead.[7]

Minton's close friend and former colleague in the Senate, Lewis B. Schwellenbach, wrote: "So far as the election was concerned, there was only one black spot in it. I was so glad to have that wiped out, in some measure at least, by your selection by the President and we are sure that at some time during the next four years the opportunity will be given for work for you along legal lines."[8]

The position to which Minton was appointed was one of six authorized in the government reorganization act passed by Congress in 1939. The act was the result of the Brownlow Committee Report on administrative efficiency, which recommended the expansion of the White House staff and the creation of the Executive Office of the President. These changes laid the foundation for the modern presidency and marked the beginning of that complex of offices and positions known today as the White House Office. In Roosevelt's day the members of the president's staff served as advisers and "trouble shooters." Their modern-day counterparts, with their direct access to the Oval Office, are often more trusted and influential than members of the president's cabinet.

Because Roosevelt insisted that his executive assistants remain in the background, the exact nature of Minton's responsibilities is vague, but letters and correspondence offer a glimpse of his duties. Although Roosevelt had insisted that Minton would not be a liaison between the White House and Congress, Minton did function in that capacity, especially as a conduit for the wishes of prominent senators. Few people knew better than Minton how the game of legislative politics was played, particularly in matters pertaining to patronage. For instance, in urging Roosevelt to make an appointment desired by

Sen. Joseph F. Guffey of Pennsylvania, Minton wrote that "Guffey is one of our most loyal friends, and we cannot be calling upon men on the Hill for help without reciprocating."[9]

On occasion Minton urged the president not to make certain appointments out of deference to a member of the Senate. Concerning an appointment to the Labor Mediation Board, Minton told the president: "This appointment would be very displeasing to Senator [Harry S.] Truman, who has always been our friend. Several of his friends have called me about it and expressed the hope that this would not be done. The appointment would give Sen. [Bennett Champ] Clark, whose support we never have, an excellent opportunity to work on Truman."[10]

In his White House post Minton watched for developments that had election implications for Roosevelt and the Democratic party. He was concerned about the outcome in 1941 of a municipal election in St. Louis in which a solidly black ward voted Republican. Minton expressed his concern to Roosevelt, calling the election results a straw in the wind. "I fear we are losing our Negro support," he said. Not surprisingly, Minton saw patronage as a way to counteract the loss of black support. He suggested that certain government jobs not be covered by civil service because "Negroes have difficulty in getting appointed to Civil Service."[11]

Serving in the White House also provided Minton with an opportunity to go to bat for old friends in Indiana. He tried, unsuccessfully, to keep his friend Meredith Nicholson, who was ambassador to Nicaragua, from being removed from his post. "I understand Meredith Nicholson . . . is to be relieved to make way for a career man. Indiana would be very appreciative if he could be saved. Can it be done?"[12] This was one request that the president was unwilling to grant. Nicholson, who had served in ambassadorial positions since 1933, was replaced by a career diplomat in February 1941.

Although patronage issues appear to be the bulk of what Minton handled as an executive assistant to the president, that was not all he did. Minton's most rewarding role was in helping his friend Truman become chairman of a Senate committee investigating defense plants and related activities. Several senators had authored resolutions regarding the investigations. Minton was instrumental in getting Roosevelt to back Truman's resolution, ensuring that Truman would be chair of the committee. After talking with James F. Byrnes about the matter, Minton wrote a memo to the president: "Unless you disagree he will report at once for passage of the Truman resolution to investigate defense activities. This is a matter of strategy to keep the investigation in friendly hands in the Senate and away from unfriendly House fellows like Cox. Barkley agrees with Jim. I agree with them. The Truman resolution is the best out. What shall I tell Jim?"[13] At the bottom of the memo in pencil Roosevelt wrote: "S.M. O.K. FDR."

Minton had been serving as executive assistant to Roosevelt for four months when Walter Treanor, judge of the Seventh Circuit Court in Chicago, died on 26 April 1941. As soon as he learned of Treanor's death, James Rowe sent a memorandum to Roosevelt reminding him that "Sherman Minton is very anxious to be put on the Circuit bench. You told me at the time of Minton's appointment that was your intention." Rowe also reminded Roosevelt that a bill creating an additional judgeship had passed the Senate but was held up in the House. He advised the president that if he planned to appoint Minton to the circuit bench "it would probably be a better strategy to appoint him to this vacancy since there is some talk that the new judgeship bill was just to take care of Minton." In a notation at the bottom of the memorandum the president wrote: "J.R. Can we do it right away? FDR."[14] Shortly thereafter, when Minton was delivering a memorandum to the Oval Office, Roosevelt casually asked, "By the way, Shay, would you be interested in that vacancy on the Seventh Circuit?"[15] It was the only time that Roosevelt ever spoke to Minton about the appointment.

On 29 April Roosevelt sent a memorandum to Attorney General Robert Jackson enclosing a telegram from F. Ryan Duffy, a United States District Court judge from Wisconsin, urging Minton's appointment to the Seventh Circuit. The president noted, "Will you speak to me about this?"[16] On 5 May Jackson sent the president a favorable recommendation, and on 7 May Minton's nomination was sent to the Senate. That same day Minton wrote to thank Roosevelt and promised that "my ambition shall be to prove worthy of your friendship and confidence."[17]

Minton's appointment to the Seventh Circuit was viewed widely as the repayment of a debt that Roosevelt owed Minton for his loyalty. Early confirmation was predicted, in part because Minton's former Senate colleagues felt that he had "taken the rap for the New Deal." Even Frederick Van Nuys, with whom Minton had sparred over political differences and who was now chair of the Senate Judiciary Committee, thought Minton deserved something from Roosevelt, and he promised early Senate confirmation. Exactly one week to the day after his nomination Minton was unanimously approved by his former colleagues. Although he still had his detractors in the Senate, the rules of senatorial courtesy, which applied to former as well as current members, guaranteed that no serious questions would be raised about Minton's suitability for a judgeship.

Letters of congratulations poured in. Among the Indiana friends who wrote were Gov. Henry F. Schricker, Indianapolis mayor Reginald Sullivan, and Herman B Wells, president of Indiana University. One of the most touching letters came from Treanor's widow Aline. She told Minton that her husband had said many times before his death, "I must write Shay," but that he kept putting it off until he felt better. "He was always much interested in your fortunes and looked forward very much to your being the next appointee on the court and serving with him. I feel that you will find that your colleagues are princely men."[18]

Those princely men to whom Aline Treanor referred included Chief Judge Evan Evans, judges William Sparks, James Earl Major, and Otto Kerner. Each wrote to offer his congratulations and assistance. Their letters confirmed what Aline Treanor had written and were the first indication of the camaraderie among the Seventh Circuit judges that awaited Minton. Chief Judge Evans wrote, "I feel sure we will be greatly helped by your association. We have a very congenial group on this court and a very happy place to work in. There is no more interesting position in the United States than of Judge of the United States Circuit Court of Appeals."[19] Judge Sparks said, "I wanted to express my welcome immediately, as one Indianan to another. I know you will like all of my associates on the bench, and I covet a small part of that estimation."[20]

On 29 May 1941 Minton was sworn in as a judge of the Seventh Circuit Court of Appeals. The swearing-in ceremony, laden with symbolism of the past and a foreshadowing of the future, was conducted in the office of Col. E. A. Halsey, secretary of the Senate. Minton had been one of the senators who frequented Halsey's office, which Minton's crowd called Halsey's Saloon, a not too subtle reference to the activities that took place there. Justice Hugo L. Black, whom Minton succeeded as chair of the Lobbying Committee and who had been named to the Supreme Court in 1937 instead of Minton, performed the swearing-in ceremony with Justice William O. Douglas at Minton's side. Among the hundred people attending the ceremony were many former senators, including Vice President Henry A. Wallace and several of Minton's political allies and foes from Indiana: Frederick Van Nuys, Frank McHale, Raymond Willis, Paul V. McNutt, and Wayne Coy.

Lew Schwellenbach, who was unable to attend, sent a telegram to Truman expressing regret that read: "Never so much disliked declining an invitation but I am what Joe Guffey would call a run-of-the-mill judge busily engaged in attempting to reconcile illogical, inconsistencies between various circuit courts of appeal. Fortunately after Minton assumes office there will be one circuit the decisions of which I can justifiably ignore."[21]

On the day that he left the White House a member of Roosevelt's staff delivered a signed photograph of the president that Roosevelt had promised to Minton. The inscription read, "For Shay Minton with the affectionate regards of his old friend, Franklin D. Roosevelt."[22]

Although Minton once described his time in the White House as the richest of his life, that time was not his most rewarding. Despite the fact that he met daily with the president, Minton never became one of Roosevelt's close confidants, nor was he part of the inner circle of advisers upon whom Roosevelt relied. Had his time in the White House been longer, perhaps his relationship with Roosevelt might have been different, but it is not likely. Roosevelt and Minton were too different in background and temperament to develop more than a cordial relationship, and Minton's close association with Paul McNutt may have affected Roosevelt's trust of Minton.

Roosevelt's own agenda at the time also may have diminished Minton's usefulness to the president. As Roosevelt sought to prepare the country for war, he needed different kinds of people. When Roosevelt's focus had been on domestic issues Minton's loyal dedication to the cause of the New Deal had been useful, but Minton's dogmatic partisanship could prove to be a liability as the president sought to forge a bipartisan coalition to wage war.

When Minton was sworn in as appellate court judge, the Seventh Circuit was finishing its spring term, and Judge Evans had written Minton that there was not much he could do before the fall term. The Mintons stayed in Washington until early June in order to attend their daughter Mary Anne's graduation from Immaculata Seminary in

Washington. They returned home to New Albany, placed their belongings in storage, and moved in temporarily with cousins since they had lost the lease on their home in the Silver Hills area of New Albany. During the summer Minton purchased a large, Tudor-style home at the top of Cherry Street hill in the same Silver Hills neighborhood. This remained the family home until a few years after Minton's death, when Mrs. Minton sold it and moved to Bethesda, Maryland, to live with her daughter Mary Anne Callanan and her family.

Mrs. Minton was present on 7 October 1941 when her husband took his seat on the Seventh Circuit bench; however, she spent little time in Chicago during his tenure on the bench. She preferred to live in New Albany, which meant that Minton had to commute home on weekends to be with his family. His usual routine was to catch the train on Friday nights for New Albany and return to Chicago on Sunday evening. The train to New Albany left late at night so Minton often worked in his office at the court building until it was time to leave for the train station. Minton's secretary, Frances Kelly, who had worked for him since 1937, worried about his working so much. She persuaded a guard at the court building to turn off the lights in the early evening so that he could not work late. When Minton asked the security guard about the lights, the guard feigned ignorance, but he continued to turn the lights off just as Kelly had asked him to do.[23] Minton never suspected the real reason why the lights were turned off.

When Minton joined the Seventh Circuit he went to great lengths to eschew his political past. On his first day on the bench he claimed that he was "forever through with politics" and expressed his pleasure at being back in the profession of law. "I'm doing what I always wanted to do," Minton said. "Ever since I was a boy I've been interested in the law. I'm happy now."[24] His words probably reflected his best intentions, but Minton was too addicted to completely remove himself from politics.

He expressed his true feelings about leaving politics in his private correspondence. When James A. Farley wrote to congratulate Minton on his appointment, Minton responded with candor about his regrets over leaving politics. "I look forward with pleasure to my new assignment; although I leave here with a tinge of regret, and I do not anticipate with too much pleasure the divorcement from politics that this appointment will require. However, it will not take away from my interest and I will be sitting on the side line cheering."[25]

He said the same thing to others. Before he left Washington he wrote to Mississippi senator Theodore Bilbo that he was leaving the scene of politics "with much regret, as I have loved the give and take of the conflict."[26] Even before taking his seat on the bench, Minton felt the constraints of being a judge. In June James Rowe wrote, "I am amused by your resentment of the fact that the robe has already muzzled you."[27]

Although the transition to the bench was hard for Minton, it was made more palatable by his fellow judges on the Seventh Circuit, a close-knit group of men with whom he developed strong friendships. The tradition of camaraderie that Minton encountered was well established before he arrived and was sufficiently recognized to warrant mention in a history of the court:

> There existed among the members of the court mutual respect and genuine friendship which seemed to go well beyond the formal courtesy men in high office extended toward each other. The friendships cut across party and ideological lines and manifested themselves in various ways—from entertaining each other at their homes to tongue-in-cheek letters circulated around the court before, during and after baseball season.[28]

One practice that helped cement the bonds of friendship among the judges was their daily lunches together in the chamber's dining room. A former clerk recalls that when lunchtime rolled around one of the judges, J. Earl Major, who was also a farmer, would call them all to lunch as if calling hogs to feed.[29] The lunches provided an informal setting in which the judges could discuss anything from business to their favorite topics—baseball and politics. Minton enjoyed the casual atmosphere of these lunches, and after he joined the Supreme Court he expressed regret that the justices did not dine together, feeling that such practices allowed the judges to "resolve their differences and to establish an *esprit de corps* which facilitated smooth functioning of the court as a whole."[30]

Although the members of the circuit court shared a strong interest in politics, they did not share a common point of view. All of them had either held elective office or been active in party politics. Evans was a lifelong Democrat from Wisconsin who belonged to the progressive wing of the state party. His commitment to the progressive philosophy was stronger than his loyalty to his party, at times he had supported Republican senator Robert La Follette and the economic reforms of his progressive organization. Major, also a Democrat, served eight years as state attorney and eight years in the United States House of Representatives. Sparks, the only Republican, had been a political activist, and Kerner, a Democrat, had been Illinois attorney general.

Ideologically, Sparks and Major were the conservatives on the bench, and as such they had doubts about many aspects of the New Deal. Both believed that the federal government should play a limited role in economic and social matters, and they had strong reservations about Congress delegating broad regulatory powers to federal agencies. As ardent New Dealers, Kerner and Minton believed in an activist government and the necessity of broad regulatory powers for administrative agencies, which in turn required broad administrative discretion. Being a progressive, Evans was philosophically closer to Kerner and Minton than to Major and Sparks.[31]

The philosophical differences among the judges often resulted in split decisions on the court, but they never let those differences interfere with their personal relationships. They shared other interests that helped to cement the bonds of friendship. One of those was a love of sports, especially baseball. Judge Major, with whom Minton developed a particularly strong relationship, was an ardent fan of the St. Louis Cardinals. Judge Evans, who had no strong attachment to any team, liked to needle Major by predicting a poor season for the Cardinals, and at the end of the season Evans took great delight in reminding Major how accurate he had been. However, Evans's predictions did not always come true, so he had to find a

GARY YOHLER/FREDERICK VOLLRATH, TIFFANY STUDIO, *INDIANAPOLIS TIMES* COLLECTION

Sherman Minton peruses information in an almanac about his favorite sport, baseball.

way to save face gracefully. Minton's compatibility with these men was something he did not fully appreciate until he joined the Supreme Court, where the atmosphere was much more restrained and the personal relationships more strained.

One of the common bonds uniting the Seventh Circuit judges was a concern about the fate of their rulings when they were reviewed by the Supreme Court. By the time Minton joined the Seventh Circuit, the Supreme Court was more sympathetic to New Deal policies with their broad grants of administrative discretion. That meant that the decisions of Major and Sparks, who were more inclined to rule against enforcing an agency order, were more likely to be overturned than those of Minton, Evans, or Kerner.

The matter of affirming or reversing decisions was often the source of good-natured kidding or bragging among the judges. In 1945, when Minton was in Walter Reed Hospital in Washington, D.C., recuperating from a heart attack, Evans wrote him about Major's displeasure over being overturned by the Supreme Court. Evans described Major as being "madder than a hatter" and "ready to cite the Supreme Court," along with Wiley B. Rutledge who was the suspected villain, for vacating a decision and returning it to the Seventh Circuit for reconsideration.[32]

Minton and his colleagues prided themselves on the heavy caseload that they carried in comparison to the other circuit courts. In 1942 the Seventh Circuit had the heaviest caseload of any of the appellate courts, averaging annually nearly forty cases per judge.[33] Like a good soldier Minton handled his share of the caseload and was known to complain on occasion if he thought others were not doing their fair share. He appeared to others to enjoy his work on the court. In a letter to Minton in December 1942 Supreme Court Justice Robert H. Jackson commented on Minton's decisions: "I always read your opinions with interest, and from them I gather, although it is only from between the lines, that you are really enjoying judicial work. It is quite a violent change from the kind of life you and I had been leading, but it certainly has its compensations."[34]

The lure of politics remained strong for Minton, although his role now was that of adviser rather than active participant. He frequently offered his opinions to Roosevelt and later Truman on a wide range of issues and on his recommendations for presidential appointments.

In November 1941 he wrote to Roosevelt about the national coal strike, led by John L. Lewis, whom Minton and Schwellenbach called "Brows." Minton was no admirer of Lewis, who had been a thorn in Roosevelt's side since 1936. The tensions between Lewis and Roosevelt escalated to full-scale warfare in 1940 when Lewis declared his support for Republican presidential candidate Wendell Willkie. The estrangement was exacerbated when the coal miners struck in 1941. Minton advised the president to avoid using troops. "Labor never forgives or forgets," he said. "Have Congress pass speedily such legislation as would make it unlawful to strike a defense industry during this emergency." Minton also thought Roosevelt should attack Lewis. "You don't want to make it a controversy between you & Labor. The C.I.O. and A.F.L. in recent Conventions have supported your policies by resolutions unanimously adopted. It isn't Labor. It is Lewis. He is hated like no one else in America. Now is the time to clip his wings."[35]

Minton also wrote to the president about political appointments. In April 1942 he urged Roosevelt to reappoint a friend, John S. Scott, to the Federal Power Commission, which the president did. After Sen. George W. Norris of Nebraska was defeated in November 1942, Minton recommended that Roosevelt appoint Norris to the vacancy on the Supreme Court created when James F. Byrnes resigned at Roosevelt's request to serve as director of economic stabilization. The nomination went instead to Wiley Rutledge, the last of Roosevelt's appointees to the Court, and the man whom Minton would replace in 1949.

Minton and Truman, who started their Senate careers sitting next to each other, had continued to keep in contact after Minton left Washington. Their letters were usually about their days in the Senate. In June 1942 Minton wrote to Truman about a visit he had in Milwaukee with Ryan Duffy, former Wisconsin senator, and with Schwellenbach. He told his former Senate seatmate that "if your ears burned, you will know the reasons. . . . I still read good things about you in the newspaper, and in all of this I take an especial pride."[36]

Truman wrote to Minton in April 1944 complaining about Minton's failure to attend a reception for Duffy. Truman added, "I wish you would let us know some time when you are in Washington so we could have a round table session and discuss how the Senate has gone to hell

UPI/CORBIS-BETTMANN

Harry Truman, Sherman Minton, and Lewis Schwellenbach (left to right) attend the 1944 Democratic National Convention.

since you and Duffy and Lew Schwellenbach have left it."[37] Within six months of that letter Truman had been nominated as Roosevelt's running mate, and Minton wrote to wish him well in the campaign. Expressing confidence that Truman would win in November, Minton said, "I want to come down and see you inaugurated and strike a blow for liberty in the old familiar haunts."[38]

Fate, in the form of pernicious anemia, intervened to deny Minton the opportunity to savor his friend's victory. Minton had been diagnosed with the disorder as early as 1943, and the symptoms became progressively more pronounced. The ailment was severe enough in late 1944 that he was forced to go to his brother's home in Fort Worth to regain his strength. He did not recover in time to attend the inauguration. Minton described his forced absence to Truman as "one of the keenest disappointments of my life that I could not see my old friend and seat mate on this historic occasion and journey to the White House to see my beloved leader sworn in for the fourth time."[39] Minton explained that he was suffering from an anemic condition, caused by poor blood corpuscles, which resulted in below-normal body temperatures and a "coffin color." The new vice president promptly responded and urged Minton not to "let the lack of red corpuscles get you down."[40] Although he never fully recovered from the anemia, Minton's health gradually improved, and in March he reported to Truman that he was making headway with his health. "I am on a strict diet and I haven't had a tasty morsel of food in three weeks. Eating was *one* of the things I lived for! The other one is about gone too."[41]

When Truman became president in April 1945, Minton did not hesitate to use his new access to the White House. He was not sure, however, how Truman's status as president affected their relationship. On 19 April Minton wrote to White House assistant Les Biffle saying that he did not "know how to reach Harry now" and asking Biffle to give Truman some thoughts he had about cabinet appointments. Minton suggested that Truman appoint Jim Byrnes as secretary of state and name Lew Schwellenbach as secretary of labor. After Biffle passed the recommendations on to Truman, the president wrote Minton that "you don't have to get at me through any secondhand route. As far as you are concerned, I am just as approachable as I was when we sat together in the Senate."[42] Truman named Schwellenbach his labor secretary, reportedly with an agreement that he would be appointed to the first Supreme Court vacancy.[43]

In 1945, amid speculation about his own appointment to Truman's cabinet, Minton was named to head the newly created War Department Clemency Board. The board was established by Under Secretary of War Robert Patterson to assist him in reviewing court-martial sentences. The five-member board was to review cases in which clemency had been recommended for convicted soldiers.

The task of the clemency board was formidable; there were over thirty thousand cases to be reviewed. To assist the board several three-member groups were formed in order to process the cases as quickly as possible. The smaller boards, which met daily, handled the bulk of the cases but passed the complicated cases to the larger board. The clemency board set general policies for different types of offenses and handled the precedent-setting or more difficult cases.

The work of the clemency board, which met every two weeks, along with his judicial responsibilities and his anemia, taxed Minton's health to the limit, and in September 1945 he suffered a major heart attack. It came just days after he had been passed over by Truman when Truman named Harold H. Burton, a Republican, as his first Supreme Court nominee. Concern about Minton's health was given as a reason why he was not selected.[44]

Minton spent four months at Walter Reed Hospital. During that stay he came to appreciate more fully than before the kindness and generosity of his fellow judge Evan Evans, who was worried about Minton's physical and financial well-being. Evans wrote to his colleague in January offering to do anything he could to help. He said: "I don't believe I ever made such an offer, although the willingness has always been there and I assumed that you knew it. It is at this time of the year when taxes and expenses are high that it came to me the other day that I might be of assistance, any and all kinds. If you should need any financial help, I will be glad to advance it. It has been quite a long hard pull, but I'm sure it is going to get better this year, and by next summer all will be fine and dandy."[45]

After being dismissed from Walter Reed and before returning to New Albany to recuperate, Minton stopped for a visit at the White House, where Truman gave him a gold-headed cane to help him get around. It was early April when Minton returned to Chicago and his duties on the Seventh Circuit, although he was still physically weak. His condition concerned his former Senate colleague Carl A. Hatch, who wrote to Truman that "poor Old Shay may be out of the running physically but he continues to think democratically always."[46] Truman, in his reply to Hatch, also expressed concern. "He is the same old Shay mentally and I'd give anything in the world if there was something we could do to make him physically the same Shay."[47]

Though physically weak, thoughts of Washington politics were never far from Minton's mind. When Chief Justice Harlan F. Stone died on 22 April 1946 Minton was alarmed that the president might fill the vacancy with a Republican, as he was being urged to do in newspaper editorials. Minton wrote to Truman: "Many of our friends are disturbed because they fear you might appoint a Chief Justice who is a Republican. . . . I am firmly convinced that the Court must be kept liberal. Don't let us be responsible for another Court controlled by the moneybags of the country."

Minton recommended that Truman elevate Black to chief justice and appoint Schwellenbach in Black's place.

PHOTOGRAPH BY HARRIS & EWING, COLLECTION OF THE SUPREME COURT OF THE UNITED STATES

Federal Judge Sherman Minton, who was head of a three-man presidential fact-finding board looking into a nationwide coal strike, reads a letter from John L. Lewis on 29 March 1948.

UPI/CORBIS-BETTMANN

On 31 March 1948 President Harry Truman received the report from the federal fact-finding board on the coal strike. At right is Minton; the other board members were George W. Taylor (rear left), former War Labor Board Chairman, and Mark Ethridge, publisher of the *Louisville Courier-Journal.*

"Black is a liberal," he said, "and is to that Court a breath of fresh air in a musty, damp cellar." He described Schwellenbach as "a liberal in the best sense of that word, and able and courageous."[48] Truman's response was noncommittal, but warm: "I often wish you and I were again sitting beside each other in the back row of the Senate. There are a lot of things going on there now that I believe the two of us could remedy."[49]

In the end Truman did not follow Minton's advice. Bitter disagreements had erupted among the members of the Court over the possibility that Truman would select one of their own to be chief justice. Two of the justices who might have been considered, Black and Jackson, were at war with each other. It was rumored that Black had told Truman he would resign if Jackson were named chief justice. Jackson, along with Felix Frankfurter, had written a memorandum fiercely attacking Black for participating in a decision in which one of the litigants was represented by Black's former law partner. When the conflict became public in an article in the *Washington Star* it eliminated both Black and Jackson for consideration. Steering clear of these internecine battles on the Court, Truman chose his longtime friend Fred M. Vinson, a former member of Congress who was then serving as secretary of the treasury. Vinson also had served five years on the United States Court of Appeals for the District of Columbia. Truman thought Vinson would be able to calm the turmoil on the Court, and he also expected Vinson to be supportive of strong executive action.[50]

Minton wrote to Black expressing his disappointment over the appointment. In his reply Black acknowledged that the president "was faced with a hard situation. Like you, I am very fond of Fred Vinson, and I can think of no reason why he will not be a good Chief Justice. At any rate, I anticipate that I shall enjoy working with him." Black also expressed hope that "Lew will get up here sometime."[51]

While Minton had been promoting his friends for Supreme Court appointments he was being promoted as a possible senatorial nominee. The idea that Minton might return to Indiana to seek the nomination reached a high pitch in May 1946, when Minton attended a meeting of Democratic newspaper editors. According to newspaper reports Minton was "receptive" to the idea, but by the June convention he had put an end to the speculation.

Although Minton did not run for the Senate seat he still maintained an active interest in Indiana politics. It was widely believed that he played a role in getting New Albany native F. Shirley Wilcox named collector of Internal Revenue for Indiana in the fall of 1945, replacing Will H. Smith, who had held the job since 1933. Questioned about the propriety of a federal judge engaging in patronage affairs, Minton denied any involvement. "I know nothing about the Smith situation," he said. "I haven't got anything to do with it."[52]

Minton's name logically surfaced in speculation over what happened because of his close relationship with Wilcox and because in the late 1930s Minton had tried to get Smith ousted as collector and replaced by Minton's longtime crony Pleas E. Greenlee. Not only was Minton rebuffed in his attempt, but his entreaty in Greenlee's behalf also prompted Treasury Secretary Henry Morgenthau to launch an investigation of the income tax returns of several Hoosier politicians, including Greenlee and Paul V. McNutt. Furthermore, the Wilcox appointment might have been a consolation prize since it was announced one day after Truman named two Republicans to positions for which Minton had been considered: Harold Burton to the Supreme Court and Robert Patterson as secretary of war.

Two years after Wilcox was named revenue collector Minton asked Truman to consider appointing Wilcox to the Federal Communications Commission (FCC). Truman did appoint a Hoosier to the commission, but it was not Wilcox. Instead, he named Wayne Coy, former head of the Indiana

Works Progress Administration (WPA) and political ally of Paul McNutt, to be FCC chairman.[53]

In March 1948 Minton's turn came to help Truman when a nationwide strike by the United Mine Workers (UMW) posed a threat to the nation's coal supplies and a disruption of freight haulage. Truman wanted to issue an injunction to stop the strike, but under the Taft-Hartley Act he first had to convene a board of inquiry into the dispute. The president appointed a three-man board to investigate the dispute; Minton was named chairman. The other members were Dr. George W. Taylor of the Wharton School of Finance at the University of Pennsylvania and Mark Ethridge, publisher of the *Louisville Courier-Journal* and *Louisville Times*.

His role on the coal board pitted Minton against UMW president John L. Lewis, whom Minton had long disliked because of Lewis's open hostility to both Roosevelt and Truman. Lewis, who was subpoenaed to testify before the board about his role in instigating the strike, denied any role in ordering the strike, claiming it was purely an independent action. The board of inquiry, however, reached a different conclusion. Within a week a report was submitted to the president blaming Lewis for the strike. Three days later a federal judge issued an injunction ordering the coal miners to return to work. Lewis initially defied the order, an action for which he was later tried for contempt of court. After a strike of nearly five weeks, Lewis did order the miners back to work, but only after he won concessions from the coal operators over pension benefits for the miners.

After helping Truman deal with Lewis, Minton sought the president's help with judicial appointments for the Seventh Circuit. The court had experienced major changes, beginning with the death of senior judge Evans in July 1948. Sparks became the senior judge for four months before retiring, because of ill health, to his home in Rushville, Indiana. When Sparks resigned Earl Major became chief judge of the circuit. Minton wasted no time in lobbying Truman to fill the two vacancies. Following the 1948 election Minton wrote to Truman about "the emergency on our court." Noting that the death of Evans and the retirement of Sparks had left the court with only three judges to handle the heaviest caseload in years, he urged the appointment of Judge Ryan Duffy of the Eastern District of Wisconsin. Minton had a high regard for Duffy, a loyal New Dealer whom Minton knew well from his Senate years. On more than one occasion Minton had singled out the quality of Duffy's opinions when they were reviewed by the Seventh Circuit. Minton told Truman that Duffy is "one of our best District Judges. . . . Please make his appointment the first message you send to the Senate so he can be confirmed promptly. We need him badly."[54] Truman finally appointed Duffy to the Seventh Circuit to replace Evans in 1949.

For the other vacancy on the court Minton urged Truman to appoint United States Judge Walter C. Lindley of the Eastern District of Illinois, probably the only time in his life that Minton supported a Republican. He and the other judges of the Seventh Circuit knew Lindley particularly well since Lindley frequently was called into service by the Seventh Circuit when the caseload became excessive. In 1948 when the vacancies first occurred, Minton pressed Truman to elevate Lindley to the appellate court. Truman was slow to respond. In January 1949 Minton wrote to the president urging him to expedite the appointment to the court: "I cannot overemphasize how important it is for the good of this court that Judge Lindley be appointed and promptly in order that we may have again a full court."[55] Although Truman indicated that he would "get the Judge for the Court of Appeals straightened out in the manner which you and I discussed,"[56] he did not. In April Minton wrote Truman that they were "disappointed you couldn't give us Lindley on our Court, but we think we understand the predicament you were in."[57] Truman eventually came through for Minton. Lindley was finally appointed to the

Seventh Circuit to fill Minton's vacancy when he was elevated to the Supreme Court.

In his final months on the Seventh Circuit, before he had an inkling of how his own life was about to change, Minton once again asked Truman for help in an Indiana patronage dispute. This one involved the position of United States district attorney, which was being vacated by B. Howard Caughran, who had held the position for nine years. The extent of Minton's involvement with this issue reveals much about the man. It reflects how deeply ingrained his ties to Indiana politics were, no matter how far removed they may have been from his professional concerns as a federal appellate judge, or how inconsequential they were for his own political fortunes.

Many names surfaced as possible successors when Caughran's retirement was first announced. Among them were Alan T. Nolan, a former Minton law clerk on the circuit court and son of Minton's close friend Val Nolan; John Cody, also an old friend and law partner; and William Steckler, who held Minton's former position as public counselor to the Public Service Commission. From the very beginning it was clear there would be a fight over the nomination.

Minton's efforts to prevent the nomination of John Hurt, a Martinsville attorney, and to promote the nomination of Marshall Hanley, a Muncie attorney, were widely publicized. Hanley, a New Albany native, had served as Minton's law clerk on the circuit court, as well as in his New Albany law office. He also had been active in the Democratic party and, at the time of the dispute, was just stepping down as president of the Indiana Young Democrats.

The conflict over the appointment stemmed from the continuing factional rivalries in the Democratic party, from which Minton never extricated himself. Hurt was backed by the McHale faction of the party, which then included state party chairman Ira Haymaker. Hurt, who had formed a law partnership with Haymaker, had been secretary of the state Democratic party and was Gov. Henry Schricker's chauffeur and personal aide during the 1948 campaign. Hurt had the public support of many prominent Democrats, including Governor Schricker, Herman B Wells, president of Indiana University, and three Democratic congressmen: James E. Noland from Bloomington, Winfield K. Denton from Evansville, and Andrew Jacobs, Sr., from Indianapolis.[58] Through the support of Haymaker and McHale, Hurt had been endorsed by both the state and national party organizations.

Hanley had the support of the younger members of the party, who rallied behind his cause in what one newspaper described as the battle between the "young politicos" and the "graybeards." The Young Democrats, resentful that so few of them had been given any posts of responsibility within the party or in state government, passed a resolution demanding Hanley's appointment to the position. The resolution was sent to the state party organization as well as to President Truman and Attorney General Tom C. Clark.[59]

Hurt's appointment was opposed not only by Minton but also by Cong. John Walsh, a Martinsville attorney, who formerly had been Hurt's law partner. Walsh was upset over not being consulted on patronage matters. Minton, writing to Truman about the matter, claimed, disingenuously, that "I don't intrude myself into the political picture in Indiana as a general thing." Still, he wanted Truman to know that while Hurt's character and integrity were above reproach, he believed Hurt lacked the necessary experience for the position.[60]

Truman answered that the congressmen in question had confirmed that they were not "satisfied with the situation," and he invited Minton to talk with him about the subject if he arrived in Washington any time soon.[61]

In July both Minton and Walsh called upon Truman at the White House to try to prevent Hurt's appointment. Minton was still behind Hanley. He told reporters after his meeting, "I'm always glad to put in a good word for an old friend." Minton went to great lengths to emphasize that his visit with Truman was purely a "side door" affair because he did not want it to appear that he was approaching Truman on behalf of his own candidacy for the Supreme Court vacancy created by the death of Justice Frank Murphy. Minton told reporters that he did not have a "Chinaman's chance" of getting the job, adding "It's been that way for 20 years."[62]

While Minton and Walsh were lobbying the White House, McHale was continuing to push Hurt on another front. One of McHale's political allies and former law partner, Alexander Campbell, was assistant attorney general in Washington. Campbell was instrumental in expediting the necessary FBI investigation of Hurt, and he confidently assured Hurt that "if the investigation is completed favorably, as I know it will be, the Attorney General will then formally recommend you and your name will be sent to the President, who will of course, follow the Attorney General's recommendation and send your nomination to the United States Senate."[63]

Campbell's confidence was misplaced. Attorney General Clark, with whom Minton had spoken about the appointment, did not recommend Hurt. In fact, before the matter was settled Clark had been nominated by Truman to fill the Supreme Court vacancy.

The affair ended with a compromise appointment. Truman nominated Matthew E. Welsh of Vincennes, Seventh District Democratic chairman, who later became governor. Welsh's appointment meant that Minton had accomplished only part of his goal. Although Minton prevented Hurt from becoming the United States district attorney, he had not succeeded in getting his protégé Hanley appointed. By the time Welsh's appointment was made Minton was already on the Supreme Court.[64]

Minton rarely questioned the wisdom of meddling in political affairs, but when Schwellenbach died in June 1948, Minton expressed regret over the part he played in returning his good friend to the grind of national politics. His sorrow over Schwellenbach's death was reflected in a letter to Carl Hatch. Minton wrote: "I have been unhappier about the hand I may have had in getting him back to Washington, D.C. than most anything in my life. I think he would be alive today if he had not gone back."[65]

Minton's inability to extricate himself from politics, even as a judge, came from a deep-seated need, almost a survival instinct. His involvement in politics may have kept his spirit alive during his years away from Washington, but he had to do more to keep his hopes for the Supreme Court alive. His chances for an appointment to the Court could not rest on political ties alone, even if those ties were with the president of the United States. Minton needed more than connections. He needed respectability as a judge, and he needed a record that would withstand scrutiny, not so much by his political supporters but by his would-be critics, both in Congress and in the media.

CHAPTER SEVEN

A Faithful Disciple of Judicial Restraint

Sherman Minton took up his judicial responsibilities on the Seventh Circuit in 1941 without much fanfare. When he arrived at the court he was shown directly to his chamber, donned his robe, and joined Judges Otto Kerner and William Sparks on the bench. I am "here to work," he told reporters.[1] And work he did. During the next eight years he wrote over 250 opinions, on par with his fellow judges on the Seventh Circuit and better than average for an appellate court judge. He managed to keep pace despite bouts with poor health and special assignments from Roosevelt and Truman.

Minton assumed his judicial role at a highly charged time. The federal courts were just beginning to wrestle with cases resulting from several pieces of legislation that Minton helped pass in the Senate, including the Selective Service Act, the National Labor Relations Act, and the Robinson-Patman Act, which dealt with price discrimination. In addition, legislation passed before Minton's Senate term, especially the Sherman Antitrust Act and the Clayton Act, continued to generate legal controversies about permissible business practices. War-related issues also began coming before the Seventh Circuit. Among these were cases involving civil liberties and individuals who resisted military service on the grounds of their religious beliefs.

Minton's approach in dealing with these issues and the host of others that came before the Seventh Circuit during his tenure reflected the dominant influences of his life—his legislative experience and his populist temperament. The judicial style he developed was characterized by restraint, pragmatism, and common sense, coupled with a philosophical and political deference to the will of the majority expressed in legislative enactments.

Judicial activism was anathema to Minton—he took a dim view of judges interfering with legislative and administrative prerogatives. As a senator he had been an outspoken critic of a Supreme Court whose interpretation of the Constitution regarding the powers of the states to regulate economic activity became an obstacle to New Deal legislation. Minton frequently had denounced the Court for standing in the way of popularly elected majorities who were seeking to serve the needs of the people. Abner Mikva, former chief judge of the United States Court of Appeals for the District of Columbia and former Minton law clerk, maintains that Minton's "experiences as a United States Senator did more to mold his judicial philosophy than anything else in his career."[2] Minton carefully dissected legislative enactments so that he would "neither thwart the legislative intent nor engraft upon it unexpressed embellishments that might appeal to the court."[3]

If judicial restraint was the first lesson Minton learned from his political experiences, pragmatism was the second. This pragmatism affected both his judicial style of reasoning and his opinion writing. During his political career Minton had looked for practical solutions to problems and had found ways to put those solutions into effect. His fiery oratory in behalf of his causes reduced complex social issues to problems that had but one obvious answer—the policy he advocated. It was the same on the bench. He approached each case with one objective: to resolve the dispute at hand. As a result scholars have viewed him as being "less of a scholar than an advocate. His opinions were constructed as a debater might prepare a position. He never conducted a jurisprudential inquiry into whether the position adopted in his opinion was better than an alternative view."[4]

Those who looked to the courts for practical answers to legal issues complimented Minton's opinions. Editors of *Tax Magazine* praised him for his "direct Hoosier logic."[5] Casper Ooms, founder of the Seventh Circuit Bar Association, called Minton's opinions "clear and orderly." Ooms said Minton possessed "the simple formality of an accomplished essayist . . . [who] states the issue simply" and then "proceeds directly into an examination of the arguments, answers each question in order, and summarizes the conclusion." Minton, Ooms added, was "the master of the short sentence. His phrasing never bewilders. His conclusions never escape even the quick reading."[6]

The style of opinion writing that Minton crafted on the Seventh Circuit became his trademark. It never appealed to commentators who looked more to an opinion's intellectual and literary qualities than to its application to the law. Minton was good at coining phrases, often with a touch of homespun humor, but they were not the kind of phrases that had enduring qualities or broad application. Although he was a good writer he lacked the verbal flourish for which famous jurists are known.

Minton's commitment to the view that judges ought to stick to the law and let Congress do the legislating was an article of faith to him, a guiding principle for virtually every decision that involved a legislative statute. For example, Minton, dissenting when the majority had ignored wording in the controlling statute, wrote that the law "is plain and unambiguous, and the words eliminated by the majority are purposeful and full of meaning. As I understand it, it is not the business of the courts to seek conflicts or ambiguities in statutes in order that we may rewrite the statute to our liking. It is our business to apply the statute as written."[7]

Minton's reliance on statutory wording often made complicated cases easier to resolve, as was evident in the case of a railroad engineer who was killed when a locomotive developed an overheated axle called a hot box. The engineer had been warned by fellow railroad employees about the hot box, but he refused to heed their warnings. Finally the axle broke, the locomotive overturned, and the engineer was killed. The railroad company appealed a district court ruling that the company was liable. Minton dismissed the arguments of the railroad company purely on the basis of the statutes in question. He said that the Safety Appliance Act and the Employers' Liability Act, construed together, made the railroad company liable. He wrote that the engineer "could not be deemed to have assumed the risk, no matter how many times the engine was observed by the decedent to be defective and he thereafter continued to use it. Congress has said so."[8]

Although Minton did not dissent very often, when he did it was because he thought the court had disregarded the intent of Congress when reviewing implementation of its laws. A case in point involved two businessmen who sued the United States Postal Service to recover a refund for excess postage they had been required to pay for items shipped at third-class rates. The district court had ruled in favor of the two businessmen, a decision upheld by the Seventh Circuit. Minton dissented on the grounds that the statute in question left the decision of refunds to the discretion of the postmaster general. "Congress did not provide for judicial review," Minton wrote.[9]

Strict adherence to legislative language often led Minton to support the exercise of government power against claimed rights of individuals. In 1947 Minton wrote the majority decision in the case of Wilhelm Hack, a German enemy alien who was ordered deported by Attorney General Tom C. Clark on the grounds that his presence was dangerous to the public peace and safety. Hack claimed that he had been denied due process of law in the proceedings. The district court had upheld the attorney general, and Hack appealed. Minton wasted few words in upholding the district court and the attorney general, declaring that the only question to be answered was whether Hack was an enemy alien. "If he is, that ends the proceeding. He may not contest in the courts of the host nation when or under what circumstances he, an enemy alien, shall be ordered to depart." Minton said it was not for the court to decide whether "the country from whence he came is still at war with the United States or is still in existence as a sovereign power; that is a political question to be answered only by . . . the executive and legislative branches."[10]

Minton's philosophy of restraint also meant that he accorded administrative agencies the same wide latitude he did legislative statutes. Agency rulings normally are appealed when aggrieved parties, usually businesses, believe that either the agency has exceeded its statutory authority or that the agency lacked sufficient evidence on which to rule. Minton would not review decisions of administrative agencies unless Congress explicitly provided for such review in its authorizing statute. When he did review administrative action it was unusual for him to conclude that an agency had exceeded its discretion in carrying out the law.

The National Labor Relations Board (NLRB) was one of the agencies Minton treated with deference. As a senator he had been one of the most enthusiastic supporters of the National Labor Relations Act, which created the NLRB. When two of his fellow judges voted to overrule an NLRB order against the Marshall Field Company, Minton vehemently dissented. "The stick-in-the-bark legalisms of courtroom practice," he said, "were not intended to be permitted to control the procedure of the Board. I do not think this Court can prescribe or veto the Board's procedure in a proceeding of this kind. Congress may, but it has not done so."[11]

When administrative decisions were appealed on grounds that the agency lacked sufficient evidence for its order, Minton was strongly inclined to give the benefit of the doubt to the agency, just as he did to trial court judges. A frequent refrain in Minton's decisions was that agencies need only look to evidence favorable to the board's findings. This is the norm for appellate courts, but Minton clung to this view even more fervently than some of his colleagues.[12] Minton's tendency to support the decisions of administrative agencies more so than his fellow judges was equally evident when he reached the Supreme Court.[13]

There were times, however, when even Minton could not bring himself to support an agency finding. He was particularly worried about cases where he felt that agencies were making inferences too far removed from the facts. In one case, chastising the NLRB for a strained interpretation, he wrote that "an inference cannot be piled upon an inference, and then another inference upon that, as such inferences are unreasonable and cannot be considered as substantial evidence. Such a method could be extended indefinitely until there would be no more substance to it than the soup Lincoln talked about that was 'made by boiling the shadow of a pigeon that had starved to death.'"[14]

While judicial restraint clearly directed Minton's actions on the bench, he was also guided by his populist philosophy. Even before he assumed a public career Minton believed that the power of government should be used to improve the health and well-being of its citizens. Specifically, he felt that government should regulate and mandate the behavior of business to serve the public good and that government revenues should be used to help people in need.

Nowhere was Minton's populist bias more obvious than in the area of monopolistic practices. His interest in monopolies dated to his high school days where he voiced concern about how the concentration of economic power affected the lives of the common people. As counselor to the Public Service Commission he sought to curb the greed of a particular kind of monopoly—utility companies. Throughout his senatorial career some of the main targets of his political attacks were powerful economic interests such as media monopolies and utility holding companies.

During his service on the Seventh Circuit Minton wrote many opinions involving governmental efforts to restrain unfair business practices. Prominent among these were the antitrust suits brought under the Sherman Act, which prohibited practices that threatened to destroy business competition. Antitrust litigation increased in the late 1940s due to the Supreme Court's interpretation of the scope and applicability of the Sherman Act. Because significant economic interests were at stake, antitrust rulings in the trial courts were appealed as a matter of course. Minton got more than his fair share of these cases, to the extent that the publication *United States Law Week* described antitrust litigation as the main emphasis of his eight years on the circuit bench.[15]

Those who expected Minton to be an economic reformer on the court were not disappointed with his antitrust rulings. Unfair business practices and monopolies were automatically suspect in his eyes. Ruling against such practices was, of course, consistent with his populist philosophy, which sanctioned the use of public power to rein in the abuses of private power. His decisions in these cases were also consistent with his judicial deference, for there were numerous statutes making monopolistic practices illegal. Most prominent among these statutes were the Sherman Antitrust Act, the Clayton Act, and the Robinson-Patman Act.

One of Minton's best-known opinions regarding monopolies was in *United States* v. *New York Great Atlantic and Pacific Tea Company*, which found A&P guilty of violating the Sherman Antitrust Act.[16] A&P, the largest retail food chain in the country, was accused of conspiring to restrain and monopolize trade in the grocery business. One way it did so was through dictating the terms and conditions for suppliers who wished to sell food products to the company. A&P, Minton said, used its mass buying power "to coerce suppliers to sell to it at a lower price than to its competitors." A&P even dictated the terms under which these suppliers could sell or not sell to A&P's competitors; the company also threatened to blacklist and compete with suppliers who resisted. Such heavy-handed tactics allowed A&P to reduce the costs of products in its retail stores. Minton, summoning up Portia's speech in Shakespeare's *The Merchant of Venice,* wrote:

> This price advantage given A&P by the suppliers was, it is fairly inferable, not "twice blessed" like the quality of mercy that "droppeth as the gentle rain from heaven." It did not bless "him that gives and him that takes." Only A&P was blessed, and the supplier had to make his profit out of his other customers at higher prices, which were passed on to the competition A&P met in the retail field.

A&P used these blessings gained through coercion to stymie its competitors. For example, if one of its stores was having difficulty in a highly competitive locale, A&P lowered that store's gross profit percentage, which in turn lowered the price at which the goods could be sold. In some cases the gross profit rate was so low that the store ran below the cost of operating. Minton noted that "some local grocers were quickly eliminated under the lethal competition put upon them by A&P when armed with its monopoly power." Writing for a unanimous majority, Minton concluded that there was substantial evidence that A&P was guilty of conspiring to restrain and monopolize trade and therefore affirmed the judgment of the district court. That became the final word in the matter as the Supreme Court refused to consider the case on appeal.[17]

Minton's position on monopolistic practices restricted by the Sherman Act was not unyielding. In a 1947 case, Cargill, Incorporated, a large grain dealer that entered into grain futures contracts, sued the Chicago Board of Trade for suspending trading for a day because of impending changes in government price controls. Cargill claimed that the board had interfered with free and open trading in violation of the Sherman Antitrust Act. The board justified its actions under established rules pertaining to emergencies. Cargill was denied injunctive relief against the Board of Trade by a federal district court and therefore appealed to the Seventh Circuit. Minton affirmed the lower court ruling. In the majority opinion he wrote that the "Board owed a duty to the public and to all parties trading upon the market to act in the utmost good faith in the general interest." He did not consider the board's actions to be either price fixing or an illegal restraint of trade. The actions by the board, he said, "rather than being in restraint of commerce, were in aid of commerce in facilitating future trading on the market."[18]

In the *Cargill* opinion Minton's opinion was brief and to the point. He made a complex issue relatively easy to comprehend, a trait recognized by Chief Judge Evan Evans when he assigned him the case. In a memo to Minton and James Earl Major, Evans said he chose Minton to write the majority opinion because "[the Board of Trade cases] are the hardest ones I have sat in. They are going to be hard to answer satisfactorily."[19]

Discriminatory pricing schemes represented another example of monopolistic practices that had been regulated by legislative acts. The Clayton Act, which prohibited many forms of price discrimination, allowed discriminatory pricing between different purchasers of the same commodity provided that such discrimination was "made in good faith to meet competition." Large corporations took advantage of this loophole and thus evaded the intent of the act. The Robinson-Patman Act, for which Minton had voted in 1936, sought to close the loophole. It said that setting a lower price to meet competition could no longer be used as an absolute defense against a charge of price discrimination. Instead, the practice was merely one factor to be considered by the Federal Trade Commission (FTC) in price discrimination cases. The act also placed the burden of proof on the company. Uncertainty as to the scope and application of the act plagued not only the FTC, which was responsible for enforcing its provisions, but also the businesses responsible for complying with them and the judges who had to interpret them.

Minton's first interpretation of the Robinson-Patman Act came in 1943 when he upheld the basing point price system used by A. E. Staley Manufacturing Company and other manufacturers of corn syrup or glucose.[20] Staley was located in Decatur, Illinois, while its chief competitor was located in Chicago. Under the basing point system, the manufacturer took the price of the commodity in Chicago and added the cost of freight to the place of destination. This meant that a buyer in Decatur, where Staley was located, would pay the Chicago base price plus freight from Chicago to Decatur, even though the goods originated in Decatur. As a result Staley's Decatur customers paid as much as 16 percent more for a commodity than buyers in Chicago.

The FTC found the discriminatory basing point system to be a violation of the Robinson-Patman Act, but Minton felt it was justified in this instance to meet the competition. He said that Staley's competitors were using the basing point system when they went into business, and that "to get into the Chicago market under that system, they had to absorb the freight from Decatur to Chicago. The bulk of their business was in the Chicago market and their product was sold at a price to meet competitors' lower price in Chicago."[21] Minton felt that the evidence demonstrated Staley had used the system in good faith in order to be competitive and refused to enforce the commission's order.

A unanimous Supreme Court reversed Minton on appeal. Chief Justice Harlan F. Stone wrote the opinion that overturned Minton's interpretation of the statutory defense of meeting a competitor's price. As one observer noted later, "Staley may not have appreciated the irony of Coolidge's former Attorney General telling the former New Deal Senator, who had voted for the Robinson-Patman Act, that Congress had not intended to be as easy on businessmen as Judge Minton had concluded."[22] The lesson of the Staley reversal was not lost on Minton, as was demonstrated in his opinion overruling a pricing scheme of Standard Oil in 1949.

Like Staley, Standard Oil defended its discriminatory pricing scheme as a good faith effort to meet its competition. Standard Oil had discriminated in its prices by charging less to four wholesale customers in the Detroit area than it charged to its retail customers. These wholesalers sold directly to the public through retail service stations that they owned and operated. Standard Oil offered convincing evidence that the discriminatory pricing was made in good faith to meet the low prices of its competitors. Both the FTC and the Seventh Circuit conceded that. However, Minton said that the injury to competition was felt farther down the chain of commerce. He determined that "the petitioner's favored wholesalers were in a position to do and did do injury to competition."[23]

Coming three weeks after the A&P decision, Minton's opinion in the Standard Oil case reinforced his antimonopolistic reputation. The basis of the Standard Oil ruling was similar to the A&P opinion in that Minton's concern was with the effect of the discriminatory practice on competitors, especially the smaller ones who could not compete with the lower prices.[24]

Monopolistic trade practices came in many forms, but regardless of form Minton was always skeptical of their legitimacy. Cases involving trademarks and patents, which have the effect of restricting trade, proved no exception to Minton's antimonopolistic bent. Because they were limited monopolies Minton demanded that patents "must show originality and the exercise of inventive faculty. It is not sufficient to take old designs or forms and adapt them to new purposes."[25] He once ruled a hydrometer device was not patentable because it contributed nothing new. The inventor had found a way to stabilize a hydrometer, a device which measures gravity, by putting a base on it. The invention in question was not the hydrometer but the base upon which it rested. Minton was not impressed. "If something without a base will not stand upright and steady, what is the first thing that one would think of? A base, of course. Is that invention? If it is, then the human family has not understood what has been perfectly apparent ever since the first baby sat upright upon its own bottom."[26]

Minton's language in this case illustrates another characteristic of his opinion writing—the application of common sense notions, often with a sarcastic humor, to technical legal questions. It was as if he were writing for a general audience, in the style of a politician, rather than for lawyers who must wrestle with the complexities that characterize the area of patent law.

Minton considered trademarks to be monopolistic agents that served the interests of large, corporate entities and not the consumer or the small entrepreneur. Generally he was skeptical of the claims companies used to support a trademark defense, once denying protection to a firm that asserted confusion would result if another company were allowed to use a similar name. "Mere confusion," was not enough, Minton said, adding the court needed proof of some "wrong added to incidental confusion in the use of similar names, such as fraud, deception, or palming off."[27]

In similar fashion Minton had little patience with the California Fruit Growers Exchange, which sold citrus fruits under the trademark "Sunkist," when it tried to prevent a bakery in Illinois from using the trademark "Sunkist Bread." It was obvious to Minton that fruits and vegetables were not in the same general class of merchandise as bread. He wrote, "Unless 'Sunkist' covers everything edible under the sun, we cannot believe that anyone whose I.Q. is high enough to be regarded by the law would ever be confused or would likely to be confused in the purchase of a loaf of bread branded as 'Sunkist' because someone else sold fruits and vegetables under that name."[28]

Minton came under strong criticism for his *Sunkist* opinion. A law review article, arguing that certain monopolistic practices are socially valuable, said that "rooting them out with excessive zeal may have deleterious economic consequences. The Trade Mark Act of 1946 . . . does not give legislative sanction to the tinge of 'monopoly-phobia' which affected this court's evaluation of the factors involved."[29]

Minton's "phobia" about trade names had been apparent long before the *Sunkist* case. He granted Quaker Oats the right to use the trade names "Oaties" and "Quaker Oaties," even though General Mills said it infringed on its product named "Wheaties." Minton said, "The names themselves suggest two different kinds of products. One suggests a product made of wheat, and the others a product made of oats." He was unmoved by General Mills's argument that Quaker Oats had infringed on a family of names, those ending with "ies." Minton's flair for sarcasm was evident when he wrote: "Our sympathy for the family ties was greatly diminished when we recalled that at the time [General Mills] was ready to market its ready-to-eat breakfast cereal of oats, it sent it forth into the cruel competitive world not as 'Oaties' but as 'Cherrioats,' wholly deprived of its family name."[30]

Minton felt so strongly about monopolies granted through trade names that he was compelled on several occasions to dissent from the majority when they provided protection for trademarks that he felt were not justified. He believed, for example, that Horlick's Malted Milk Corporation should not have been allowed to force Charles

Horlick, who sold Horlick's Dog Food, to alter the wording on his packages of dog food to prevent any confusion with Horlick's that sold malted milk.[31] In the same vein he could not see why a company that sold solid fuels should be prevented from using a name similar to a business that sold fuel oil.[32]

Minton's decisions about monopolistic practices were consistent with his long-standing bias against economic concentrations of power. By the same token his decisions about the rights of labor were consistent with his strong commitment to labor legislation while he was in the Senate. Appeals in cases concerning labor usually involved three pieces of legislation—the National Labor Relations Act (NLRA), the Fair Labor Standards Act (FLSA), and the Federal Employers' Liability Act (FELA)—two of which, NLRA and FLSA, Minton ardently supported while he was in the Senate.[33] Some judges in similar circumstances might have declined to participate in cases involving acts with which they were so closely identified, but Minton apparently felt that he could be objective in reviewing cases arising under these statutes. His record tends to bear out that assumption.

The NLRA was passed in 1935 to permit and encourage American workers to bargain collectively about wages and working conditions. The act established the right of employees to organize, to join the labor unions of their choice, and to have these unions represent them in collective bargaining. Employers were prohibited from interfering in these rights in any way. Specifically prohibited were such tactics as supporting a company union and firing union organizers. The NLRA created the National Labor Relations Board (NLRB) to oversee collective bargaining activities and authorized it to take action against employers who interfered with workers' bargaining rights.

The NLRB's efforts to prevent unfair labor practices increased significantly after the Supreme Court declared the NLRA constitutional in 1937. The courts were soon flooded with appeals from decisions of the NLRB that found employers guilty of unfair labor practices. Sometimes the appeals raised questions about the interpretation of the act, but most of the cases involved factual questions about the motivations of employers in dealing with union employees.

As one of the strongest supporters of the NLRA, Minton was expected to make decisions favorable to the NLRB. In general these expectations were borne out, but his record "surprised those who had assumed that Judge Minton would carry his New Deal partisanship to his new job."[34] His labor decisions have been called "invariably fair,"[35] and indeed they were. While his general inclination was to support the NLRB, because he thought that was the intent of Congress, he did not hesitate to rule against the NLRB when he thought that the agency's rulings did not square with congressional intent.

The NLRB was zealous in its efforts to root out unfair labor practices. Employers were equally zealous in defending themselves against NLRB orders to cease and desist their practices. Appellate courts such as the Seventh Circuit became arbiters of these disputes because, as the court of first instance in NLRB appeals, only they had the power to enforce an order of the NLRB. In resolving these conflicts between two sets of adversaries, Minton returned time and again to the purpose of the NLRA.

In one of his very first opinions written on the Seventh Circuit, Minton ordered the enforcement of an NLRB order against a manufacturer of transmission machinery because he found that company management had interfered with the employees' rights to organize. Minton said that the employer "has no more right to intrude himself into the employees' efforts to organize . . . than the employee would have to intrude himself into a stockholders' meeting to interfere with the election of the company's directors."[36]

The above opinion, written in November 1941, signaled that Minton would have little patience with employers who violated the law by their anti-union tactics. Chastising one company for its intransigence in collective bargaining with its employees, Minton said: "It was the duty of the company to meet the representatives of the union not with a closed mind but with an open mind, with the purpose and intention in good faith to try by an exchange of views to reach an understanding and a conclusion if possible." Quoting Edmund Burke, who observed that "all government . . . is founded on compromise and barter," Minton said that "faith in this democratic doctrine led Congress to pass the National Labor Relations Act."[37]

In another strongly worded opinion Minton reminded a company confronted with an NLRB order that it had no business interfering with the efforts of employees to form a union. Minton was emphatic that "the question of organization by the employees for the purpose of collective bargaining is the exclusive business and concern of the employees. The slightest interference, intimidation or coercion by the employer of the employees in the rights guaranteed to the employees by the statute constitutes an unfair labor practice."[38]

Minton reiterated the same point after the NLRB found the Sunbeam Electric Company guilty of unfair labor practices because of its vigorous campaign among employees to make sure the election went against the union. A company superintendent had summoned two employees to his office and asked them what they expected to get out of the union that they could not get out of management and informed them of a company plan to increase wages all along the line. Minton took a dim view of the company's tactics, which he said "had created a false issue between the employees and their employer. That false issue was that the employees were to choose between the company's executives and the union. That was not the issue. The issue was whom would the employees have for their bargaining agent. Obviously, the company's executives could not be. Who is to represent the employees as bargaining agent and the manner of selection are matters which belong exclusively to the employees. The statute has made it so, and it is the duty of the employer to keep hands off and maintain a strictly neutral attitude."[39]

Minton felt that the NLRA not only protected employees who wanted to form a union for collective bargaining, but that it also protected workers who did not so choose. Minton backed the NLRB when it found that a company had discriminated against an employee who was discharged because he would not join the union. There was no closed shop, or unionship, agreement, and the board held that in the absence of such a pact the employee could not be compelled to join a union. Minton agreed that "to coerce or force an employee to join a union . . . is to encourage membership," which is not protected by the act.[40]

Frequently the judges of the Seventh Circuit were asked to determine if the NLRB had exceeded the authority granted to it by Congress. These types of labor appeals often divided the court.[41] Minton, naturally, was usually on the side of giving the NLRB fairly broad discretion in carrying out the NLRA. In so doing he was well within the mainstream of judicial opinion in the 1940s, which interpreted the powers of the board liberally.[42]

Following what he thought to be the intent of Congress led Minton to uphold an NLRB order against the Marshall Field Company, which the board found guilty of discrimination in the firing of two employees. The NLRB ordered Marshall Field to give the employees back pay but allowed the company to exclude from the amount owed the employees their "net earnings" from other employment during the period in question. Marshall Field sought to exclude not only such wages from the settlement but also unemployment compensation. Minton said that "only by distorting the English language could we say that unemployment benefits are 'earnings.'"[43]

A year later, in another labor case involving Marshall Field, Minton again sided with the NLRB, only this time he was in the minority. He dissented from the court's decision to deny enforcement of an NLRB order that regrouped Marshall Field employees into different bargaining units after a union election. The majority concluded that the NLRB lacked the power to take such action. Minton, in his dissent, wrote, "What is an appropriate unit and the representative of that unit are to be determined by the Board and not by us or by the Marshall Field Company."[44]

While Minton went to great lengths to uphold the NLRB he did not automatically side with the agency. He often gave the board a wide berth as he did in sustaining an NLRB decision that two employees had been fired for union activity even though the paucity of evidence might lead a "fair-minded person [to] conclude that the Board was prejudiced in its action." He added, "We do think that the Board's decision in this case has reached the limit to which a court might go to sustain it."[45] He was not so generous, though, in the matter of workers fired by Western Cartridge for conducting a "wildcat strike." In reversing the board, Minton ruled that the company had not engaged in unfair labor practices because the strike was not authorized by the union. In fact, Minton noted, the "employees through their leaders had pledged themselves not to strike" because the country was at war and the company was a munitions manufacturer. "In violation of that solemn pledge they struck, instead of resorting to the ample machinery set up by the Government to settle labor disputes," Minton wrote.[46]

Minton firmly believed that the NLRA was specifically limited to unfair labor practices pertaining to labor's right to bargain collectively and not to unfair treatment of employees in general. He sought to make this point clear to the board in an opinion that overturned the board's order to reinstate a worker who had been discharged because he was uncooperative and failed to do his work properly. In a sternly worded opinion Minton said that "when honorable men, wholly unimpeached, testify under oath to their reasons for discharging a man and such reasons are supported by all the evidence in the case and are not in any way connected with the discharged employee's union activities, the Board is not justified in . . . finding the employer guilty of an unfair labor practice."[47]

Minton's record in labor cases that arose under the Fair Labor Standards Act and the Federal Employers' Liability Act bore striking similarity to his record in NLRB cases in that he usually upheld the administrator's discretion. However, Minton was somewhat more liberal in interpreting the power of the NLRB than he was in actions taken to enforce the other two labor-related laws. Minton rejected numerous claims from workers under these acts on the grounds that Congress did not intend to grant the rights in question.[48]

Minton's almost single-minded determination to resolve issues by relying on legislative intent often cast him in an unfavorable light, especially to liberals who thought the New Deal senator had abandoned his principles. As long as Minton's judicial deference resulted in upholding policies that permitted governmental regulation of the private sector in order to promote social and economic reform, his decisions met with the approval of liberals. However, Minton's judicial deference also extended to legislative policies that limited individual rights to promote order and security. For that, Minton, the political liberal, was branded a conservative, creating one of the great paradoxes of his life.

In reality Minton was the victim of a shifting paradigm of what it meant to be liberal. When New Deal programs were being invalidated by the Supreme Court one of the tenets of liberalism was judicial restraint. While conservatives praised the Court for striking down legislative policies that encroached on property rights, liberals attacked the Court for obstructing needed economic changes. They argued that the Court ought to show greater deference to legislative prerogatives. However, once the supporters of the New Deal joined the Court, the justices' commitment to judicial restraint diminished. As it turned out, their support of judicial restraint was more of a tactical position designed to thwart attacks on New Deal policies than a true philosophical commitment. Many of them became activists, especially in the area of civil liberties, although they continued to extend less protection to property rights. Minton, however, remained committed to the philosophy of judicial restraint in both areas.

Minton, however, was a firm believer in majority rule, and because of his legislative experience he well understood the role of elected representatives in responding to the will of the people. Confronted with threats, real or imagined, to the social and political order, Minton's ideological commitment to majority rule made him much more willing to accept limits on freedom of speech and to curtail procedural guarantees to those accused of criminal acts and of being enemy aliens. On these issues Minton's judicial philosophy of restraint and his strong majoritarianism combined to produce a record that earned him a reputation of being against civil liberties.

Although legal scholars may differ as to exactly what comes under the broad umbrella of civil liberties, generally the liberties are thought to consist of two types of enumerated rights. The first type includes those individual freedoms specified in the First Amendment—freedom of religion, speech, press, and association. The second type consists of procedural rights guaranteed in other amendments in the Bill of Rights that were established to ensure that individuals would be treated fairly in government tribunals where their life, liberty, or property might be affected. Among these are protection against unreasonable searches and seizures, self-incrimination, double jeopardy, the right to counsel, the guarantee of just compensation when private property is taken for public purposes, and other rights required by the guarantee of due process.

The United States Supreme Court has not always treated these two types of individual rights the same. Distinctions were made first in what is known as the "doctrine of incorporation," one of the most fundamental doctrines governing the interpretation of individual rights under the Constitution. The doctrine is a judicial response to the question of whether the freedoms guaranteed in the first eight amendments of the Bill of Rights protect citizens from state action as well as from action by the national government. While it was clear that the Bill of Rights prohibited the national government from interfering with these freedoms, not until the twentieth century did most jurists consider the question of whether the Bill of Rights prohibited the states from doing the same.

As early as 1897 the Supreme Court held that the just compensation requirement of the Fifth Amendment was applicable to state government,[49] and in 1925, in *Gitlow* v. *People of New York,*[50] the Court extended the speech and press protections of the First Amendment to the states. The vehicle through which these restrictions were applied to the states was the Fourteenth Amendment, which stipulated, among other things, that a state may not "deprive any one of life, liberty or property without due process of law." In the landmark case *Palko* v. *Connecticut*[51] the Court sought to determine the extent to which the first eight amendments were incorporated into the due process clause of the Fourteenth Amendment. In *Palko,* the Court ruled that the rights previously designated as applicable to the states—free speech and just compensation for private property—were so essential to "a scheme of ordered liberty" that states could not interfere with them. The rights of the accused, however, were viewed differently.

While the guarantee of a fair trial in itself was considered essential to liberty and therefore protected by the Constitution, specific guarantees, including protection against double jeopardy and self-incrimination, and even a trial by jury, were not automatically incorporated. Instead, what constituted a fair trial was determined by the court on a case-by-case basis. As legal historian David Bodenhamer points out, there were both advantages and disadvantages of the fair trial approach. It meant that the values and attitudes of individual justices rather than some objective standard would determine "which state procedures created such a hardship or so shocked the conscience that they denied fair treatment." At the same time, says Bodenhamer, the fair trial approach "also provided a method for modernizing the Bill of Rights by inviting justices to extend liberties if modern conditions required it."[52]

This bifurcated view of individual rights prevailed in the judicial system the entire time Minton was on the Seventh Circuit and throughout his tenure on the Supreme Court. Minton's strong penchant for judicial restraint and strict adherence to precedent meant that he would be no pioneer in defining individual rights.

Civil liberties cases before the Seventh Circuit during Minton's tenure were much more likely to raise questions about the fair trial or procedural protections guaranteed by the Bill of Rights than about First Amendment freedoms of speech or religion. When appellate judges review trial proceedings they have to determine not only whether errors did occur, but also whether the errors are serious enough to reverse a verdict. Judicial reputations sometimes rest on how willing a judge is to tolerate errors. Minton had a reputation for being "willing to tolerate extensive errors in a trial before he would conclude that in its overall context it had been unfair." The decisive criterion for Minton was guilt. If the fact of guilt was not contested in an appeal, Minton "rarely concluded that any conviction had been unconstitutionally obtained, regardless of the injustice which the appellant alleged he was dealt in the course of his apprehension or prosecution."[53]

The question of how much scrutiny the appellate court should give to the evidence presented at a trial was a matter of debate among the Seventh Circuit judges. Chief Judge Evans, in particular, was concerned that appellate courts were too passive in this regard. In a strongly worded memo to his colleagues Evans said he believed "that more injustices have been done out of a too slavish devotion to the rule that a finding precludes an inquiry into the facts than any other appellate court weakness."[54]

Despite Evans's concern, Minton felt that he should defer to the discretion exercised by the judge who presided over the trial proceedings. This deference to trial court judges was a product of Minton's fair trial jurisprudence. For Minton, the fair trial doctrine was the chief consideration when weighing appeals based on the Sixth Amendment right to be tried by an impartial jury. In one opinion, which concerned a defendant's claim that a trial judge erred in dismissing two potential jurors, Minton said: "The defendants were not entitled to have the case tried by any certain jurors. They were entitled to have only an impartial, legally qualified jury."[55] These words foreshadowed an opinion Minton wrote when on the Supreme Court in which he said that "a defendant is entitled to a fair trial but not a perfect one."[56]

The seeming inconsistency about the constitutionally guaranteed rights of the accused demonstrates the difficulty of the case-by-case approach that is inherent in fair trial jurisprudence. The fairness or unfairness of any single aspect of a trial depends upon its significance within the context of the trial as a whole. Those who opposed the fair trial approach, such as Minton's friend Justice Hugo Black, argued that a more objective standard was needed, one that would lead to more consistency in results. Black thought that the simplest and most consistent approach was total incorporation of the Bill of Rights into the Fourteenth Amendment's guarantee of due process. Minton's rulings in search and seizure and right to counsel cases clearly show that he did not accept the doctrine of incorporation or the necessity of a single standard of justice for both state and federal courts.

Minton's comfort within the fair trial approach—and his rejection of the incorporation doctrine—is seen clearly in the right to counsel cases. The Supreme Court had held as early as 1932[57] that failure to provide adequate counsel might be a denial of due process under the Fourteenth Amendment. But this did not mean that counsel had to be provided in all cases. To Minton this meant that "each case stands on its own bottom" and that "a failure to have counsel in one capital case may spell out a failure to provide due process" but not necessarily in another case.[58]

In one capital case the defendant's attorney was described by Minton as "an experienced, reputable attorney . . . [who] at the time of this hearing . . . was in bad health and feeble in mind." This attorney had advised his client to plead guilty and was not present in court when his client entered his plea. Despite this, Minton rejected the defendant's claim that he had been denied effective counsel because he had waived his right to have counsel present when he appeared at his trial. "That one is entitled to an attorney when charged with a crime and to a jury trial may, as a general proposition, be conceded," Minton said, "but it is equally true that such rights may be knowingly and intelligently waived."[59]

In a noncapital case a defendant claimed that the counsel appointed for him was not adequate because he was illiterate, but Minton said, "That, if true, standing alone would not be sufficient to brand such counsel incompetent."[60] According to Minton's fair trial philosophy, the true test of incompetence was how the attorney handled the case. The attorney in question had practiced law for forty years and was president of the local bar association. For Minton this evidence was enough, and he denied the defendant's appeal.

At times Minton's unwillingness to go beyond the record resulted in the sort of questionable decisions that cast doubt on the fairness of the fair trial doctrine. In one noncapital case the evidence of the attorney's incompetence was rather substantial. In fact, the district court had discharged the prisoner, Thomas Feeley, from the custody of the Illinois state penitentiary in part because the court found that he was not defended by competent counsel. When Minton heard the case the attorney in question was dead and so was the judge who had tried the case. Minton himself said that "looking upon it in cold print nine years after the event, we cannot say that some of the actions or omissions of [the attorney] could not be criticized." However, he concluded that the constitutional requirements for necessity of counsel had been met. He reasoned: "Whenever the court in good faith appoints or accepts the appearance of a member of the bar in good standing to represent a defendant, the presumption is that such counsel is competent. Otherwise, he would not be in good standing at the bar and accepted by the court."[61]

Minton was greatly troubled by the district court's intervention in the Feeley case because it had been tried originally in a state court. He was insistent that federal courts should respect the jurisdiction of state courts, and he saw the state prisoner's ability to file a habeas corpus petition in federal court as a "collateral attack" by the federal judiciary on state courts. He worried that "Federal Courts are being used to invade the sovereign jurisdiction of the States, presumed to be competent to handle their own police affairs. . . . We are not super-legislatures or glorified parole boards. When we condemn a State's exercise of its jurisdiction and hold that the exercise of its powers is not in accordance with due process, we are in effect trying the states."[62]

The *Feeley* opinion, written after Minton had been on the bench for seven years, was the strongest he wrote on the subject of federal interference with state court jurisdiction, but his opinions had long reflected a strong state bias since his earliest years on the court. He reaffirmed his intention to protect state court jurisdiction time and again. In one case he wrote: "The right of the courts of Illinois to their jurisdiction to decide the question . . . [which] depends upon the construction of the Illinois statutes, should be jealously guarded."[63] In another opinion he said: "The courts of Indiana have never passed upon a case of this kind. If we knew what the law of Indiana was on the question, we would be bound to follow it."[64]

Minton's opinions in cases arising from state courts that involved the application of state laws reflected a strong commitment to a more traditional view of federalism. This conception of federalism stresses a duality of powers in which each level of government has a separate and distinct jurisdiction over its own laws. His view was consistent with the position on diversity of jurisdiction in civil cases established in 1938 in *Erie Railroad Company* v. *Tompkins*.[65] Prior to 1938, when federal courts heard cases involving litigants from separate states about contracts and other instruments of a commercial nature, the courts were permitted to develop a uniform national law of commerce, superseding individual state laws. The *Erie* case reversed that trend by requiring federal courts to apply state law in diversity cases.

Minton's respect for the rights of states to interpret their own constitutions' statutes was not unique. It was the standard practice of judges, but Minton's commitment to state powers was rooted not only in legal precedent but also in his more general political philosophy about states' rights. Like Justice Felix Frankfurter, Minton's reluctance to support total incorporation of the Bill of Rights into the Fourteenth Amendment derived from a concern that such incorporation would undermine the principle of divided power that was the basis of the federal system provided for in the Constitution.

Mindful of the predisposition of the law in favor of trial court judges, Minton rarely voted to overturn their decisions. In an appeal from a case where the district court had denied a motion for a new trial, Minton backed the trial court. "We do not have the right . . . to substitute our findings or judgment for that of the trial court. We determine by the record only whether the trial judge might reasonably have reached the conclusion which he did."[66]

There were occasions, however, when Minton ruled in favor of a defendant who claimed a denial of due process. In his last year on the Seventh Circuit he sided with Sotero Tovar, an alien Mexican worker, against both the IRS and the district court. Tovar was a man of limited means. He earned fifty-five dollars a week in a steel mill and was paying a mortgage on a four thousand dollar house in south Chicago where he lived with his wife and children.

Tovar ran afoul of the law when Chicago police officers, without a warrant, entered his home and found marijuana, which he had picked in the alley behind his home and which he intended to smoke. Tovar was arrested and taken to jail. Even though he spoke no English he was interviewed by a federal narcotics agent who spoke no Spanish, a situation which Minton said in his opinion was "a bit difficult to understand." The agent took possession of the marijuana, which had been illegally seized, and reported to the commissioner of the Internal Revenue Service in Washington. Tovar was indicted on two different charges, but the district court judge suppressed the evidence in each instance because Tovar's constitutional rights had been violated. When the government could not prosecute him for criminal conduct it levied a seven thousand dollar tax assessment against him. This action was based on a statute levying tax at a rate of a hundred dollars per ounce on the transfer of marijuana to a person who has not registered and paid the special tax. Tovar was given no notice of a hearing.

The district court, which had thrown out the previous indictments because of the illegally obtained evidence, nonetheless dismissed Tovar's petition for a temporary injunction against the government's tax lien. Minton wrote the majority opinion that reversed the district court and ruled that a temporary injunction should have been issued. He wrote that Tovar was in effect assessed a penalty without a hearing and that the tax levy was in fact a punishment and not a revenue-raising measure. "Is it not perfectly plain," Minton asked, "that what the Government is trying to do is take this plaintiff's property and turn him and his family out on the street for not having a license to do something the Government did not want him to do? This the Government claims the right to do without notice or hearing and by means of its tax techniques when it could not convict for the same offense by a fair trial in a criminal proceeding."[67]

Although the large majority of cases regarding individual rights that Minton heard were related to the rights of criminal defendants, a number of cases involved First Amendment rights. In these cases Minton was no absolutist. He viewed individual rights in relative terms and rejected the position that the Constitution conferred an absolute right to their exercise. Minton wrote in a 1942 case that the right of free speech guaranteed by the Constitution "is not an absolute right. It is a relative right that may be modified in its interplay with the rights of others."[68]

The most common First Amendment issues that Minton reviewed were libel and slander cases, which involved not only freedom of speech but also freedom of the press. The First Amendment does not protect libel or slander, and in each case the court must determine if the words in question were libelous or slanderous. Publishers may have been a little jittery over how Minton might rule when it came to issues of freedom of the press. They no doubt remembered his ill-fated attempt in the Senate to prohibit newspapers from publishing information known to be false.

Despite his previous hostility to the press, Minton's rulings did not always go against publishers, as was demonstrated in a libel suit brought by Montgomery Ward against McGraw-Hill Publishing Company, publisher of *Business Week*. Montgomery Ward, the second largest mail-order business in the country at the time, claimed that it had been libeled in a *Business Week* article. The article described the company's union policies in an unfavorable light and made the company appear guilty of violating the National Labor Relations Act. Minton sided with McGraw-Hill. "To charge one with being unfair to labor is a much broader charge than to charge one with unfair labor practices. If it were libelous simply to say of another that he is unfair to labor, every picketer who carries a banner with such a legend would be guilty of libel. To say that one is unfair to labor is not a statement of a fact, but of an opinion."[69]

During his tenure on the Seventh Circuit Minton heard several appeals concerning individuals who were enemy aliens. Perhaps best known was the case of Paul Knauer, whose certificate of naturalization had been revoked by the government on the grounds that it had been obtained fraudulently and illegally. Knauer was a member of the German-American Bund, an organization overtly and actively committed to Adolf Hitler and the Nazi cause. When Minton wrote his opinion upholding the government he could not contain his intense disdain for Knauer and his organization. He said: "This was no beer drinking, song singing gab-fest in Deutsch by a group of nostalgic old burghers. This organization had a serious purpose, a tragically serious and sinister purpose. It was, as the defendant said, 'Hitler's grip on America.'"[70]

Knauer appealed his case to the Supreme Court. Minton's fellow judge Evans kept Minton posted on the progress in the case while Minton was recuperating from a heart attack at Walter Reed Hospital in the spring of 1946. In March Evans told Minton that after postponing arguments in the case the Court would hear arguments in the spring term. He said, "I am still hopeful about the case, but probably it will be too much to expect unanimity by the

PHOTOGRAPH BY HARRIS & EWING, COLLECTION OF THE SUPREME COURT OF THE UNITED STATES

Minton leaves the White House on 5 October 1949 after visiting President Harry Truman to thank him for the Supreme Court nomination.

Supreme Court."[71] Evans's prediction proved correct. Justice William O. Douglas, Minton's friend from his New Deal days, wrote the majority opinion of the Court, which not only upheld Minton's opinion but also relied heavily on Minton's own words. Justices Frank Murphy and Wiley B. Rutledge dissented.

Minton's opinion in the Knauer decision was well within the mainstream of legal opinion of the day and can be understood best in the climate of public opinion that prevailed at the time. A fear of people such as the Bundists was understandable and widely shared, yet Minton's fears "gradually became transformed into a somewhat rigidified bias directed at aliens in general." As a result, his record on the Supreme Court in regard to aliens "was more illiberal than that of any other justice with whom he sat."[72]

After eight years on the Seventh Circuit Minton finally received the nomination to the Supreme Court that had eluded him for so many years. Truman nominated Minton to the Supreme Court following the sudden death of Justice Rutledge. Many speculated that Truman was rewarding Minton mainly for his party loyalty and personal ties and not because of his distinguished record as a jurist. Minton himself may have been in that category. Minton noted on occasion that he had helped Truman's career in 1941 when he convinced Roosevelt to support Truman as chairman of the Senate committee investigating allegations of wasteful defense spending, and that Truman in turn had made Minton a Supreme Court justice.[73]

Yet to attribute Minton's appointment purely to partisan politics unfairly deprecates his performance as an appellate court judge. Minton had proven himself to be competent and impartial. His consistent adherence to judicial restraint caused him to rule both for and against business, for and against labor, for and against the exercise of administrative discretion, and for and against the rights of individuals. His rulings were as likely to displease liberals as conservatives. While many judges may be assigned more readily to one camp or the other, Minton defies easy classification.

Minton's opinions, reflecting his own brand of pragmatism, offered clear and practical answers to the issues before the court, even though they often lacked a clear theoretical underpinning and made no lasting contributions to legal theory. He was conscientious about his judicial responsibilities. Despite the demands placed upon him by special assignments on the War Clemency Board and the board investigating the labor dispute in the coal industry, and his own poor health, he did not shirk his responsibilities for opinion writing, which in volume, if not in length, matched that of his fellow judges. He heard every type of case that came before the court, and he established a reputation for being especially adept at reducing complex, technical issues to comprehensible dimensions.

Throughout his term on the appeals court Minton sought to downplay his partisan reputation, and, indeed, it is impossible to detect any partisan influence in over 250 of his decisions. Yet, in the Senate confirmation hearings for his nomination to the Supreme Court, his partisan past, rather than his decisions as appellate court judge, proved to be the most controversial aspect of his nomination. The debate over his partisanship slowed but did not block his confirmation. Minton's supporters in the Senate, in particular Scott Lucas of Illinois, sought to focus the confirmation hearings on Minton's record on the appellate court. Republicans, however, insisted on dredging up Minton's dogmatic support of the Court-packing plan and his proposed libel law. When requested to testify before the Senate Judiciary Committee, Minton wrote a letter refusing to do so on the grounds that it was not appropriate. Ultimately the request was withdrawn and Minton was confirmed by the Senate. Although Minton had been confirmed unanimously when he was appointed to the Seventh Circuit, sixteen senators voted against confirming his nomination to the Supreme Court.

As Minton assumed his seat on the Supreme Court in October 1949 his supporters and critics waited to see what kind of justice he would be. To those who knew Minton well there was no reason to expect him to be any different than he had been on the Seventh Circuit. Yet there was an air of expectation about where he would align on the Court. The institution itself was in the midst of change, and Minton's arrival would have important implications for the direction that the Court would take on the vital issues facing the country in the next decade.

CHAPTER EIGHT

Vinson's Ally on the Court

In May 1952 Sherman Minton, in conference with his fellow Supreme Court justices, pounded the table excitedly and declared, "There can be no vacant spot in power when the security of the nation is at stake. It rests with the president. There is an emergency. Truman seized the plants because the defense of the country required it. The president had to act."[1]

Minton's tirade came as the justices debated what became known as the steel seizure case, a case that posed one of the most important constitutional questions of the twentieth century: did the president of the United States have inherent powers to seize private property to protect the nation's security? To Minton the issue was simple. In conference he lectured his fellow justices about the necessity of deferring to the president in times of emergency in the same way that he had lectured to his fellow senators about the evil Supreme Court that repeatedly thwarted Franklin D. Roosevelt's efforts to deal with the economic emergency of the Great Depression. Minton's reaction to both situations was similar. The country was faced with peril, and the well-being of the nation required strong action. The difference, of course, was that in the spring of 1952 Minton was a Supreme Court justice.

PHOTOGRAPH BY HARRIS & EWING, COLLECTION OF THE SUPREME COURT OF THE UNITED STATES

Official photograph of Sherman Minton at the beginning of his tenure on the Supreme Court.

Minton's experiences in the 1930s, especially his New Deal antipathy to the "Nine Old Men" on the Supreme Court, strongly influenced his behavior on the federal judiciary. He had developed a dogmatic commitment to judicial restraint and thought that the Court should be extremely reluctant to intervene in the prerogatives of the elected branches of government. The steel seizure case presented a dilemma for Minton as well as the other restraint justices since it pitted one elected branch of the government against another. At issue was the constitutional separation of powers.

The case posed fundamental constitutional questions, but to the pragmatic Minton the issue rested simply on the rightness of the president's cause and the practical consequences of the Court's decision. "The Korean War was on and I couldn't think of anything worse than men on the firing line reaching back for munitions that weren't there," Minton said, talking about his vote years later. "I believed that government had the right to defend itself in an emergency."[2]

Hugo L. Black, who wrote the Court's opinion in *Youngstown Sheet and Tube* v. *Sawyer,*[3] saw the issue in starkly different terms. Black argued that in the American system of separated powers the president lacked any constitutional authority "to take possession of private property in order to keep labor disputes from stopping production." The authority to seize property was a legislative power that only Congress could exercise, and it had not done so.

That Black and Minton took such divergent views on constitutional questions about the steel seizure and in so many other cases was surprising to many contemporaries. Prior to joining the Court Minton was personally closer to Black than to any of the other justices. Both were self-proclaimed populists, coming from humble origins and rural communities. During their Senate days together they were allies in their support of Roosevelt and the New Deal.

Minton and Black relentlessly pressed the president's opponents while serving together on the Lobbying Committee, and they were leading advocates of Roosevelt's Court-packing scheme.

On the Court, however, they were often poles apart. While both shared the belief that the Court should refrain from interfering with economic and social legislation that affected property rights, they differed over the power of the Court to intervene when legislative bodies passed laws restricting other rights of the individual. Black was known as an absolutist who believed that certain individual rights, especially First Amendment guarantees, were beyond the reach of congressional regulation. He also was the Court's premier advocate of total incorporation, the position that the Bill of Rights in its entirety applied to the states through the due process clause of the Fourteenth Amendment. Minton once expressed his approval of this doctrine in a review of a Black biography, asserting that it was "illogical" for the Court to secure some but not all of the freedoms in the Bill of Rights against state action.[4] Once on the Court, however, Minton not only refused to adopt Black's absolutist position, but he also once described Black as a "demagogue" to Felix Frankfurter.[5]

That these two men, so alike in background and outlook at the outset, took such divergent paths to the Court was largely a function of how they viewed the Constitution and how they interpreted the powers of the Court. Black took literally the admonition that Congress make "no law" restricting First Amendment freedoms. Protecting First Amendment rights was a logical extension of Black's populist philosophy. He believed in the capacity of people to govern themselves, and these fundamental rights, such as freedom of speech and of the press, were essential to effective self-governance.[6]

Minton's brand of populism, however, contained a much stronger attachment to the will of the majority than Black's, even when the majority will sought to curb individual rights. Whereas Black looked constantly to the Constitution for answers, Minton was guided more by his pragmatic and political instincts. The rhetoric of his famous "You can't feed a hungry man the Constitution" campaign speech in 1934 was an early indication that Minton saw the Constitution as malleable. He reiterated the same point in 1937 in a nationwide radio broadcast in which he defended Roosevelt's Court-packing bill. Roosevelt, Minton said, was seeking to use the Constitution "not to destroy government, but to make it work for the masses of the people."[7] Minton's vote in favor of Truman's seizure of the steel mills was guided by the same kind of pragmatic view. To Minton the critical concern was how government could serve best the needs of the people, and the Court had to accommodate whenever possible the judgments of elected officials seeking to serve those needs.

Although they voted on opposite sides in the steel dispute, Minton's views about judicial power and the role of the Court were closer to those of Frankfurter, the former Harvard law professor, who was the Court's most articulate and thoughtful advocate of judicial restraint. Frankfurter believed that judicial invalidation of statutes was basically undemocratic. He felt the best remedy for unwise legislation or executive action lay with an informed electorate, which could remove officeholders whose policies were disliked.

But Minton's belief in judicial restraint was hardly as carefully developed or well reasoned as the learned Frankfurter's. Minton's version rested on a simple principle that the Court should not undo the actions of the political branches of government. While Frankfurter's philosophy was sophisticated enough to permit him to rule against political majorities when he thought the Constitution so dictated, Minton's more simplistic approach led him to read the Constitution almost exclusively as a document for majority will. The complexities of constitutional cases posed an intellectual challenge for Frankfurter; for

Minton the cases represented problems that needed to be simplified so that a decision could be reached.

From Minton's very first day on the Court, Frankfurter sought to make Minton his ally. He was particularly eager to keep Minton from joining the colleagues he despised—Black and especially William O. Douglas—and to that end his personal memoranda to Minton were voluminous. These messages indicate that Frankfurter used the same condescending strategy with Minton that he used with the other junior justices, especially those he considered to be his intellectual inferiors, courting them with flattery and instructing them about their votes and opinion writing.[8] Although Minton was sometimes irritated with Frankfurter's patronizing overtures, he generally bore them with good grace and responded warmly to Frankfurter. He did not, however, always side with his senior colleague.

As restraint justices, both Minton and Frankfurter faced a dilemma in the steel case. To rule in favor of the president's seizure of the steel mills meant ruling against Congress, since several laws provided the president with less radical alternatives to prevent a strike detrimental to the nation's war effort. The Taft-Hartley Act, passed over Truman's veto, allowed the president to order an eighty-day cooling-off period when strikes posed a threat to national security.

In the end Frankfurter reluctantly sided with Congress. The provisions of the Taft-Hartley Act convinced him that Congress had specifically denied seizure authority to the president. Like Minton, Frankfurter agreed that the president had acted only for the good of the nation, but unlike Minton he concluded that the "structure of the American government at times foreclosed swift action in emergency situations, and it was important to the future of freedom in the United States to adhere to constitutional restrictions."[9]

Minton's own views about presidential powers were closest to those expressed by Chief Justice Fred M. Vinson in his vehement dissent in the steel case. Vinson argued that given the nature of the emergency and the imminent threat to national security the president had the authority to act without a specific direction from Congress. Although all the Truman appointees held similar views on most of the critical issues of government power, only Minton and Vinson had supported the president in *Youngstown,* along with Stanley F. Reed, a Roosevelt appointee.

The voting records of Vinson and Minton were more alike than any two justices serving on the Court, and the two men were similar in other ways. Both had served in Congress as well as the executive branch, and these common experiences made them more sympathetic to both legislative and executive prerogatives. Minton and Vinson shared one other common experience that made them unique among the court members: prior judicial experience at the federal level. Vinson had served for five years as judge of the United States Court of Appeals for the District of Columbia. This common judicial experience predisposed Minton and Vinson, more so than any of the other justices, including Truman appointees, to maintain a limited judicial role for the Court. They were inclined to follow precedent, to find practical solutions to complex issues, and to defer to legislative and executive authority. Justice Black once commented that his differences with Minton on the Supreme Court were the result of Minton's experience on the Court of Appeals. It made him, Black said, "a bit more hidebound on precedent and procedure than I would have liked."[10]

While following precedent is consistent with judicial restraint in that it serves to limit judicial discretion and promotes stability in the law, it also can lead to results that are inconsistent with judicial restraint, such as the invalidation of a legislative statute. After all, the Supreme Court that Minton had attacked while in the Senate was following established precedent.

The fragmentation of the Court, revealed sharply in the steel case by the multiple opinions, was a source of great concern to Minton throughout his tenure on the high bench. Minton always had been a team player, and he thought that the opinion expressed by the Court or by its majority was far more important than the expression of his personal views. For that reason he wrote comparatively few dissenting or concurring opinions. Minton's behavior in *Youngstown* is a case in point. He had begun to draft his own dissent following a discussion with Reed, the Court's other dissenter in the case, about what should be said by the minority. In the meantime, the chief justice circulated his dissenting opinion. And while neither Minton nor Reed agreed fully with Vinson's reasoning, both decided that a coherent and unified dissent would be more effective. Consequently, Minton suppressed his draft opinion.[11]

Minton's position in the steel seizure case is further evidence of the difficulty of labeling his judicial philosophy. His decision to side with the president over Congress, especially in view of existing policies that provided the president with alternative courses of action, is inconsistent with Minton's long professed belief in following the majority will. The legislative branch offers a greater opportunity for the majority to work its political will than the executive branch. An explanation for Minton's departure from his usual stand may be found in views he expressed earlier in his political career. Minton thought that the Court should not tie the president's hands in an emergency situation. In 1937 he had argued that "the greatest Presidents in this Nation's history, developed in the stress of great emergencies, have been at grips with the power of the Court, as they sought to serve the masses and the common people and found their purpose thwarted by the opinions of the Court."[12] Minton was particularly disturbed that Robert H. Jackson, another of the Court's judicial restraint justices, had voted with the majority to limit the president's power in the steel case. As United States attorney general, Jackson had justified Roosevelt's seizure of the North American Aviation plant in order to use the airplanes for the war effort. When Minton confronted Jackson on this apparent about-face, Jackson replied, "But I was Attorney General then and I'm a Justice now."[13]

Partisan considerations also played a role in Minton's decision in the steel suit as they did in other cases he participated in as a Supreme Court justice. While a senator, Minton had promoted the idea that justices should carry out the wishes of the president who appointed them. Defending Roosevelt's Court-packing scheme in 1937, Minton pointed out how the size of the Supreme Court had changed six times in its history "in an effort to make the Supreme Court's opinions conform more nearly to the policies of the administration in power." If it was all right to change the size of the court to help previous presidents achieve their policy objectives, Minton asked, "what's wrong with changing it . . . to help Roosevelt meet his problems?"[14]

Partisan considerations were never far from Minton's mind, even as a justice, and 1952 was no exception. Throughout the steel seizure episode Minton was growing anxious about the president's political fortunes. Truman, undecided about running for reelection,[15] had allowed his name to be entered in the New Hampshire primary. It was an unfortunate decision; he was beaten handily by Sen. Estes Kefauver, who had achieved notoriety for hearings on gambling and organized crime that he had held around the country. It was a humiliating defeat for the president, and Minton took the results personally.

A day after the New Hampshire primary, held while efforts to resolve the labor dispute in the steel industry were under way, a discouraged Minton wrote to Vinson, who was in the hospital. "The New Hampshire thing should not have happened," he said. "I wish the President had followed his own good judgment and stayed out of there. This can only serve to embarrass him."[16] Two and a half weeks later at a Jefferson-Jackson Day dinner, Truman informed his party, and the nation, that he would not seek reelection. A week later he wrote to thank Minton for the note he sent about Truman's decision not to run again. "You and I have been 'through the mill,'" he said. "Most politicians never know when to quit. All this 'weeping and wailing and so forth' convinces me that no mistake has been made."[17] Truman wrote his letter to Minton the same day that he ordered the seizure of the steel mills. In the final analysis, the most plausible explanation of Minton's position in the steel case may be that his loyalty to Truman overrode his normal inclination to defer to the popular will.

The steel seizure case, "one of the few which discuss at length the powers of the President,"[18] had lasting constitutional significance. Not only did it help to redress the balance of power among the three branches of government, but, more important, it also "served as a prelude to a more activist period for the Supreme Court."[19] The Court abandoned its traditional reluctance to resolve cases on constitutional issues if the cases could be decided on other grounds. The Court's willingness to tackle constitutional issues head-on in disputes involving school desegregation, reapportionment, and the Pentagon Papers can be attributed to its newfound assertiveness in the *Youngstown* case.[20] It was perhaps this aspect of the steel case that had the greatest import for Minton, for in making the ground fertile for a more activist Court, this assertiveness planted the seeds for his own eventual estrangement from the Court majority.

Minton had other opportunities to demonstrate his loyalty to Truman besides the steel seizure case. The Cold War politics of the Truman administration, which had helped fuel the steel seizure case, also propelled other highly visible controversies onto the agenda of the Supreme Court. Beginning in 1947 Truman initiated a series of anti-Communist measures that were driven not only by a legitimate concern for the nation's security but also by political considerations for the upcoming presidential election.[21] Truman had been under fierce attack by the Republicans for not doing enough to combat Communism at home, and when the congressional elections in 1946 put the GOP in control of both houses the president fought back. In response to Republican charges that Communists were running rampant in government agencies, Truman issued an executive order establishing the country's first loyalty program for government employees.

A second anti-Communist strategy followed by the Truman administration was the prosecution of the leaders of the Communist party of the United States. The prosecutions had begun in earnest in 1948 when Attorney General Tom C. Clark was stung by a question from the Republican-controlled House Un-American Activities Committee as to why he had failed to use the Smith Act against the Communist party.[22] In rapid time the Justice Department succeeded in getting indictments and convictions of the eleven top party leaders for violations of the Smith Act. The trial, highlighted by disruptive and dilatory tactics by the defendants, was presided over by Judge Harold Medina, who was less than sympathetic to the defendants and their legal strategies. The convictions were announced on 14 October 1949, just three days after Minton took his seat on the Supreme Court. His arrival on the Court helped to seal the fate of United States Communist party leaders.

The sudden deaths in 1949 of Justices Frank Murphy and Wiley B. Rutledge removed from the Court two staunch defenders of civil liberties. The vacancies were filled by Clark and Minton, who, like the other Truman appointees, were much more inclined to subordinate individual rights to governmental policies promoting order and security. Truman had chosen men with whom he worked closely in the Senate or the executive branch and with whom he maintained close personal ties. Such practices often led to charges of "cronyism" being leveled at Truman's appointees. Schooled in practical politics, they shared Truman's beliefs in a limited judiciary. He expected his appointees to defer to the legislative and executive branches or, in his words, "to stop making the law up there."[23] Truman, with few exceptions, got what he wanted from his appointees.

Guided by their philosophy of judicial restraint, the Truman appointees deferred to the legislative view as to what was reasonable in the area of national security. They sought to avoid, whenever possible, declaring either state or federal legislation unconstitutional by employing the balancing test—weighing the rights of the individual against society's need for order, security, and stability. These characteristics formed the foundation of Minton's approach to constitutional issues.

GARY YOHLER/FREDERICK VOLLRATH, TIFFANY STUDIO, *INDIANAPOLIS TIMES* COLLECTION

Paul V. McNutt (left), former Indiana governor and political ally of Minton's, and J. Emmett McManaman (right), attorney general of Indiana, at a reception in honor of Minton when he was sworn in.

The two Communist conspiracy cases, both of which are titled for Eugene Dennis, general secretary of the United States Communist party, offer clear examples of Minton's judicial philosophy. In his first term he wrote the majority opinion in *Dennis* v. *United States*,[24] the first appeal lodged by the Communist party leaders against United States government actions. The appeal stemmed from the conviction of party leader Dennis for his failure to respond to a subpoena from the House Un-American Activities Committee, which was carrying out its own investigation of Communist activities. Dennis challenged his conviction on the grounds that seven members of the jury were government employees who were, by virtue of the government loyalty program, biased against him.

Agreeing with the majority, Minton believed that the government loyalty programs could not be used to disqualify jurors in a trial. Minton relied heavily on his interpretation of a congressional statute that declared government employees eligible for jury duty in the District of Columbia and on two Supreme Court precedents.[25] The statute had established a doctrine of general eligibility of government employees for jury duty, except in special circumstances. Minton did not think that the Dennis situation presented special circumstances. "While one of an unpopular minority group must be accorded that solicitude which properly accompanies an accused person," Minton observed, "he is not entitled to unusual protection or exception." Furthermore, he said that "a holding of implied bias to disqualify jurors because of their relationship with the Government is no longer permissible. The Act makes no exceptions for distinctive circumstances."[26]

Minton had refused to find any exceptions for members of the Communist party even though Frankfurter urged the other justices to reconsider this decision before Minton wrote his opinion. Dennis's plight presented a special circumstance that the Court should consider, Frankfurter insisted. Recognizing "the existence of what is characterized as a phobia against a particular group," Frankfurter argued, "is not to discriminate in its favor." Popular hostility against a group is bound to affect jurors, he said, and to exclude potential jurors who might be susceptible to such pressures "is not to pay regard to political opinions or affiliations but merely to recognize . . . the facts of life."[27] Frankfurter's views about *Dennis* reveal how differently he and Minton viewed issues about procedural fairness. To Frankfurter the guarantee of a fair trial was essential to an ordered scheme of justice, and he was able to elevate his concern for due process over his normal tendency for judicial restraint. Minton was much more unyielding.

Typically, Minton refused to look beyond the record in the case. In *Dennis* he asserted that no question of actual bias was before the Court, adding "vague conjecture does not convince that Government employees are so intimidated that they cringe before their Government in fear of investigation and loss of employment if they do their duty as jurors."[28] Even though in his private correspondence Minton concluded that "Dennis was really being tried for being a communist [and] not for refusing to appear,"[29] this perception did not persuade Minton to treat the defendants in *Dennis* any differently.

Following the announcement of the Court's *Dennis* decision, the Communist party stated its intention to move for a reconsideration, but before that happened it was caught up in another battle with the government—this one led by Truman's Justice Department. The second *Dennis* decision,[30] the most noted of the Communist conspiracy cases, reached the Court in 1951, during Minton's second term. It sought to appeal the convictions of the Communist party leaders for violating the Smith Act, which had been won by the Justice Department in October 1949.

The Communist defendants argued that their convictions for advocating the violent overthrow of the government violated their freedom of speech and also that the conspiracy provisions of the Smith Act were unconstitutional. The Court's response to the appeal rested on its interpretation of the "clear and present danger test." According to this standard, first adopted by the Court in *Schenck* v. *United States,* the question of whether speech is protected by the First Amendment depends on whether the words "are used in such circumstances and are of such a nature as to create a clear and present danger that they will bring about the substantive evils that Congress has a right to prevent."[31] Between 1937 and 1948 the Court had applied the "clear and present danger" rule in fourteen cases, and in each had ruled against the government.[32] Minton's presence on the Court in 1949 helped to insure a new interpretation of "clear and present danger." This new interpretation relied on Judge Learned Hand's "gravity of the evil" variation of the "clear and present danger" rule. According to this standard the crucial consideration was "whether the gravity of the 'evil,' discounted by its improbability, justifies such invasion of free speech as is necessary to avoid the danger." Embracing this modified version of "clear and present danger," which afforded less protection for free speech, the Vinson majority upheld the constitutionality of the Smith Act.

Minton's vote was predictable. He had voted for the Smith Act as a senator in 1940, a time when the country was anxious about the possibility of war. Among other things the act established penalties for advocating, abetting, advising, or teaching the violent overthrow of the government and for organizing or knowingly joining a society that conspires to overthrow the government. These provisions clearly impinged on the First Amendment freedom of speech and right of free association but, as a senator and as a justice, Minton thought that national security concerns overrode individual rights.

To Minton the Communist conspiracy posed a serious threat to national security and was the kind of "grave evil" that Congress sought to prevent. He was not oblivious to the public hysteria over Communists infiltrating government. Indeed, while contemplating the second *Dennis* case, the Court also was deciding the fate of Alger Hiss. On 12 March 1951 the Court let stand the conviction of Hiss, a former high-level State Department official, found guilty of perjury but also presumed to be guilty of espionage, by denying his petition for review. Two weeks later, in federal court in New York, Ethel and Julius Rosenberg were found guilty of passing atomic secrets to the Soviet Union and were sentenced to death. Their subsequent appeals were rebuffed by the Supreme Court in the following term. These events served as reminders to Minton of the potential danger of the Communist conspiracy. So when Vinson, the author of the majority opinion in the second *Dennis* case, concluded that the First Amendment did not mean that "before the Government may act, it must wait until the *putsch* is about to be executed, the plans have been laid and the signal is awaited," Minton agreed wholeheartedly.[33]

During the summer recess Minton wrote to reassure the chief justice, who had received sharp criticism for his opinion in *Dennis,* that the decision was "receiving highest praise out here. I think we rendered a service to our country and that opinion of yours will come rapidly to be recognized as one of the Court's greatest. I am proud to have been with you all the way."[34]

Of course Minton was wrong. The *Dennis* decision, widely denounced in 1952 and still denounced today, is commonly criticized for watering down the "clear and present danger test" and exaggerating the extent to which an imminent danger existed.[35] As one scholar observed, the Court had applied the "clear and present danger test" in such a way that it was "unlikely any legislative action could fail to meet its requirements."[36] In *Dennis,* "restraint and deference were . . . carried to their extreme."[37]

The notoriety surrounding the appeals of the Communist party leaders was exceeded a year later when the public's attention was captured by the relentless efforts of the Rosenbergs to stay their executions. The imposition of the death sentence for spying during peacetime generated pleas for clemency from all parts of the country and around the world. Numerous appeals were filed on behalf of the Rosenbergs, and the case created tremendous turmoil among the justices. At least five times between 7 June 1952 and 18 June 1953 the Court considered requests for review from the Rosenbergs' attorneys. Each request turned on a slightly different issue. Minton, along with Vinson, Reed, and Clark, voted against all the petitions. Frankfurter and Black consistently voted to grant each request. Harold H. Burton, Jackson, and Douglas vacillated.

Douglas's behavior was the most peculiar and caused the most anguish for the Court.[38] In each of the five appeals Douglas had voted against the Rosenbergs. However, Douglas was finally persuaded to reconsider his position, and on 16 June 1953 Douglas stayed the Rosenbergs' execution.[39] Vinson immediately called a special session of the Court to hear the new issues raised in Douglas's stay. Minton, who was already in New Albany for the summer recess, was very upset with Douglas for granting a stay, which meant that all the justices had to return to Washington.[40]

After two bitter conferences the Court announced its decision, in an unsigned opinion, vacating Douglas's stay. The Rosenbergs' last-minute appeal for clemency was rejected by President Dwight D. Eisenhower, and on 19 June Ethel and Julius Rosenberg, still proclaiming their innocence, were executed. The Rosenberg case ended one of the most gripping episodes in the history of the Cold War. It also revealed the sharp personal and philosophical differences that remained on the Court. The lingering animosity between Frankfurter and Douglas was most apparent. Frankfurter described Douglas's sudden change of heart as grandstanding intended to enhance his libertarian image.

These bitter personal rivalries on the Court disturbed Minton. An affable, sociable man, he got along well with all factions. He even functioned as an "unobtrusive mediator" between the Black-Douglas faction and the Frankfurter-Jackson duo.[41] Minton did not believe in letting philosophical differences interfere with personal relationships. One of his law clerks said that "Minton was probably the one person who was welcome in every other Justice's chamber."[42] Minton believed that it was important for the members of the Court to spend time together outside their conference sessions, and he wanted them to eat lunch together, just as he and his fellow judges on the Seventh Circuit had done. The only justices who dined together on a regular basis were Vinson, Reed, Clark, Burton, and Minton. The others either dined alone or in the public cafeteria. Yet Minton did succeed in gathering some of his colleagues in his office in the late afternoon for what was known as "afternoon teas." Minton served beverages ranging from coffee to straight whiskey. Even Frankfurter and Douglas participated in the "afternoon teas," although not always together. Frankfurter looked forward to "those late afternoon libations,"[43] and Douglas described "those Napoleon brandy teas [as] the most refreshing and heartwarming experiences in my Court years."[44]

Although Minton and Douglas represented opposite ends of the political spectrum, they nonetheless enjoyed an amicable relationship. Both were given to earthy language and delighted in telling each other off-color stories. One exchange between them illustrates the kind of humor that permeated their written correspondence. In October 1951 Minton was hospitalized in Walter Reed Hospital with a sprained back. Reporting on his condition to Douglas, Minton wrote that he knew he had improved because when he first arrived he was unable to "wipe my own ass."

"Hell," he said, "I couldn't even find it! Now I can not only find it I can scratch it."[45]

Minton's efforts to make the Court a more convivial place may have helped soothe tensions on the Court, but the ever-present drumbeat of Cold War cases prevented the Court from being a peaceful place. A loyalty program for federal workers represented another aspect of the Truman administration's confrontation with the Cold War. Instituted by executive order in 1947, the program made allegiance of all government employees subject to investigation by their department heads, and any negative information regarding an employee's loyalty could be grounds for dismissal. In addition, the attorney general was authorized to make a list of subversive organizations, and membership in any of these organizations was also grounds for dismissal.[46]

Two direct challenges to the federal loyalty program in 1951—*Bailey* v. *Richardson*[47] and *Joint Anti-Fascist Refugee Committee* v. *McGrath*[48]—found the Court so hopelessly divided about the constitutionality of the program's provisions that it sent conflicting signals about the extent to which individuals or groups affected by loyalty program decisions were entitled to due process. In *Bailey* the Supreme Court let stand a lower court decision that allowed the dismissal of a government employee even though the identities of the persons making the charges were not given to the loyalty review board or to Bailey, the dismissed worker. Four justices, including Minton, supported the government's actions.

In *McGrath,* handed down the same day as *Bailey,* the Supreme Court upheld the complaint of two organizations that had been put arbitrarily on the attorney general's list of subversive organizations without a hearing. Five of the justices—Burton, Douglas, Frankfurter, Black, and Jackson—upheld the organizations' complaint, but no majority opinion emerged. Each of the five justices wrote a separate opinion, leaving the Court without a definitive judgment.

The dissent, written by Reed, in which Minton and Vinson joined, took the position that the petitioners were not ordered to do anything nor were they punished for anything. The "Communist" classification given them was a "mere abstract designation," and unless the petitioners were punished or enjoined in their activities they were not entitled to judicial redress.

The contradictory signals stemming from *Bailey* and *McGrath* indicated that the Court was as badly divided on the question of government loyalty programs as it was on other measures taken in the name of national security. The difference between *Bailey* and *McGrath* turned on the vote of a single justice, Burton, who sided with the government in *Bailey* but switched his position in *McGrath*. His actions created a paradox that caused Jackson to observe that the Court had turned justice bottom-side up in granting relief to the group and not to the individual.[49]

After the mixed signals in *Bailey* and *McGrath,* the Court was confronted with numerous challenges to state and city loyalty programs; most of these were sustained, but characteristically without unanimity. One of the most publicized of the Court's decisions on the subject was the opinion written by Minton in *Adler* v. *Board of Education*[50] in 1952, which upheld the constitutionality of a New York state law barring persons belonging to subversive organizations from working in the state's school system. The Feinberg Law, as it was known, made membership in any organization listed as subversive by the State Board of Regents prima facie evidence of unsuitability for any job within the school system. *Adler* generated much public interest because it was one of the first cases to deal with the issue of academic freedom. Minton's majority opinion rejected the contention that the Feinberg Law was an unconstitutional interference with free speech: "It is clear that . . . persons have a right under our law to assemble, speak, think and believe as they will. It is equally clear that they have no right to work for the State in the school system on their own terms."[51]

A critical point for Minton was the particular nature of the employment. He argued that "a teacher works in a sensitive area in a schoolroom. There he shapes the attitude of young minds towards the society in which they live. In this, the state has a vital concern. That the school authorities have the right and the duty to screen officials, teachers, and employees as to their fitness to maintain the integrity of the schools as a part of ordered society, cannot be doubted."[52]

Even Douglas, in his dissent, agreed that "the school systems of the country need not become cells for Communist activities; and the classrooms need not become forums for propagandizing the Marxist creed."[53] However, he argued that the "guilt of the teacher should turn on overt acts,"[54] and he expressed concern that the decision would wreak havoc with academic freedom. Black, who concurred with Douglas, wrote a brief dissent of his own that maintained that the law penalized schoolteachers for their thoughts and actions. Frankfurter dissented on the grounds that the Court should have rejected jurisdiction in the case because the law had not been put into effect and therefore the issues presented were abstract and speculative.

Not unexpectedly there was wide press coverage of the decision, often with banner headlines. The *New York Times* ran lengthy articles and printed the full text of all the opinions. Most editorial comment, especially from papers in New York, was favorable. The *New York Sun* said Minton had put "into plain words exactly what most loyal American parents and taxpayers have long felt and will continue to feel."[55] Even the *Indianapolis Star,* a longtime Minton critic, hailed the decision. In a letter to Indianapolis attorney Kurt Pantzer, Minton said, "I am gratified to have the *Star* approve of something I do. It is a rather unique experience for me and therefore all the more acceptable."[56]

Response from the academic legal community was mixed. A noted court scholar of the day damned the *Adler* decision with faint praise in the *University of Chicago Law Review*. "Like it or not," he wrote, *Adler* "has the great merit of candor. There is no aura of pretense to it, no seeming but insubstantial reservation of individual right, not even a conventional bow to the usages of academic freedom. It is the legal statement of the popular aphorisms, 'If he doesn't like it here, let him go back where he came from.'"[57]

Although Minton felt strongly that the state of New York had the power to pass the Feinberg Law, his private correspondence provides evidence that he did not necessarily think it was a good law. Minton frequently corresponded with a former law clerk, George Braden, who later became a professor at Yale University law school. More often than not Braden's letters were highly critical of Minton's opinions. Despite the tenor of Braden's letters, Minton always responded graciously and candidly. When the *Adler* opinion was announced Braden wrote Minton that the "opinion leaves the impression that you not only believe the law to be Constitutional, you also think it is a good law."[58] Minton took issue with Braden's assumption, saying, "I don't see why you think I approved the policy of that law. As you well know one may have a view on policy that may not agree with the Constitutional question involved. In my own experience I hotly opposed while a Senator the Hatch Act as a matter of policy. I never questioned its Constitutionality."[59]

Adler, like most controversial decisions, generated letters from citizens with strong opinions about the Court's ruling. Many justices considered it inappropriate to comment publicly about Court decisions, but Minton had no such aversion. Like a politician responding to his constituents Minton answered the letters regardless of the views they expressed. To those who praised his *Adler* opinion Minton's letters reflected a genuine respect for the opposing point of view. "It is not easy to resolve these difficult questions," he wrote to one supporter, and cautioned another that the dissenting justices "reached their opinion only upon the most conscientious consideration of the constitutional law involved."[60] Those who found fault with the *Adler* decision were less generous in their views of Minton's position than he was of theirs.

Minton never altered his position that government loyalty programs were constitutional. In fact, over the years he became even more adamant that such programs were essential to the nation's security. In 1956, shortly before he retired from the Court, Minton wrote in an unpublished opinion that Congress never "intended that any place in the federal government should be 'snug harbor' for Communists." Even in 1956, as the Cold War hysteria was dissipating, Minton insisted that "if we have learned anything from the cold war it is that old procedures to oust the disloyal were inadequate for this fast moving day."[61]

In a noteworthy exception to his normal deference to government's anti-Communist schemes, Minton acknowledged in 1952 that there were restrictions on how far such programs could go. He joined a rare, unanimous decision striking down an Oklahoma loyalty oath that failed to distinguish between "innocent with knowing association" with subversive organizations as a violation of due process.[62]

Minton, however, was not so liberal in applying due process to aliens whose rights to enter or remain in the country were governed by statutory law and administrative regulation. In every case involving noncitizens whose loyalties were suspect, Minton voted against the individual. Aliens do not automatically have the same constitutional rights as natural-born citizens. Thus, whatever procedural rights aliens may have regarding decisions about entry or deportation is a function of how generous the Court chooses to be in interpreting constitutional protections and statutory law affecting their status. In the political environment of the 1950s the Vinson Court exhibited great deference to legislative and administrative authority over the rights of aliens. One constitutional scholar called the treatment of aliens suspected of possible disloyalty or of subversive affiliation in the 1950s one of the "cruelest aspects of the cold war."[63]

The Vinson Court's view of aliens' rights was epitomized by the *Mezei* decision in 1953. Minton, along with the other Truman appointees and Reed, voted to uphold the exclusion of Ignatz Mezei, an alien who had lived in the United States for twenty-eight years and who left the country to visit his dying mother in Rumania, his homeland.[64] When he returned he was excluded as an alien entering the country for the first time, detained on Ellis Island, and subsequently barred from the country without benefit of a hearing. The Supreme Court ruled that a court could not intervene because the exclusion proceeding was grounded on danger to national security. The Court's ruling, which had the effect of condemning Mezei to a life on Ellis Island because he literally had no other place to go, was called "the most brutal shock to the moral sense of any of the [Vinson Court] opinions in this tragedy-laden area."[65]

The position taken by the majority in *Mezei* was so extreme that Frankfurter and Jackson joined Douglas and Black in dissent. Scholars have observed that in carrying judicial restraint to excess the Vinson Court succeeded in uniting the two groups of justices who normally were poles apart. This was especially true in cases involving aliens' rights and was evidenced in one of Minton's most controversial and perhaps most famous opinions, *United States ex rel Knauff* v. *Shaughnessy*. Ellen Knauff, a German war bride, was denied entry to this country by the Immigration Service on the grounds that it would be "prejudicial to the interests of the United States." She was given no notice or a hearing before being barred. Knauff petitioned the Court for a review of her case on the grounds that she was entitled to a hearing before

FABIAN BACHRACH, HARRY S. TRUMAN LIBRARY

Sherman Minton with the other members of the Supreme Court during the fall 1949 term. Front row, left to right: Justices Felix Frankfurter, Hugo Black, Chief Justice Fred Vinson, Stanley Reed, and William Douglas; back row, left to right: Tom Clark, Robert Jackson, Harold Burton, and Minton.

being excluded from the country. The Immigration Service based its action on an administrative regulation, established by the attorney general, that permitted exclusions of aliens without a hearing. The authority for this regulation was a congressional statute that allowed the president to issue "reasonable rules, regulations and orders" governing the entrance of aliens during periods of national emergency. The issue that confronted the Court was whether these rules were "reasonable" given the War Brides Act of 28 December 1945 in which Congress made it easier for wives of soldiers to enter the country as long as they were "otherwise admissible under the immigration laws."[66]

The vote in *Knauff* was almost identical to that in *Mezei*. Minton, Vinson, Burton, and Reed against Black, Frankfurter, and Jackson.[67] Minton's opinion dismissed the idea that the regulations were void because they contained unconstitutional delegations of power. He defined the power to exclude as a fundamental act of sovereignty, stemming not only from legislative power but also from the inherent powers of the executive. Minton argued that it was not necessary for Congress to supply administrative officials with a specific formula to guide their decisions in an area characterized by "infinitely variable conditions." Minton wrote: "Whatever the procedure authorized by Congress is, it is due process as far as an alien denied entry is concerned." It was sufficient for Minton that the attorney general denied Knauff a hearing "because, in his judgment, the disclosure of the information on which he based that opinion would itself endanger the public security." The majority found the rules to be reasonable "in the circumstances of the period for which they were authorized," namely, the national emergency of World War II. For further emphasis Minton added: "We are dealing here with a matter of *privilege*. Petitioner had no vested *right* of entry."[68] Having determined that the attorney general was acting within constitutional and statutory authority, Minton wrote that the "action of the executive officer under such authority is final and conclusive." He added that "it is not within the province of any court, unless expressly authorized by law, to review the determination of the political branch of the Government to exclude a given alien."[69]

The *Knauff* opinion, written in Minton's first term, was his first of any significance. It typified the deferential approach he had followed so faithfully on the Seventh Circuit, limiting judicial intervention by carefully reading the relevant statutes to determine the intent of Congress and deferring to the judgment of the administrative official. Once Minton had determined that Congress and the executive had the authority to act, he was not concerned about the outcome. Deciding a case on the issue of power rather than the result was one of the cornerstones of Minton's judicial philosophy.

While Minton was not concerned about the consequences of the *Knauff* ruling, others were. Jackson wrote in his dissent, also joined by Frankfurter and Black, that: "Congress will have to use more explicit language than any yet cited before I will agree that it has authorized an administrative official to break up the family of an American citizen or force him to keep his wife by becoming an exile."[70] Although he joined Jackson's dissent, Frankfurter also wrote a separate dissent, chastising the majority for reading too narrowly the intent of Congress in passing the War Brides Act. Frankfurter saw the War Brides Act as a "bounty afforded by Congress not to the alien who had become the wife of an American but to the citizen who had honorably served his country."[71]

Outrage at Minton's *Knauff* opinion poured from every segment of American society. Newspaper editorials critical of the opinion were numerous. The *Chicago Sun Times* lamented that it was "a pretty raw deal to hand a soldier's bride. Congress passed the War Brides Act for the purpose of relaxing certain immigration restrictions." The editorial chided Minton for "choosing a literal rather than a strict interpretation of the issue in his first time out."[72] Minton wrote to Russell Stewart on the staff of the *Sun Times* about the editorial. "Where I line up," he said, "is not of much importance, but it is important as to whether I am right in what I decide." Minton responded to the editorial's description of the decision as "a raw deal," saying "if it was a 'raw deal,' it is something Congress fully authorized. I have always believed that this Court has no power to legislate, and I certainly believe it now as strongly as when I fought the old Court because we thought that it was using its power to legislate."[73]

Minton sent a similar letter in response to an editorial in the *Louisville Courier-Journal*. Publisher Mark

Ethridge, who had worked with Minton on the courts-martial review board in 1945, was persuaded by Minton's letter and opinion. In his reply Ethridge said that "reading the opinion creates an entirely different impression than we gained from the news story. In fact, the decision was so inadequately—if not inaccurately—reported that I have asked our editorial people to get a text of a decision in an important case before we comment on it. Certainly in this instance we did you and the Court an injustice."[74]

To citizens who wrote letters of criticism, and there were many, Minton wrote the same kind of response, stressing that as a senator he had fought against the Court using its power to legislate and nullify acts of Congress and thus usurping its power. To one citizen he wrote: "However appealing the case may be, we must declare the law as we see it."[75]

Minton was convinced that in this case Congress had not written in the War Brides Act an explicit exception to the power of the executive over immigration rules, and he had no intention of writing one for Congress. He said as much in a letter to George Braden, his frequent critic. Braden, a self-proclaimed liberal, claimed that the day the *Knauff* decision was handed down was known in liberal circles as "Black Monday," because the Court "moved so far to the right that Frankfurter and Jackson found themselves on the left." Braden continued: "I feel very strongly about the *Knauff* case. It is grimly ironical that Congress undoubtedly meant the result that you reached, but I feel that in these days when the Legislature leaves a loophole, and they certainly did here, the court has a good opportunity to insist that where Congress wants to do anything as unfair and unjust as this seems to be, they must say so in very clear language."[76]

In Minton's mind that was exactly what Congress had done and that left the Court with little choice. Following Braden's advice, he said, would have resulted in the Court legislating. Minton added, "I do not see how this Court could have reached any other conclusion. Congress said that under wartime regulations an alien seeking admission to this country could be excluded on security grounds, which the Attorney General was authorized to find. He found such grounds, he was authorized to find them, and for me that was enough. It was not for me to enlarge the scope of the War Brides Act to make this alien admissible. I have not yet been able to reconcile myself to the view that this Court should amend acts of Congress."[77]

Not all issues of due process tackled by the Court in the 1950s involved matters of loyalty and subversive activities, but even when procedural rights were not tied to security questions Minton was inclined to support government action against the claimed rights of citizens. One of Minton's deep convictions was that in balancing society's need for order and the rights of the individual, courts must not tip the scale against the government. This was especially true in cases involving the rights of defendants in criminal proceedings, where Minton demonstrated a belief in the need for unhampered law enforcement.

Minton's record on the Seventh Circuit placed him squarely in the center of "fair-trial jurisprudence," the case-by-case approach of deciding the rights to which a defendant is reasonably entitled. In an opinion upholding the conviction of a man who claimed that the state of North Carolina had violated his protection against double jeopardy, Minton reiterated his view that the requirements of due process are not a fixed concept. "As in all cases involving what is or is not due process," he said, "no hard and fast rule can be laid down. The pattern of due process is picked out in the facts and circumstances of each case."[78]

On the Seventh Circuit Minton had shown little sympathy for defendants who claimed their rights had been violated if he could determine from the record that the defendants were guilty. So it was on the Supreme Court. He once permitted testimony otherwise inadmissible because, he said, "this record fairly shrieks the guilt of the parties," and "we cannot conceive how this one admission could have possibly influenced this jury to reach an improper verdict." After all, Minton said, "A defendant is entitled to a fair trial but not a perfect one."[79]

Minton believed that in criminal proceedings the Fourteenth Amendment did not restrict the states to the same extent that it restricted the federal government. He subscribed to the "silver platter" doctrine, under which evidence seized illegally by federal officials could be introduced in state trials as long as it was allowed under the state constitution.[80] Minton's 1952 majority opinion in a case where wiretapped evidence was admitted illustrates his deference to state court proceedings. Although Congress specifically outlawed the use of wiretapped evidence in court proceedings in the Federal Communications Act, Minton concluded that a federal statute could not be presumed to "supersede the exercise of the power of the state unless there is a clear manifestation of intention to do so. The exercise of federal supremacy is not lightly to be presumed." Douglas, dissenting in the case, considered wiretapped evidence inadmissible under the Fourth Amendment, but Minton thought otherwise. "Indeed," he said, "evidence obtained by a state officer by means which would constitute an unlawful search and seizure under the Fourth Amendment to the Federal Constitution is nonetheless admissible in a state court."[81]

Among the most troublesome issues for the Court was determining the extent of protection afforded by the Fourth Amendment against unreasonable searches and seizures. On these issues Frankfurter was more likely to be in opposition to Minton and the other Truman justices while Black was more likely to be on their side. Black's experience as a prosecutor and Senate investigator made him construe the Fourth Amendment more narrowly than Frankfurter, who "saw it embodying the right most prized by civilized men—the right to be let alone."[82]

The Court's difficulties in interpreting the limits imposed by the Fourth Amendment on searches by law enforcement agents were manifested in its erratic pronouncements. Before 1946 a search without a warrant incidental to arrest could extend only to objects in plain sight of the arresting officers. In 1946 the Court established a more permissive standard in *Harris* v. *United States,*[83] in which it sustained an arrest that followed a five-hour search of the defendant's apartment without a warrant. The search turned up evidence related to illegal activities other than those for which he was arrested, and this evidence was used later to convict the defendant.

Two years later the Court modified the *Harris* ruling in the *Trupiano* case.[84] The former opinion required police to obtain a warrant if there was reasonable opportunity to do so. In *Trupiano* the Court invalidated the seizure in question because the government agents could easily have obtained a warrant, even though the evidence they seized was in plain sight at the time of the arrest. Against this confusing backdrop of legal precedents about the Fourth Amendment, Minton wrote the *Rabinowitz* decision,[85] without question one of his most controversial. Minton was joined by the other Truman appointees and Reed in the *Rabinowitz* case, which was viewed as "a symbol, as good as any, of both a changing face of the nation and the changing direction of a reconstituted Court."[86] *Rabinowitz* signaled a new hard-line approach to procedural requirements in criminal matters.

Rabinowitz was convicted of dealing in forged postage stamps with evidence taken from his business office without a search warrant. Minton did not think that the defendant's protection against *unreasonable* searches and seizures under the Fourth Amendment had been violated. "It is not disputed," he said, "that there may be reasonable searches, incident to an arrest, without a search warrant. Such searches turn upon the reasonableness under all the circumstances and not upon the practicability of procuring a search warrant, for the warrant is not required."[87]

A second issue in *Rabinowitz* was whether the search violated a precedent established in the *Trupiano* case in 1948, which required police to obtain a warrant if there was reasonable opportunity to do so.[88] The majority opinion overturned *Trupiano* and declared that "the relevant test is not whether it is reasonable to procure a search warrant, but whether the search was reasonable. That criterion in turn depends upon the facts and circumstances—the total atmosphere of the case."[89]

The *Rabinowitz* decision produced strong dissents on the Court, the most noteworthy of which was a lengthy opinion by Frankfurter, which was eight pages longer than Minton's majority opinion. Frankfurter charged that "it makes a mockery of the Fourth Amendment to sanction search without a search warrant merely because of the legality of an arrest."[90] Prior to the publication of his dissent, Frankfurter had written Minton a lengthy memorandum lecturing him on his and the other justices' disregard for the "Fourth Amendment and the great place which belongs to that Amendment in the body of our liberties as recognized and applied by unanimous decisions of this Court long before there were 'New Deal' justices."[91] The content of the memorandum became the basis of Frankfurter's dissent, and although it did not dissuade Minton from his own point of view, it impressed upon him Frankfurter's fervent commitment to the Fourth Amendment. In a reply to his ever-frequent critic George Braden, Minton observed: "Frankfurter's dissent was quite vigorous, especially as delivered from the bench. I think it took me a little less than 10 minutes to announce the opinion of the court, and he took thirty-five or forty minutes to announce his dissent. So you can see he was very much in earnest about it." Minton, defending his own opinion, told Braden that *Rabinowitz* was "not off the beam as far as the law had been laid down in preceding opinions by this Court, except Trupiano, which we overruled. I remember what a shock Trupiano was to the bench and bar when it came out."[92]

Frankfurter was not the only one with sharp criticism of Minton's opinion. Of particular concern to many legal scholars was Minton's position that what constitutes a reasonable search "is not to be determined by any fixed formula. The Constitution does not define what are 'unreasonable' searches and, regrettably, in our discipline we have no ready litmus-paper test."[93] Critics said that Minton's opinion constituted "a fundamental change in fourth amendment theory." In establishing reasonableness as the basis for deciding the legality of a search without a warrant, Minton provided no "formula or test to guide reason."[94]

There were those who found merit in Minton's opinion, more so for the way in which it was written than for the substance of the decision itself. *Rabinowitz* was cited in an *Indiana Law Journal* article as an example of Minton's ability to write an excellent, informative opinion. "This is honest, good opinion writing."[95] It was called Minton's best opinion in his maiden year on the bench, one "which, overruling an earlier opinion on searches and seizures, does so with great care and precision."[96]

Once again Minton received angry letters from the public about his opinion, and as usual he patiently answered them. In one letter he explained that the decision was "based upon the authorities handed down by the Court and the states which apply the Federal rule. You will also notice that the case is limited to the narrow factual situation presented by the record in this one."[97]

Not everyone was critical. One writer described Minton's decision as being "as 'American' as pop corn and ice cream," and added that "no honest person fears the power of any police (local, state, or federal) if he has nothing to hide or who makes an honest living because if the police do make a 'mistake' they can be held accountable."[98] Minton's decision may have dismayed legal scholars, but it found acceptance among many Americans, the people with whom Minton identified.

The *Knauff* and *Rabinowitz* opinions, both written in Minton's first term on the Court, cast a shadow over his judicial career, at least in the minds of judicial scholars, and seemed to color forever their views of him. Indeed, it is impossible to find a review of Minton's tenure on the Supreme Court that does not mention these two decisions.

Critics took aim not only at the substance of Minton's decisions but also his style of opinion writing. The most frequent criticism of his opinions was that he had "a little of the legislator's tendency to make a case easier than it is by stating the questions so that it admits only one answer."[99] One of Minton's law clerks, who had a firsthand look at his opinions, confirmed that Minton tended to write "as an advocate," which led him to "state the facts not as the record had revealed them but as would best support the decision."[100]

George Braden drew attention to this trait in an article in the *Indiana Law Journal,* assessing Minton's first year on the bench. Braden wrote Minton to prepare him for the critical nature of the article. He said: "You write in the style of Roberts and Sutherland. That is, you assume the answer then ask how anyone can decide contrary to the assumed answer."[101] Minton, unabashed by Braden's criticism, responded that he was looking forward to Braden's article and added, "I shall not be at all sensitive about whatever you say. I only do my best in my 'pedestrian' sort of way and maybe my writing does smack of Roberts and Sutherland. Frankly . . . while I never agreed with what Sutherland had to say as a general rule, I remember that he was the easiest fellow in the books for me to read. When I finished his opinions, I at least understood them."[102]

Despite the weaknesses in Minton's opinion writing there was some virtue in its simplicity. Even his critics claimed that his opinions were "very much to the point, and leave no doubt for the lower courts as to what they are supposed to do."[103] Indeed, Minton's style was welcomed by many lower court judges. A case in point was a letter from a federal district court judge in Arkansas who wrote to thank Minton for his "common sense and direct approach" to the law. "It is refreshing for a 'Country Lawyer' or a 'Country Judge' to read an opinion of the highest court in our land which clearly and succinctly states the problem and then answers it in plain everyday language that cannot be construed three or four different ways."[104]

The harsh criticism over his first-term dissents were no doubt troubling to Minton. As the session was nearing its end he wrote to his son Sherman that he was anxious to get home for a rest. "This has been an interesting experience. To sit on this top Court is an awesome experience and I am troubled by everything I do. I cannot be as relaxed as I was in Chicago."[105]

Minton's doubts about his first-year performance were also expressed in correspondence with Frankfurter. Frankfurter's friendship had been a source of moral support to Minton in his first term. Although the attention Frankfurter showered on Minton was not without ulterior motives, he nonetheless helped Minton feel at home on the Court. Minton told Frankfurter he would always remember "the cordial manner in which you received me into the circle," adding, "maybe I did disappoint some of my colleagues—if you were among them you concealed it with a gracious tolerance."[106]

Vinson tried to take the sting out of the criticism directed at his junior colleague, for whom he had obviously developed a genuine affection. He wrote: "You will never know what a tower of strength you were during your first term on the Court. I never had any doubt as to your ability to do the fine job that you did, but it was difficult for me to visualize in advance the extent of the comfort I would receive in your just being around. We certainly had some tough ones, and we will have many more confronting us."[107]

Minton, who received Vinson's letter in New Albany where he spent the Court recess, was grateful for Vinson's confidence. "You made me feel most welcome and by your confidence gave me more assurance," he said. As an indication that he had been hurt by the criticism aimed at his opinions, he added, "I shall preserve your letter to offset the [negative media comments] that my family could not quite understand."[108]

While Minton's opinions about individual rights drew the most attention and evoked the sharpest criticism, his strengths were often overlooked. Minton exhibited a strong competence in the fields of economic regulation, administrative law, and labor law, and he wrote a large share of the Court's opinions in those areas. Because of his experience on the Seventh Circuit handling cases of government involvement with business, Minton had a special interest in this field and was respected by the other justices for his expertise.[109]

Minton was particularly skilled in issues involving statutory interpretation and factually complex situations. *Alabama Great Southern Railroad Co.* v. *United States*[110] is illustrative of Minton's technical competence. In this case he spelled out for the Interstate Commerce Commission the factors it had to consider in setting differentials between rail and barge rates—not the type of issue to stir a lot of public interest. Nonetheless, a *Harvard Law Review* article called the opinion one of the excellent performances of the year,[111] and it was praised in the *University of Chicago Law Review* as "a cogent opinion" that handled the problem with considerable skill.[112]

In addition to the approval Minton received for his deft handling of technical economic policy, his commitment to end racial discrimination was also highly regarded.

"When it came to the Equal Protection Clause," Douglas wrote in his autobiography, "no one was more adamant than Minton in insisting on equality in the treatment of blacks. He was indeed one of the great mainstays in the early school-desegregation cases."[113] Three cases decided unanimously in Minton's first term provide a clear indication that Minton

MARY ANNE CALLANAN COLLECTION

Sherman Minton and his wife Gertrude relax at home.

was not sympathetic to state actions that denied equal rights based on race. In *McLaurin* v. *Oklahoma State Regents*[114] the Court held that Oklahoma could not engage in "nominal segregation" by designating special sections for students in the classroom, cafeteria, and library once they had been admitted to the university. In *Sweatt* v. *Painter*[115] the Court ruled that a separate law school established for blacks did not conform to the equal protection clause of the Fourteenth Amendment. In yet a third case, the Court overruled discrimination in railroad cars, although it did so by ruling that the Interstate Commerce Act forbade this type of discrimination rather than it being prohibited on constitutional grounds.[116] Although in 1950 the Court was not ready to attack the *Plessy* doctrine of "separate but equal" head-on, nonetheless the Court took significant steps to eliminate discrimination based on race.

The school desegregation cases as well as others pertaining to equal rights represent the one area of law where Minton deviated from his philosophy of judicial deference. Minton thought the Court had an obligation to intervene where racial discrimination occurred because he believed that the Fourteenth Amendment was written to prohibit the states' practices of racial discrimination. Nowhere is this belief more clearly demonstrated than in *Barrows* v. *Jackson,*[117] one of Minton's most memorable opinions, and one for which he received much acclaim. With only Vinson dissenting, the Court moved to make restrictive covenants virtually unenforceable in state courts by ruling that state courts cannot award damages when a restrictive covenant is violated because it is tantamount to the state itself discriminating on the basis of race, which it may not do under the Fourteenth Amendment.

Barrows closed a loophole that remained after the *Shelley* v. *Kraemer*[118] decision in 1948 held that state enforcement of restrictive covenants amounted to discriminatory action and thus was a violation of the Fourteenth Amendment. Although state courts could not enforce racially restrictive covenants, covenants remained legal and cosigners could still sue violators for damages. This was the problem Minton had to address in *Barrows,* and to solve it he had to find a way around the requirement of standing, a rule allowing only those persons directly affected by a situation to have their concerns addressed by the Court.

In the *Barrows* case one white property owner sued another for damages because she violated the terms of a restrictive covenant by selling her property to a non-Caucasian. In her defense the second property owner claimed that for the state to award damages against her would be a violation of the Fourteenth Amendment since in so doing they were upholding a policy that discriminated against nonwhites. The claim made in behalf of a third party not immediately embroiled in the suit raised the issue of standing. Unless that issue could be addressed, discrimination resulting from restrictive covenants would continue. Minton resolved the problem by relying on precedent from another case, *Pierce* v. *Society of Sisters,*[119] in which private schools were allowed to challenge an Oregon statute requiring all parents to send their children to public schools as a violation of the parents'constitutional rights. Even though no parent affected by the statute sought redress from the Court, the schools were granted standing to assert their constitutional rights.

The *Barrows* opinion probably brought Minton more positive reviews from the legal community than any other decision he wrote. He was praised in law review articles for his imaginative approach in addressing both the issue of state action and the issue of standing. His fellow justices also were lavish with their praise. Burton congratulated him for "a difficult constructive job admirably done." Black called it a "firm, forthright, opinion." Frankfurter noted in the margin of the circulated draft of the opinion, "Shay—this is a true, lawyer-like job. Greater praise is not in my vocabulary."[120] Minton had lived up to Black's expectations who, as the senior justice on the majority side, had assigned the case to him. The delicacy of the case required as much unanimity as possible, and Black thought Minton could devise an opinion that would satisfy most of the justices. Oddly, he satisfied all but Vinson, whose lone dissent contended that the requirement for standing had not been met because rights were being invoked in behalf of those who had no direct stake in the case before the Court.

The *Barrows* opinion represents one of the few times in which Minton took a liberal approach in broadening the meaning of "state action" under the Fourteenth Amendment. Usually he was adamant that the Fourteenth Amendment was not a remedy against private discrimination, no matter how reprehensible that discrimination might be. Three weeks earlier Minton had written a dissent that was more consistent with his view about "state action." *Terry* v. *Adams*[121] invalidated a preprimary election by an all-white association, known as the Jaybird Association, whose winners were placed on the Democratic party ballot in the regular primary. By a majority of seven to one the Court ruled that such an election, even by a private association, amounted to state action and therefore was unconstitutional under the Fifteenth Amendment, which prohibits states from discriminating in voting. Minton, the only dissenter, wrote one of his longest and most vehement dissents. He challenged the conclusion of the majority that the actions of the private Jaybird Association equated with state power. He said, "I am not concerned in the least as to what happens to the Jaybirds or their unworthy scheme. I am concerned about what this Court says is state action within the meaning of the Fifteenth Amendment to the Constitution. For, after all, this Court has power to redress a wrong under the Amendment only if the wrong is done by the State."[122]

Minton's unusually spirited dissent may have been in reaction to pressures from other justices to get him to conform to the majority view. Frankfurter, author of one of the three opinions on the majority side, wrote his junior colleague a reassuring note about his refusal to change his position. Frankfurter assured Minton that more important than their differences on the merits of problems was their "agreement about the duty to express convictions and not yield merely on the score of prudence or good fellowship or whatever the reason may be by which convictions that matter are suppressed and their opposites are embraced."[123]

Minton's reply indicated that no hard feelings existed over their differences in the Jaybird case. He thanked Frankfurter for his "generous remarks about my dissent in the Jaybird case," and added: "Since I have been here, you have comforted me more than a little, not only by your attitude towards my work but in our personal relations. I know you will always feel free to criticize as well as approve, and I assure you I shall appreciate both—as I have your friendship."[124]

Minton's comments to Jackson about the Jaybird case were more characteristic. Jackson sent Minton a bar association article that discussed whether the Supreme Court was influenced by election returns. In reply Minton noted, "When the Jaybird opinion comes down, there may be some question as to which election returns the Court follows. It will be damn clear they aren't following the law."[125]

Six years after the Jaybird decision, when Minton was retired, the subject of the Jaybird decision was recalled in a letter from Black. As a senator, Black wrote, "you were not afraid to follow that hard course if your honest judgment told you that was right. You followed that same guide on the Court. You showed that in your dissent in the Jaybird case—a dissent which expressed views with which I wholly disagreed. I cannot think of one case in which you participated during your Supreme Court service where you lowered your flag because of any effect your decision might have on Shay Minton."[126]

The Court handed down other important civil rights decisions in the 1952–53 term, but none was more significant than the Court's actions in the school desegregation cases. Although the oral arguments were heard in December, the Court delayed its response in the desegregation cases until the end of the term. On 8 June 1953 the Court announced that the cases would be reargued in the next term and outlined the questions that opposing counsel was to address. One week later the Court adjourned. No one knew that when it reconvened there would be a new chief justice.

Vinson died unexpectedly of a heart attack at his home in Washington on the morning of 8 September, while Minton was still in New Albany. Just two weeks earlier Minton had written to welcome Vinson to the "Ancient and Decrepit Order of Grandfathers," and to discuss the most recent events in politics and baseball.[127] Vinson's reply was the last letter Minton ever received from the chief justice. "I miss you a lot," he said.[128]

In their four years on the Court together Minton and Vinson had developed a strong affection for one another. Their private correspondence indicates that they counted on each other for mutual support against an often hostile environment. Minton once told Vinson that "my greatest satisfaction is to be associated with you and to have the comforting assurance that I can always depend on you come hell or high water."[129]

Upon learning of Vinson's death Minton had nothing but words of praise for his friend and colleague. "Fred Vinson was a great Chief Justice," he said, "because he was a great lawyer with a background of experience in government unexcelled by anyone. He was a prodigious worker with a capacity for friendship which gave him leadership. He was ever kind and considerate, which endeared him to all. His death is a great loss to the Court and the country and I grieve for the death of a great friend."[130] Expressing his grief to Vinson's widow Roberta, Minton said that "outside of his family, no one loved him more than I."[131]

Minton's view is not shared by legal scholars who fault Vinson for his inability to unify the Court and his weak record in defending civil liberties. As Vinson's closest ally on the Court, Minton is tarred with the same brush. By the 1950s judicial deference to governmental actions, which both Vinson and Minton practiced, was increasingly out of step with a newfound faith in judicial activism held by many prominent legal scholars.

The most positive legacy of the Vinson Court is its record in civil rights, but even in this area of law Vinson has been criticized for his ambivalence about how far and fast the Court should proceed in confronting the constitutionality of the separate but equal precedent established in *Plessy*.[132] Minton did not share Vinson's reticence about overturning state laws requiring separation of the races in public schools, but their differences on this issue were never a source of tension between them.

Vinson's death had profound consequences for Minton. He had lost the person on the Court to whom he was closest philosophically and personally. Vinson's absence had an important impact on the balance of power on the Court, and no one would feel that impact more than Minton. In Vinson's final term there were already signs of dissension within the Truman bloc. Minton, along with Black and Douglas, albeit for different reasons, was increasingly in dissent, while Reed and Jackson were more and more frequently voting with the majority. It was clear at the outset of the 1953 term that the new chief justice would usher in a new era for the Court.

CHAPTER NINE

Just an Echo

President Dwight D. Eisenhower moved quickly after Fred M. Vinson's death to appoint a successor. Eisenhower chose Earl Warren, the popular governor of California who was considered a moderate, with the expectation that Warren would use his political skills to bring more unanimity to the Court. The transition affected Minton both personally and in his role on the Court. Although he missed Vinson, he quickly developed a warm relationship with Warren. However, just as quickly it became apparent that the new chief justice would move the Court back in a more activist direction, a direction that did not fit with Minton's views about the role of the Court and its relationship to the other branches of government.

Because the Senate was in recess Warren's appointment was an interim one, which meant he could take over the reins of the Court right away, even before his confirmation hearings were held. Warren had many of the same personal characteristics as Minton—he was warm, friendly, and a good politician. In addition he loved baseball, and he and Minton frequently attended games together. Once they sat through eight hours of a doubleheader between the Senators and the Yankees at Griffith Stadium in Washington. Socially, Warren interacted with Minton more so than with

MARY ANNE CALLANAN COLLECTION

Sherman Minton in his Supreme Court office in 1951.

any other justice on the Court at the time,[1] even though they did not share the same view about the Court and many of the cases before it.

During the fall term of Warren's first year, 1953–54, Minton wrote to Homer Bone, a former Senate colleague, then a judge on the Ninth Circuit Court of Appeals in San Francisco, about his life on the Court. Minton praised Warren's appointment, saying we "hold him in the highest esteem," and predicted that "he is going to measure up here in every respect. Certainly a finer personality could not have been found." Minton was less optimistic about his own situation. "I keep plugging away here," he wrote, "trying to keep up my end at the Court, with rather indifferent success, but I still keep plugging."[2]

In the fall of 1953, besides adjusting to changes on the Court, Minton was still adjusting to the changes on the national political scene. Republicans, in full control of the White House and Congress, were already gearing up for the 1954 congressional elections. In mid-November Republicans announced that "Communism" was going to be one of the big issues they would use against the Democrats. They planned to use the case of Harry Dexter White, a member of both the Roosevelt and Truman administrations, who had been cited in an FBI report for alleged spy activity, as an example of how the Democrats were soft on Communism. Charges and countercharges flew over Truman's handling of the White affair. A combative Truman defended himself in a nationwide radio address. After listening to Truman's speech Minton wrote to congratulate him for "the greatest performance of your remarkable career." Minton accused the Republicans of creating a diversionary tactic so that people would not notice the problems in the economy.[3]

Politics aside, the change that had the most profound effect on Minton was the shifting direction of the Court. Although Warren began as a centrist on the Court, he frequently voted with William O. Douglas and Hugo L. Black, the Court's staunchest supporters of individual liberties. Minton, Harold H. Burton, and Stanley F. Reed still tended to vote together, but they were unable to maintain the influence over cases that they once had without Vinson and Tom C. Clark, who began to desert them. As the Court became more activist in behalf of individual rights, Minton found himself increasingly out of sync with the Court's judicial philosophy with the result that his substantive contributions declined. Although he maintained the same level of productivity in the quantity of opinions written, they were generally cases of lesser visibility. Warren chose others or himself to write opinions in more prominent cases, even in cases in which Minton voted with the majority.[4]

Minton's tendency to vote with the government against the claimed rights of defendants did not diminish under the new chief justice. Minton and Felix Frankfurter continued to have differences when the Court ruled against the rights of a defendant, especially if the case involved evidence obtained through questionable searches and seizures. Minton kidded Frankfurter about this tendency, prompting Frankfurter to defend himself. "I may be deluding myself," he said, "but I do not think I am any 'softer' about crime than you are. I think such differences as we have derive from our different experience in regard to criminal justice."[5] Minton answered that sometime "you and I may discuss our respective views about criminal justice—with the concession before we start that yours are the more enlightened." Frankfurter returned the letter to Minton with the "yours are more enlightened" phrase underlined. Then at the bottom he wrote: "S.M. You are saying it's not!!"[6]

Leyra v. *Denno,* a case decided during Warren's first term, is a good example of the differences between Minton and the Court's new perspective on criminal matters. The majority opinion held that confessions obtained through the help of a psychiatrist amounted to mental coercion and therefore resulted in a denial of due process and thus overturned convictions that rested on those confessions. Minton's dissent, joined by Reed and Burton, the frequently dissenting trio under the new regime, maintained that there was sufficient evidence to support the voluntary nature of the confessions. Further Minton argued that it was not a denial of due process since the issue of whether the confessions were voluntary was submitted to the jury.[7]

One of Minton's frustrations with criminal cases was the lengthy appeals process relied upon by defendants. He expressed his irritation in a dissenting opinion where the majority had overturned the conviction of a person who was tried in federal court without counsel. The defendant had been tried twelve years before he filed the appeal and had completed his sentence eight years earlier. Minton showed little sympathy for the defendant. He wrote: "The respondent doesn't say, nor does he suggest how a lawyer might have helped him unless he picked the lock on the jailhouse door." Showing an impatience with a system that allowed the defendant to appeal his conviction after so many years, Minton continued that "at some point a judgment should become final—that litigation must eventually come to an end."[8]

On occasion Minton found himself dissenting from the majority in antitrust cases. As an appeals court judge he had interpreted broadly the commerce clause of the Constitution and antitrust legislation, such as the Sherman Act, in favor of government regulation of business and industry. On the Supreme Court, however, he sometimes construed narrowly antitrust provisions, with the result that fewer activities were considered to be subject to regulation. Consequently, Minton had no trouble supporting the Court's per curiam decision in *Toolson* v. *New York Yankees* in 1953, reconfirming that baseball should be exempt from the interstate commerce clause.[9] *Toolson* rested solely on the basis of an earlier decision, *Federal Baseball Club* v. *National League,*[10] exempting baseball from the Sherman Act.

Unlike the rest of the Court, however, Minton thought all sports should be excluded from coverage of the act, and he dissented in 1955 when the Court refused to grant boxing the same exemption it had granted baseball. Minton reasoned that "when boxers travel from State to State, carrying their shorts and fancy dressing robes in a ditty bag in order to participate in a boxing bout, which is wholly intrastate, it is now held by this Court that the boxing bout becomes interstate commerce. What this Court held in the *Federal Baseball* case to be incident to the exhibition now becomes more important than the exhibition. This is as fine an example of the tail wagging the dog as can be conjured up."[11]

Minton sometimes interpreted the provisions of the Sherman Act so literally that it thwarted the intent of Congress. This happened in the case of *United States* v. *Employing Plasterers Association.*[12] The Court's majority determined that an association of plasterers in Chicago, charged with conspiring to suppress competition, came under interstate commerce because many of the materials used by the association members had been shipped through interstate commerce, making the materials subject to antitrust regulation. Despite this interstate connection of the building materials, Minton's dissent deemed the association's activities to be purely intrastate and therefore not subject to the Sherman Act because "commerce ends when the plaster and lath reach the building site." Therefore, he concluded "the construction of a building and the incorporation therein of plaster and lath are purely local transactions."[13]

Minton's interpretation about what constituted interstate commerce was contrary to the body of judicial opinion that extended back to 1937 when the Court ruled in *NLRB* v. *Jones and Laughlin Steel Corporation*[14] that Congress could regulate activities that had an indirect effect on commerce, such as labor relations, as well as a direct effect. Following the *Jones and Laughlin* case, as more Roosevelt appointees joined the Court, the interpretation of interstate commerce was extended to allow Congress to regulate important aspects of state and local economies by removing the distinction between direct and indirect effect. By 1946 the Court had extended the reach of the commerce clause to the point that "the concept of intrastate commerce was drained of any substance."[15]

His shift to a more narrow definition of what constituted interstate commerce did not necessarily mean that Minton had abandoned his New Deal beliefs. Although he was reluctant to upset state and local regulations whenever they were not expressly forbidden or were not in direct conflict with a federal statute, he consistently upheld federal regulation of commerce when he thought the wording and legislative history of the statute clearly conveyed congressional intent to preclude state regulation.

In one of his more famous opinions concerning federal power to regulate business, *Phillips Petroleum Company* v. *Wisconsin*,[16] Minton interpreted the Natural Gas Act as authorizing a power for the Federal Power Commission (FPC) that the commission itself did not want. Phillips Petroleum maintained that natural gas, produced and sold to interstate pipeline companies, was exempt from regulation under the Natural Gas Act. The FPC also claimed that it had no authority to determine the wholesale rates charged to interstate pipeline companies. In a ruling that clearly favored consumers, Minton and the majority disagreed, saying that Congress did not intend to exclude these transactions from regulation.

The initial reaction to the *Phillips* decision was positive because it favored consumers over producers, but not everyone shared that view. Clark, who dissented in the case, later referred to "Minton's opinion as the most important, if unfortunate, one he wrote because of its serious long term effects on the country's energy supply."[17] Some members of Congress also criticized Minton's ruling. In 1956 measures were introduced in Congress to exempt interstate resales of gas from the Natural Gas Act, opening a round of protracted deliberations. In Senate debate on the measure, William Fulbright of Arkansas accused the Supreme Court of "writing its own Natural Gas Act against the intent of Congress" in the *Phillips* decision. Referring specifically to Minton, Fulbright said: "I don't think he ever regulated an oil or gas well in his life. He's a great Justice, but sometimes great justices are wrong."[18] It was ironic that Minton, the advocate of judicial restraint, was charged on the floor of the Senate with rewriting the laws of Congress.

In the 1953–54 term the Court rendered its historic *Brown v. Board of Education* decision that outlawed segregation in public schools. After nearly two years of preliminary maneuvering the Court finally came to terms with the issue of whether state-mandated segregation violated the provision in the Fourteenth Amendment prohibiting states from denying to anyone "equal protection of the laws."

The first arguments in the desegregation cases were scheduled originally for 14 October 1952. However, in an attempt to prevent the matter from becoming an issue in the 1952 presidential campaign,[19] the Court postponed the arguments until 8 December, safely after the election. The arguments in the desegregation cases ended on 11 December, and on 13 December the Court held its first judicial conference to deliberate the case. At that meeting Minton, Black, Douglas, and Burton indicated a willingness to end the practice of segregated schools.[20] Minton made his position known in no uncertain terms. "Classification by race is not reasonable," he said, "[and] segregation [is] per se unconstitutional."[21] Other members of the Court were less certain. Unable to resolve their differences over this great constitutional issue that had far-reaching consequences, the Court announced that the case would be reargued in the 1953–54 term. Little did the justices know at the time that they would have a new chief justice when the case came back to the Court.

In rescheduling the oral arguments the Court issued instructions about specific issues that counsel for the two sides should address. The most important question was whether there was any evidence that the framers of the Fourteenth Amendment specifically intended the equal protection provision to extend to public education. In 1896 in *Plessy* v. *Ferguson,* the Court had established the doctrine of "separate but equal," which meant that as long as facilities or accommodations were equal, it did not violate the Fourteenth Amendment if they were separate. The *Plessy* doctrine would have to be overturned for the Court to rule that segregation in the public schools was unconstitutional.

The second round of arguments, originally scheduled for mid-October 1953, did not take place until 7 December. The arguments lasted for two days, and on the following Saturday the justices met in conference to decide the *Brown* case. Black was absent because of an illness in his family but left word that he still supported overturning the practice of separate but equal. Warren led with a forceful argument that the time had come to end racial discrimination in education. After Warren, each justice spoke in order of his seniority. By the time it got to Minton, the junior justice, only Warren, Douglas, and Black were solidly behind overturning segregation by judicial decree, with Burton leaning strongly in that direction. Reed was definitely opposed. Frankfurter, Jackson, and Clark were sympathetic but had reservations about the power of the Court to bring an end to segregation. Frankfurter and Jackson especially had strong philosophical reservations.

In his epochal study of the desegregation cases, Richard Kluger wrote that Minton "was hardly less forceful than either Warren or Douglas" in advocating an end to desegregation. Minton said that the separate but equal doctrine "had been read into the Constitution by the Court in *Plessy*, and was 'a weak reed today' and now it should be read right out of it." Minton said that in the 1950s "no justification remained for racial barriers except, as the Chief Justice had said, an avowed belief in Negro inferiority."[22]

Minton's position meant that at least a majority of five was committed to overturning *Plessy*, but Warren was convinced that the decision to overturn segregated schools had to have the moral force of a unanimous decision. For the next few months Warren worked on two levels—the personal and the conference—to get that unanimity. Minton, of course, was a good candidate for helping with the personal strategy. The luncheon grouping, fostered by Minton when Vinson was chief justice, proved a valuable tool since Reed, the most reticent justice, was one of the regular participants. At these gatherings Warren, Minton, and Burton worked on Reed to join with the majority. Minton, along with Burton, was the most congenial with Reed and the most likely to influence Reed's vote. As the Court's strongest team player, Minton no doubt stressed to his colleague the unfortunate effects of a split decision.[23]

Court proceedings leading up to *Brown* were shrouded in secrecy. Regarding all the Court's business, but especially pertaining to *Brown*, Minton was adamant that neither he nor his law clerks would discuss the deliberations of the Court with outsiders, either then or in the future. One clerk, recalling the drama surrounding *Brown*, acknowledged that "the Court generally maintained much stricter confidentiality even with respect to law clerks in regard to *Brown* than in regard to the general run of cases." For example, following a conference Minton would usually provide his clerks with his record of how the justices voted and who was assigned to write the opinion of the Court. He did not do that in *Brown*. The strict confidentiality pertained to the clerks for other justices as well, who often, over lunch, would discuss particular pending cases, including the views of the justice for whom each worked. Minton's clerk could not recall any law clerk discussing such information before the *Brown* decision, but he noted that none of the clerks with whom he spoke had any real doubt that *Plessy* would be overturned given the general trend of segregation decisions in the years prior to *Brown* and the very fact that certiorari, or review, had been granted in *Brown*.[24]

No one, however, could know for certain that the decision would be unanimous. Sometime in March or April, the exact date is not known, the justices met to take their final vote on the case, reaching a compromise that resulted in a unanimous decision. On 17 May 1954 the Court announced its decision, with Warren reading the relatively short majority opinion he had written for the Court. The Court had concluded that school segregation deprived minority students of equal protection of the law and was therefore unconstitutional. In the most moving passage from the opinion, Warren said: "To separate [children] from others of similar age and qualifications solely because of their race generates a feeling of inferiority as to their status in the community that may affect their hearts and minds in a way unlikely ever to be undone."[25]

Warren's opinion made clear that the Court had relied heavily on the results of psychological testing that demonstrated the effect of segregation on minority students.

The Court's reliance on social science evidence was one of the more controversial aspects of the decision. After he retired from the bench Minton confirmed that the sociological data were persuasive. In an interview in *Ebony* magazine Minton said: "Education shapes the thinking of our citizens. Segregated education has its impact on the psychological makeup of the colored child. One of the reasons the Court ruled against segregation in education was that it was a discrimination against the colored school child that was psychologically detrimental."[26]

The press coverage of *Brown* reflected its monumental importance. Banner headlines heralded the news of the decision, and the full text of the opinion was printed in most major newspapers. The *Christian Science Monitor* called *Brown* "the decision of the century," and it was. Minton echoed the same opinion, calling *Brown* "the most important decision of the century because of its impact on our whole way of life."[27] He also said many times thereafter that it was the decision of which he was most proud. Ironically, the *Brown* decision was one of the few times in Minton's judicial career when he abandoned his commitment to judicial restraint. The Court's decision had all the characteristics of activism. Ignoring its own precedents, the Court had overturned the laws passed by popularly elected legislatures and in doing so had relied heavily on sociological evidence rather than legal reasoning. The Court was in effect legislating, something Minton avowed previously it should never do. Nonetheless, Minton's vote was consistent with his previous votes on civil rights, which reflected his firm conviction that the Fourteenth Amendment was written specifically to protect blacks against state discrimination.

When the Court handed down the *Brown* decision in May 1954, it did not make any provisions for implementation of the ruling. Instead, it delayed making a decision on that aspect of desegregation until the 1954–55 term. On 11 April 1955 the Court heard arguments about how the decision should be implemented. In the conference that followed Minton was still forceful in his views, stating it was vital for the Court to be unanimous in its second decision. Also, he said it was important that the Court "not talk big in the opinion and small in the decree—that would be weaseling." To Minton the main goal was "to get the desegregation process started without, in the process, revealing its own impotence to make it happen."[28]

On 31 May 1955 the Court announced its decision. The responsibility for implementing the order was placed on the shoulders of the federal district court judges in each state. Since the Supreme Court could not render a decision that bound all school boards, the initiative in bringing an end to segregated schools had to be taken by litigants for minority students through filing suits against individual school boards. Any board that was sued had to formulate a desegregation plan that would be reviewed by a federal district court judge to determine if it followed the guidelines established by the Supreme Court. The process amounted to desegregation on a case-by-case basis, which proved to be very slow and costly. Significant headway in desegregating the schools did not come until after 1965 when Congress passed the Elementary and Secondary Education Act, which provided aid to education and prohibited the allocation of funds to segregated schools. The act gave the federal government a new carrot-and-stick approach to ending racial discrimination in public schools. Minton did not live to see the goal achieved.

After *Brown* there was no longer any doubt that Warren's leadership meant major change was in store for the Court. He had demonstrated a capacity to unify the Court, even on such an emotional issue as school segregation, that Vinson never exhibited. The long-term implications of Warren's leadership for the Court could not have been lost on Minton. Although Minton joined the Court in its unified commitment to end racial discrimination, he did not share its activist commitment to restrict the power of government in other areas of individual rights. Near the end of the

1953–54 term Minton was giving some thought to retiring. After hearing a Drew Pearson broadcast that Minton might retire because of his health, Judge Homer Bone wrote to Minton: "I want you to know that I have always felt the warmest affection for you and you have my most sincere sympathy if you find yourself swimming in troubled waters in respect to your health."[29]

Contrary to Pearson's prediction, Minton did not leave the Court, but his longtime secretary, Frances Kelly, did. She had earned her law degree by attending night courses at George Washington University, and she left her Supreme Court position in 1954 to work as a lawyer for the Department of the Navy. Kelly's departure was a tremendous personal loss to Minton. Officially she had been his secretary since 1937, but more accurately she was his right hand. Her wise counsel helped keep him on an even keel. After her departure Frankfurter wrote Minton that he would miss her "around the Court almost as much as you will. In character and ability she is a very superior person. She certainly brought uncommon intelligence to her job."[30] Minton's reply to Frankfurter was uncharacteristically pessimistic. "I shall miss Frances Kelly [to] no end," he said. "Her kind is hard to beat. She no doubt thought I was on my last legs, and the ship I mastered was about to go down so she took to the rafts. I hope she prospers."[31]

Minton's ship, if not actually sinking, was certainly drifting, and the waters became more troubled when Jackson, an ally on the question of judicial review, died of a heart attack in October 1954. Jackson's replacement, John Marshall Harlan, did not take his seat until the following March. Although Harlan also was committed to judicial restraint he often agreed with the majority, and Minton frequently found himself in the role of a dissenter. In the 1954 term Minton wrote seven majority opinions, along with a total of nine dissenting opinions, four above the Court's mean.[32] Four of his seven majority opinions were in tax law, two were in criminal law, and one was in administrative law.

Four of his dissenting opinions were in the area of criminal law, and all held against the claimed right of the individual. One in particular attracted attention because of the amusing way in which Minton chided the majority for its ruling. *Bell* v. *United States*[33] was the last case in which Minton participated that involved an interpretation of a federal criminal statute. The defendant had been convicted of two violations of the Mann Act, which prohibits transporting females across state lines for immoral purposes. Bell argued that he should be charged with only one offense, rather than two, because he had transported both women in one trip. The majority of the Court, in an opinion written by Frankfurter, found nothing in the language of the Mann Act to indicate that Congress intended punishment to be cumulative for transporting more than one female at a time. In the absence of a clear directive from Congress, the Court erred on the side of leniency.

In his dissent in *Bell,* in which he was joined by Warren and Reed, Minton said, "The statute does not seem ambiguous to me." Congress, he said, had intended to "stamp out the degradation and debauchery of women by punishing those who engaged in using them for prostitution." Minton concluded that Congress intended to punish the transportation of each female. "Surely," he said, Congress "did not intend to make it easier if one transported females by the bus load."[34] This dissent became part of the folklore of the Court. In 1961 Truman wrote to Minton about a recent trip to Washington where he had lunch with the members of the Court. They hashed over old stories, and one that they mentioned was Minton's dissent in *Bell*. Truman said, "They told me about your decision that it is cheaper to transport whores across state lines by the dozen than singly."[35]

By the end of the 1954–55 term Minton was well aware of his growing estrangement from the Court. He wrote to his former law clerk, Harry Wallace, that there was not much of importance on the 1954–55 term docket. "It was my lightest year ever," he said. "I was in dissent a great many cases, though I wrote few of the dissents."[36] At the same time he wrote Frankfurter of his frustration with the endless pleas that characterize the American system of criminal justice: "I do get a bit impatient with our system which seeks to cheat the law by some specious plea that hasn't anything to do with his guilt or innocence but is only a plea that [he wasn't tried] according to the rule without even hinting that the application of the rule would have saved him. But if law is to be respected it must be considered as something other than a game."[37]

As Minton entered the 1955–56 term the Supreme Court was beginning to lose some of its luster for him. A major factor in his disenchantment was his health. Minton wrote to Truman in December about his decision to retire the following October. "I am slipping fast," he said. "I have to carry a cane now all the time. I find my mental health keeps pace with my physical health. I find my work very difficult and I don't have the zest for the work I use to have. You know I have had pernicious anemia for ten years & it has sapped my vitality, especially mental."[38]

As his physical stamina declined Minton adjusted by slowing his pace and scheduling afternoon naps. He found it difficult to sit for long periods of time without moving about and often became irritable when oral arguments began to drag on. When Minton lost interest in the tedious arguments it showed in his body language. Sometimes he would snap several rubber bands around his stack of briefs. If the lawyer before the bench did not get the message, Minton would snap the rubber bands until he did.[39] Minton also became exasperated with Frankfurter's endless, sometimes irrelevant, questions from the bench. One of Minton's clerks wrote that when this happened, "Minton could be seen muttering and Burton, who sat next to him and was quite straight laced, would start to blush with embarrassment and shock."[40]

Even if his health had been better, Minton may have made the decision to retire from the Court anyway. As the Court adopted a more activist stance, a clash between legislative and judicial power was inevitable. Minton, who once was described as having "elevated judicial restraint to a new high," felt out of place. In 1955–56 a significant part of the Court's cases dealt with subversives and seditious activities, and the Court's new libertarian outlook estranged him even further. Minton's dissenting opinions began to attract more attention than his majority opinions.

Minton wrote only three dissents in his final term on the bench. Two of those involved the rights of defendants and the other concerned the power of an administrative agency. True to form, Minton sided with the government in each dissent. The first was in *Toth* v. *Quarles*.[41] The case involved a man who was tried in a military court for having committed murder while an airman in Korea, even though he was a civilian at the time of his trial. The majority overturned the conviction of the defendant, ruling that military trials of civilians were unconstitutional and that the federal statute authorizing military trials after discharge for offenses committed prior to discharge was invalid. Minton, Reed, and Burton dissented; both Minton and Reed wrote dissents. Not surprisingly, Minton deferred to the power of Congress to retain court-martial jurisdiction over the defendant and to try him as a soldier. He wrote: "This is the way Congress had provided for his trial. No other way was provided. That it may have provided another way is not to say the way provided is invalid."[42] *Toth* was a final affirmation that Minton had not changed his basic approach to resolving conflicting claims about government power. To him, the issue, as always, was a question of power. As long as the legislature had the power, it was not the role of the Court to judge the wisdom of the policy.

Minton issued his final dissent in the case of *Griffin* v. *Illinois*,[43] which concerned the rights of indigent defendants in state courts. A sharply divided court held that the appellate criminal procedure in Illinois was unconstitutional. A transcript of the trial proceedings, paid for by the defendant, was required before a case could be appealed. The procedure failed to provide indigent defendants with the means to bring a full appeal within the state court system. This failure, the Court ruled, violated both the equal protection and due process clauses of the Fourteenth Amendment.

Minton's last written dissent was full of symbolism. The four dissenters included Minton, Burton, Reed, and Harlan. Black, the Court's strongest defender of civil liberties, wrote the majority opinion. The majority of five, which included Warren and Clark, indicated that the Court was gradually coming to accept Black's position on the doctrine of incorporation. Minton's opinion in *Griffin* stands as his final statement that he never accepted fully the argument that the Fourteenth Amendment imposed the same requirements of due process on the states that the Bill of Rights imposed on the federal government: "It is one thing for Congress and this Court to prescribe such procedure for the federal courts. It is quite another for this Court to hold that the Constitution of the United States has prescribed it for all state courts. The Constitution requires the equal protection of the law, but it does not require the States to provide equal financial means for all defendants to avail themselves of such laws."[44]

Minton wrote one final dissent, which was never published. The *Cole* v. *Young* decision, announced the last day of the term, concerned the interpretation of the powers of the president under the National Security Act.[45] In this legislation Congress had authorized department heads in the federal government to dismiss civilians deemed to be a threat to the national security. Although Congress had listed specific agencies to which this power applied, it also authorized the president to extend the provisions to other agencies, and the president had extended it to all other agencies of government. A food and drug inspector, who was suspended from his job in the Department of Health, Education and Welfare without a hearing because of his alleged involvement with a subversive organization, challenged the government's action. The majority ruled that Congress had intended to restrict the provisions of the National Security Act to sensitive positions and therefore the president had acted contrary to the will of Congress.

Both Minton and Clark wrote dissenting opinions. Minton's was a very spirited argument about the usurpation of the power of Congress and the power of the president. Minton did not think that Congress had intended to limit the National Security Act to sensitive positions. Instead, he said, Congress left to the president the decision as to which other agencies the act should be extended. Therefore, Minton said, it was the president's judgment "not ours, nor that of anyone else." In his final statement about limits on judicial power Minton wrote: "This is substituting our judgment for that of the President." Minton's dissent was never presented. As he had done in the steel seizure case four years earlier, Minton decided to suppress his own opinion and concur with Clark's for the sake of effectiveness.[46]

The *Cole* decision was presented on 11 June 1956, the last day for announcing opinions. Minton's dissent represented that side of him which drew the sharpest criticism—the willingness to elevate the power of government, even in its most arbitrary fashion, over the rights of individuals. On that final day, however, Minton also displayed the other side of his philosophy—populism. He wrote the majority opinion in two cases involving the application of an amendment to the Federal Employers' Liability Act to employees of carriers in interstate and foreign commerce.[47] In each instance the Court held the amendment extended the coverage of the act to the employees in question. One was an employee engaged in the construction of new railroad cars and the other was a blueprint file clerk. Minton rejected the argument that the amendment covered only employees engaged primarily in transportation because no language in the act contained such a limitation. Finding no language for limiting the liability of the railroad, Minton concluded: "The benefits of the Act are not limited to those who have cinders in their hair, soot on their faces, or callouses on their hands." Frankfurter, dissenting, chided the majority for ignoring the history of the act and predicted that its interpretation would lead to a "new series of sterile litigation."[48] When the Court session was over Frankfurter slipped Minton a handwritten note, like the many that Minton had received from him during their seven terms on the Court. "That on your last day of announcing opinions I would be dissenting without a scratch of feeling between us, is a good example of the unbroken warm relationship between us. Difference of creed means nothing to harmony of affection."[49]

When the Supreme Court held its last session of the term, Minton had already informed his fellow justices of his intention to retire. Clark wrote to Minton on 3 May, the last day of oral argument for the 1955 term: "I write my regrets that you will not be here next year. During the seven terms we have served together we have never been apart personally and seldom on decision day. I have enjoyed your company immensely and the five years we sat side by side in conference were my best days."[50]

Black, his Senate ally but Court opponent, paid tribute to Minton in the last conference of the term. Black's words touched Minton so deeply that he could respond only in writing. He did so in a moving tribute to Black, which shows that their sharp differences on the Court had not diminished their affection for one another. "The sentiments you expressed concerning me are reciprocated a hundred fold," Minton wrote Black. "I have never ceased in my admiration for you as one of the ablest men of our time—Indeed our history." Minton acknowledged retirement was attractive to contemplate, "but when it comes to the consummation there is much pulling at the heart strings and wonder at what it will be like to leave you cantankerous fellows with whom it has been a priceless privilege to serve."[51]

In order to qualify for a full pension, which would provide him with the handsome sum of $35,000 a year for the rest of his life, Minton had to remain on the Court until October 1956. Rather than spending a quiet summer in New Albany, as they usually did, he and Gertrude sailed to Europe for a six-week tour. Whatever respite the trip offered them from the harshness of politics in Washington, it was quickly dissipated upon their return. While still on board the luxury liner, Minton, the "pathological Democrat" as Frankfurter once called him, answered a reporter's question about the 1956 election. Letting his guard down Minton offered opinions about both Adlai Stevenson and Dwight Eisenhower. "Stevenson," he said, is "a very able man," and added as for Eisenhower, he is "terribly handicapped physically." When Minton was asked whether it was appropriate for a Supreme Court justice to express his partisan bias, he responded: "Hell, I wasn't speaking judicially."[52] A Minton spokesman said later that the justice was not expressing a political preference but was merely commenting on Stevenson's qualifications.

Minton's remarks did not go unnoticed in the press, where most editorial comments criticized him for showing his partisanship. In mock outrage Carl Hatch, who authored the Hatch Act prohibiting federal employees from engaging in partisan activities, wrote to say that he was "chagrined, shocked and horrified to read in the press of the nation" about Minton's comments. "What pernicious, political activity this is. It should have been prohibited by a certain law sponsored by a Senator from New Mexico and valiantly, if not gallantly, opposed by a Senator from Indiana."[53] Minton replied to his good friend that he accepted the judgment of the "world's greatest authority on pernicious political activity," adding, "I do not consider that I have spoken judicially. I had not thought it beyond the right of a justice of this Court to express his choice as between candidates."[54]

Minton's comments about the 1956 presidential campaign were just one indication that he had not fully divorced himself from partisan politics while sitting on the Supreme Court. Although he tried to downplay his partisan image in public, he occasionally failed. During his first term on the Court Minton attended a Jefferson-Jackson Day dinner sponsored by the Democratic party. One of his fellow justices asked him if he thought it was proper for a member of the Court to attend such a political function. In response Minton smiled and said, "What is political about the Democratic Party?"[55]

The most compelling evidence of Minton's inability to extricate himself from the political thicket occurred during his first year on the bench, in the midst of the furor over the *Knauff* decision. James Earl Major, chief judge of the Seventh Circuit, had written to Minton about the urgent need to replace the retiring federal district judge from Indiana, Robert Baltzell, and asked for Minton's intervention with Truman. Minton wrote Truman, who in turn replied that he hoped to "get these things straightened out as they should be." At the bottom of the letter Truman wrote in hand, "Shay: If the President didn't have to make appointments to office he could spend all his time kissing horse's asses to make the government run and he could have a grand time! Maybe?"[56]

The issue of Baltzell's replacement became the source of a dispute within the Indiana Democratic party. The feud that broke out between Minton and Frank McHale, longtime political kingpin, over the appointment really represented a battle for control of the state party by different factions.[57] Minton was criticized in Indiana by those who contended that it was improper for a Supreme Court justice to play a role in the selection of a federal judge. Minton's actions were defended by the *Indianapolis Times,* which noted that he was the member of the Court in charge of the district courts in the Seventh Circuit and that he knew the lawyers of the district better than anyone else in Washington. Besides, the *Times* said, Minton "has no axes of his own to grind."[58]

Following these incidents early in his Court tenure, Minton's political concerns were expressed mainly from the sideline, as he encouraged his friend Truman through the ups and downs of his administration. After the 1952 election, which brought the Republicans to the White House, and up until his public comment about Eisenhower in 1956, Minton's political opinions were expressed exclusively to his friends in private correspondence. Like them, he was moving farther from the seat of power.

On 7 September Minton sent a letter to Eisenhower stating that he planned to retire on 15 October. Speaking with reporters after the announcement of his retirement, Minton explained that his health problems made it difficult for him to perform the exacting work of the Court. It was hard for him to walk more than a block, even using a cane. "My knees buckle and I lose my balance," Minton explained. "It's pretty depressing. This thing keeps pecking away at me. Worst of all, it's gone to my brain. It affects my power to concentrate and think and retain arguments in my mind."[59] Minton, who as a senator had railed against the Court's "Nine Old Men," did not want others telling him it was time to go.

Understandably, Minton regretted having to give up the position he had worked so long and hard to attain, but he thought the decision "was best for me and best for the court. But it is not an easy place to leave. I love it. I hate to go."[60] He especially hated to leave his colleagues on the Court, particularly Douglas, Black, Warren, and Frankfurter. Warren told reporters that Minton's retirement was "a matter of sincere regret to me. The court loses the services of a splendid justice and the members the daily association of a valued friend."[61]

History has not dealt kindly, or fairly, with Minton's role as a Supreme Court justice.[62] Whatever faults Minton had as a justice, and there were important ones, it is hard to justify the conclusion of some Court scholars that he was a failure. Those who participate in surveys that attempt to rank justices qualitatively must make judgments with only a limited knowledge of the opinions written by over a hundred justices and a limited understanding of the judicial philosophy behind those opinions. For lesser-known justices, such as Minton, judgments are based inevitably on thumbnail sketches of lives of the justices, which all too frequently offer only a superficial basis, and sometimes a biased one, for judging the record of any justice. These sketches of Minton invariably mention such opinions as *Rabinowitz, Knauff,* and *Adler,* all of which upheld government power against the claimed right of the individual. Occasionally the sketches note that Minton sided with Truman in the steel seizure case, or that he voted to uphold all-white primaries. To look at the results of only a few decisions and to ignore the reasoning behind them offers a distorted view of Minton's judicial record. Indeed, the scholars who have thoroughly examined Minton's judicial decisions do not consider him a failure.[63]

The coauthor of a study in which Minton received low ratings has acknowledged the shortcomings of judicial ranking surveys. Aside from methodological problems, these rankings are flawed because of the relatively small number of court observers expressing views as well as the academic orientation of the evaluators. Most are law professors who value "brilliance, education and a professional writing style," none of which were Minton's strengths.[64] Furthermore, there is an undeniable liberal bias to these rankings, and Minton's opinions were not consistent with the shift in liberal views about an activist Supreme Court.

The single most distinguishing aspect of Minton's judicial philosophy, and the key to understanding his Supreme Court record, was his fervent belief in judicial restraint. By the time Minton reached the Court in 1949 liberals had lost their enthusiasm for judicial deference to the legislature. Once liberals formed a majority on the Court, and conservatives gained control of Congress, judicial activism became a more appealing philosophy. Minton, however, was never able to forget his anger at the Court's assertiveness during the early years of the New Deal, and as a result he was steadfast in his belief that the Court should defer to the legislative and executive branches of government. He faithfully followed what he thought was the letter or intent of legislation, and he upheld the exercise of administrative discretion as long as there was any statutory language that could be construed as supporting that discretion. Consistent with his philosophy of judicial restraint he interpreted statutes literally, relied on a strict construction of constitutional language, and hewed closely to precedents. In so doing Minton remained more faithful to the New Deal aversion to an interventionist Supreme Court than any of his New Deal colleagues on the Court, save for Vinson and Frankfurter.

Minton once explained to Frankfurter that his approach to law was shaped by William Howard Taft, Minton's law professor at Yale and former president who later became chief justice of the Supreme Court. "He was of the 'bird dog' school," Minton told Frankfurter. "Find what the Court has said—get a 'hog' case—and stick to it. I think my training and practice were too much in that school." The virtue of following precedents, Minton said, was that it created stability, "which was a fetish with Taft."[65] The same could be said of Minton.

A second crucial dimension to Minton's approach to the law was his view about written opinions. In this regard he failed to measure up to what Court scholars hail as an essential component of greatness in a Supreme Court justice. Minton thought that the function of an opinion was to state the conclusion reached by the Court and to explain the rationale behind it. He never thought that he was "writing for the ages" and saw little value in lengthy opinions. He was adamant that opinions should not be used as vehicles to express his personal views. His opinions have been called "reasoned expositions," "technically skillful," "precise," "flat," and "colorless." They have been aptly characterized as being "like Minton himself, direct and utterly pragmatic in style; while they might satisfy the technician, they will not satisfy the theorist who wishes to know the larger social dimensions which a case might embody."[66] Warren's description of Minton's opinions at a memorial tribute following Minton's death would have pleased him: "Totally without guile and with absolute honesty of expression, he wrote for the Court or in dissent so that no one could be misled by what he said."[67]

Minton's conviction that courts should not be making the law, coupled with his pragmatic approach to opinion writing, meant that his opinions often sounded harsh. When he upheld government power to require loyalty oaths for public school teachers, or validated unfair procedures in state trial courts, or sanctioned the expulsion of aliens without a hearing, he was not necessarily saying that these government decisions were wise. He thought that as long as government had the power to do these things, it was not his place to judge the results, as he often said in his opinions. In a eulogy to Minton, Attorney General Nicholas Katzenbach said: "He was at pains to separate predispositions from the decision-making process; indeed on occasion he noted his personal distaste for the actions of parties in whose favor he felt constrained to decide."[68]

Before he left the Court Minton wrote to Frank McHale, his fellow Hoosier and sometime political adversary, his thoughts about his work on the Court. It is as honest a description and explanation of Minton's judicial approach as any he ever offered:

> Since I have been here . . . I have tried to call them as I saw them and in doing so I seem to have earned the designation of a conservative. Maybe I am. I certainly consider a job on this Court to be vastly different than that of a United States Senator. In the Senate you are part of a policy-making organization all the way, and you fight for policy. Here, while there must inevitably be some policy-making in some of the decisions involving the construction of the Constitution, policy-making, in my opinion, should be kept at a very minimum and avoided in all cases not absolutely necessary. Consequently I have upheld Government rather consistently, and have felt bound, in most instances, to follow the law as it had been laid down. At least I have tried to do what I thought was right in each case that came here, as it appeared to me on the record, uninfluenced by all extraneous matters.[69]

Assessed in the long run, Minton's most important legacy to the Court and to the nation was his role in the school desegregation cases and all the other civil rights cases in which he participated. He helped to lay the foundation for ending racial discrimination in the landmark *Brown* decision and in his *Barrows* decision, which undermined the basis for enforcing restrictive covenants in housing. With the exception of the Jaybird case, upholding the all-white primary of a private association, Minton voted with the Court in every case to strike down racial discrimination and segregation. "You can't have two grades of citizenship, first and second class, in a democracy," he once said. "Segregation is incompatible with democracy."[70]

It is ironic that Minton's most important contribution to the Court came when he deserted his philosophy of judicial restraint and joined forces with the Court's activists. If he believed that the Constitution did not permit two classes of citizens based on race, how could it allow two classes of citizens based on other criteria, such as indigence or unorthodox beliefs? His stands on civil liberties can be rationalized against the backdrop of the McCarthy era and fears that Communists were about to topple the government. Minton may or may not have truly believed that subversives might undermine the power of government, but he certainly believed that popularly elected assemblies had the power to protect the government against threats that were perceived as real.

Some of Minton's views about the rights of criminal defendants might be rationalized on the basis of his genuine belief that the law-abiding citizen had a right to be protected from hardened criminals. What is harder to explain, in view of his theory that the Constitution does not allow for two classes of citizenship, was his belief that states may treat indigent defendants differently. To deny a defendant privileges available to someone with more resources creates two classes of citizenship as surely as racial discrimination does. Perhaps Minton thought that people have no choice about the color of their skin, but they do have a choice about becoming a criminal. Although Minton was convinced that the Fourteenth Amendment was intended to remedy inequality between the races, he was not certain that it was intended to eliminate economic disparity among criminal defendants.

Minton's impact on the Court has been dismissed mainly because none of his opinions has withstood the test of time. Rarely, if ever, are they mentioned as precedents. Many of his opinions were eclipsed by rulings of the Warren Court. Even if Minton's lasting contributions to the Court do not stand as large as some, his short-term contributions warrant some consideration. Minton was a hard worker, and despite his poor health he wrote more than his fair share of opinions. During the seven years that Minton was on the Court, each justice wrote an average of fifty-five majority opinions. Minton wrote sixty-four majority opinions.[71] Furthermore, he wrote opinions in every category of the law and wrote all the opinions on tax liens heard during his seven-year tenure.

An equally important contribution to the functioning of the Court was Minton's role of peacemaker. He believed strongly in institutional harmony, as well as stability, and was willing to sacrifice his own personal distinction for the sake of institutional solidarity.[72] He often revised his opinions to accommodate other members of the Court, and on several occasions he suppressed his own written opinion to lessen the perception of court disagreements.[73] Minton was genuinely well liked by all his fellow justices, and he served as an "unobtrusive mediator" between the Frankfurter-Jackson and Douglas-Black factions.[74] Burton, thanking Minton for his contributions to the Court, said, "you have helped the morale of the Court on many occasions both in and out of conference."[75]

Minton did not delude himself about how he would be judged. Talking with reporters on the day that his retirement was announced, he expressed perhaps the most accurate view of his tenure on the Court: "There will be more interest in who will succeed me than in my passing. I'm an echo."[76] He was correct about the interest in his successor. While men such as Attorney General Herbert Brownell, Jr., Secretary of State John Foster Dulles, and Judge Stanley M. Barnes of the Ninth Circuit Court of Appeals were mentioned in the early speculation about a new justice, Eisenhower selected William J. Brennan, Jr., of the New Jersey Supreme Court. Brennan was generally considered to be a liberal judge, especially in cases concerning the rights of criminal defendants. The only vote against his confirmation was cast by Sen. Joseph McCarthy, whom Brennan had publicly attacked.

Brennan's swearing in took place during the same opening day ceremony at which Minton bade farewell to his colleagues. The exchange of Brennan for Minton, coupled with the retirement of Reed later that year, hastened the libertarian, activist trend of the Warren Court.

CHAPTER TEN

Returning to the Hills

After twenty-one years in positions of power and influence in Washington and Chicago, Sherman Minton returned home to New Albany and southern Indiana for good. Physically, the retiring Supreme Court justice bore but a shadowy resemblance to the tall, athletically trim, dark-haired, and handsome warrior who had marched off to the nation's capital in 1935 to fight the good fight for the common people. A heart attack and an enfeebling anemic condition had sapped his quick step and robust stature. Much about Minton, however, was unaltered. Time and disease could not erode the qualities within. The features that endeared him to so many—his kindness, compassion, wisdom, and humor—remained. So did his humility. Exalted status in the legislative, executive, and judicial branches of national government notwithstanding, Minton never acquired an inflated sense of himself.

Fittingly then, his departure from the Court and Washington was all but unheralded. Seventeen law clerks who served Minton on the Court of Appeals and the Supreme Court arranged a surprise party at the Mayflower Hotel in his honor and presented him with a gold watch. His last day on the Court, 15 October 1956, however, passed without ceremony. Minton took his usual place at the far right end of the bench and sat just long enough to hear the day's orders handed down and to witness the swearing in of attorneys as members of the Supreme Court bar. Fifteen minutes after the Court had convened Minton turned to Justice Harold H. Burton, who sat beside him, shook his hand, and left the bench.

Writing to Justice Felix Frankfurter in the summer of 1956 about his decision to retire, Minton said that from a distance retirement seemed attractive, "but when it comes to the hour to go it is not so easy." Minton said he would stay on were it not "for my feeling of inadequacy and decrepitude and the embarrassment which comes from this deferential treatment accorded my 'senility.'" The time had come, Minton concluded, for him to "be going home to Indiana and its hills and people I love, not 'to sit down by the silent sea and wait for the muffled oar,' but to enjoy my remaining days doing as I damned please."[1]

During his first years of retirement Minton and his wife Gertrude did just that. Once ensconced in their roomy Tudor-style brick home in the exclusive Silver Hills section of New Albany, the Mintons had some time to relax. Minton filled his days with catching up on his reading, which included Churchill's history of World War II, Truman's memoirs, and other historical and biographical works, answering a steady stream of letters, giving interviews to reporters from local newspapers, and visiting his old lawyer friends at the county courthouse. He had offers to address various civic groups, but declined such requests on the advice of his doctors, who felt public speaking might take too much effort. "Besides," Minton explained, "I've mellowed quite a bit since I've been on the court."[2]

The leisurely settling in period lasted until the end of fall, and then the Mintons embarked on an ambitious traveling schedule over the next three years. Much of the time they were visiting their three children, grandchildren, and Minton's brothers, Herb and Roscoe, in Texas. They were always eager to get back to the Washington area to visit their daughter Mary Anne and her husband, John Callanan, and their children, and then to swing south to see their son, John, who was teaching art at Clemson University in South Carolina. The Mintons went east for official and social reasons as well. He filled in for a few weeks as a judge on the United States Court of Claims, and they attended such events as an Army-Navy football game in Philadelphia as guests of Chief Justice Earl Warren and at Warren's dinner for the president.

The Mintons also took two trips to Europe during this period and in early 1959 went on an around-the-world odyssey, taken mainly to see their son Sherman, his wife, and their three daughters who were in Karachi, Pakistan. Doctor Minton, a microbiologist on the faculty of the Indiana University School of Medicine, was teaching overseas as part of a university exchange program. After reaching Karachi by way of Paris, Rome, Athens, Istanbul, and Cairo, the Mintons stayed two weeks and then steamed off to Hong Kong, stopping briefly in Bombay, Colombo, Sri Lanka, and Singapore. The voyage from Hong Kong to San Francisco had stopovers in Kobe and Yokohama, Japan. Writing about the journey to Justice William O. Douglas, Minton said it was "pleasurable all the way except crossing the Pacific by ship. Rough and cold all the way. We never saw the sun from Feb. 24th to March 18th." He added, "I think I can understand your great interest in these far away places and its people. The lives the people live seem incredible to us and the people are so desperately in need of understanding and help."[3]

Shortly after returning to the States the Mintons were off again to Washington for the birth of their daughter's fifth child—a girl to join her four boys. The pace and breadth of Minton's journeys drew admiration from his friend and former colleague on the Seventh Circuit Court of Appeals, Earl Major. He praised Minton for his courage to do such gallivanting with his physical problems, adding, "You . . . must have a terrific desire to travel."[4]

MARY ANNE CALLANAN COLLECTION

Sherman Minton at the dedication of the new law school building at Indiana University in the fall of 1956. At left is Herman B Wells, president of IU, and third from the left is Chief Justice Earl Warren. Also pictured are John Hastings, president of the IU Board of Trustees, and Leon H. Wallace, dean of the law school.

Minton's itinerary also consisted of frequent trips to the campus of his alma mater, Indiana University in Bloomington. He was appointed a professorial lecturer of the law school, a nonpaying position, and from time to time he conducted seminars with law students. He attended commencement, some home football games, and the dedication of the new law school building.[5] Minton also went to Hanover College near Madison to speak with students and presided at the University of Notre Dame's moot court in South Bend.

His in-state traveling included trips to Indianapolis—once, appropriately, for a testimonial at a Jefferson-Jackson Day dinner, and again, remarkably, to be honored by Indi-

MARY ANNE CALLANAN COLLECTION

Sherman Minton (center) with New Albany mayor C. Pralle Erni (left) and Indiana state senator Clifford H. Maschmeyer of Jeffersonville in 1962 after a bridge between New Albany and Louisville was named in honor of Minton.

ana's Republican governor, George N. Craig. Craig, using moneys from his contingency fund, had a bronze bust of Minton cast and placed in the rotunda of the statehouse. During the dedication ceremony Craig led the tributes paid to Minton, saying, "Indiana has never produced a son greater than we honor here today. His contribution to progress of the nation and to the advancement of the dignity of mankind will long be a factor in our life." Minton responded with typical modesty and humor: "Ladies and gentlemen, I'm no great man. You know I'm no great man . . . but this was an awfully nice thing for you to do." Expressing his fondness for Governor Craig, Minton said, "Why, I would do anything for him but vote for him."[6]

Other honors accorded Minton required that he travel only a short distance. In December 1956 the nearby University of Louisville, as part of its ceremonies to recognize the centennial of the birth of Louisville native Justice Louis Brandeis, awarded Minton an honorary doctor of laws degree. Dr. Philip Davidson, university president, in presenting the award called Minton "a man of good will who has abiding faith in the common man and unlimited confidence in democratic government. You have carried on the principles voiced by the man whose centennial we are celebrating today."[7]

The most enduring tribute to Minton, and the one that has made his name a household word to motorists for decades, came in 1962 when a double-deck bridge over the Ohio River between New Albany and Louisville was named in his honor. Shortly after the $14.8 million Interstate 64 span was dedicated in late 1961, New Albany mayor C. Pralle Erni, a longtime Minton friend and manager of his first run for political office in 1920, suggested to Indiana governor Matthew E. Welsh that the structure be named for Minton. Welsh got the consent of Gov. Bert T. Combs of the state of Kentucky, which assisted in building the bridge, and the Legislative Advisory Commission of Indiana gave its approval in a resolution. State senator Clifford H. Maschmeyer, of Jeffersonville, who introduced the resolution, noted that often such recognition is granted after the recipient has died, but, he said, "a more fitting policy would be, 'Let us honor the honored while they are able to appreciate the honor.'"[8] Minton certainly did. He was surprised by it and, he said, "I'm very gratified." The distinctive "tied arch" bridge itself won a top award from the American Institute of Steel Construction as the most beautiful long-span bridge opened in the country in 1961.

Minton also stayed busy in retirement by corresponding with his friends, including Truman, his former colleagues on the Court, mainly Douglas, Frankfurter,

Black, and Warren, and a former law clerk, Harry Wallace, a Milwaukee attorney who wrote a biography of Minton and law journal articles on Minton's Supreme Court years. Minton reveled in speculating about elections, discussing world and national developments, keeping up with court cases, and assessing the strengths and weaknesses of baseball teams, particularly his favorite New York Yankees.

The Minton-Truman exchanges were dominated by the subject of presidential politics: assessments of how the incumbent, either Dwight D. Eisenhower or John F. Kennedy, was handling the major domestic and international issues of the day; speculation about likely presidential candidates and comments on their campaigns; and remembrances about Truman's White House years. Not surprisingly, the two old Democratic warhorses were scathing in their observations about Eisenhower and generally complimentary about Kennedy's performance, although neither man had had much enthusiasm for his nomination in 1960.

Minton believed that Eisenhower was incompetent and incapable of leading the country, but his popularity shielded him from criticism by the Democrats and the press. Minton came under fire shortly before retiring from the Court when he publicly suggested that Eisenhower might not be physically able to complete a second term. Writing to Truman on the adverse reaction he received, Minton complained: "It seems to be profane for anyone to even suggest that Ike isn't God. I am afraid I must be a pretty profane man because I haven't the least bit of a deity complex pertaining to that fellow. If he is the great man of integrity that he is supposed to be his record belies it, and some of that record is known to you personally and will never be known to the public."[9]

"I am," Minton later wrote, "sometimes ashamed of myself for my low opinion of the President. Not since Buchanan has there been such a woeful lack of leadership in the White House." But, he said, "His lack of fitness & ability were kept covered up by the press that made him into a mythical God." He also criticized Senate Majority Leader Lyndon B. Johnson for not taking the gloves off. "I said to Johnson six months after Ike took over that the Democrats should end the honeymoon & take after him. Lyndon replied, 'Oh, it's too early.' Far as I can see it is still too early for him." However, Minton thought that Eisenhower "knocked his halo off" in the Sherman Adams affair. Adams, the president's chief of staff, resigned after his dealings with New England industrialist Bernard Goldfine were called into question. Minton said the matter "would not have been so bad if those pious bastards hadn't campaigned so righteously against lesser offenses of the Democrats."[10]

Truman did not need any priming from Minton to launch into his own tirades against his successor. "I can't help but explode once in a while on what has happened," he wrote Minton, citing what he considered failures of the Eisenhower administration and successes of his own. "The people around the halls of the Great White Jail have succeeded in making Gen. Grant and Warren Harding great Presidents! The Dirksen-Yates give away, the atomic power debauchery, and the give away of our forest reserves for fake mining claims rank almost with offshore oil in the use of public assets for payment of political debts to the special Republican interests." Continuing, he noted, "I reduced the national debt by 27 billion dollars, balanced the budget for six of my eight years, met Tito, Stalin et al in Yugoslavia, Persia and the near east, kept Stalin out of Greece and Turkey and Berlin and put the United Nations into Korea and saved that Republic. Also kept crooked old Chiang Kai-shek from being mopped up by placing the 7th fleet between him and danger." "Well to hell with it," Truman concluded. "I'm going to paste them hip and thigh in this '58 go around and then try to smash them in 1960—if we can find a candidate to do it with."[11]

The two men were ecstatic over the pounding Republicans suffered in the off-year election of 1958. Democrats, in handing the GOP its worst defeat since the 1930s, would outnumber Republicans by nearly two to one in both houses of the new Congress. Minton told Truman that he deserved "a lot of credit for that victory a week ago. You have been working & speaking among the Democrats for months & you helped to keep them up." Minton saw the results as a repudiation of Eisenhower: "The people are just beginning to learn that this man on the pedestal, so carefully screened & built up by the kept press, has feet of clay. They are beginning to find out that he is incompetent, inept

MARY ANNE CALLANAN COLLECTION

Sherman Minton and Harry Truman at a Democratic party function in Fort Wayne, Indiana, September 1958.

and what is worse, indifferent to his responsibilities. He has no conception of the presidency in our scheme of government. How could he raised in the caste of the Army & reading only Westerns?"[12]

In his response Truman said he "never attacked the halo wearer publicly because I have too much respect for the greatest office in the history of the world. But as Wayne Morse said on 'Meet the Press' when asked what the most important thing the present occupant of the White House had done, 'He has made a statesman out of General Grant!'" Assessing the party's prospects in 1960 Truman recalled the divisive 1924 Democratic convention where delegates "voted 104 times, I think, and then nominated a stripped pants New Yorker by the name of John W. Davis. Cal went in without a move on his part. Now if the Damned Democrats do that [in 1960] the same thing will happen and Tricky Dickie will take us to hell sure enough. We can't let it happen."[13]

While the two men were optimistic of the party's chances of retaking the White House in 1960, their feelings were tempered by what they considered a weak field of contenders for the Democratic presidential nomination. John Kennedy's showing in the primaries impressed Minton, but he worried about the anti-Catholic vote. Truman said of him: "I like the boy, but he's still a boy."[14] Neither man, however, had much use for Kennedy's father. Truman, who was especially bitter toward Joseph Kennedy, told Minton about a confrontation he had with Kennedy during the 1944 election. After completing an exhausting cross-country campaign trip, Truman checked into the Ritz-Carlton in Boston where he found Kennedy in his suite. According to Truman, "He began cussing Roosevelt and called him a murderer because *his* boy was killed in Germany. I stood up and told him if he would repeat that statement I'd throw him out the window. Bob Hannegan [party chairman] came in then and kept me from doing it. I haven't seen the old bastard since."[15]

Minton, likewise, had a horror story about Joe Kennedy. It occurred in December 1939 when he and Lewis B. Schwellenbach were having lunch with Kennedy, then ambassador to Great Britain. Minton told Truman that Kennedy "scared the hell out of me" when he said that "England was through. Hitler would win & we could do business with Hitler. How wrong can a man get?"[16]

Despite their misgivings about the party's national ticket in 1960, Minton and Truman, as uncompromising Democrats, naturally supported Kennedy and Johnson. "I of course accept the ticket," Minton said, adding he was encouraged by the way Kennedy had organized and campaigned in the primaries. "If he can organize for the election as well he should overcome the handicap of his religion," Minton believed. Still, he worried how many of the Humphrey votes in the West Virginia and Wisconsin primaries were anti-Catholic votes that would switch to Nixon. "On the other hand," he wrote, "my barber says don't worry—the people are tired of this administration & want a change!!"[17]

Truman, not so hopeful, replied bluntly, "We are in a hell of a fix." He was worried that Kennedy, only forty-three years old, lacked the maturity and experience for the office, and he felt that Kennedy's meteoric rise was due more to his father's millions than the candidate's ability. "What can we do? You and I will have to support the lesser of the two evils. Nixon is outside the pale. Well we'll support the Democrats as we have always done. I'm not so sure it won't be in vain. And then where do we go—God only knows." In spite of his age, seventy-six, and his feelings, Truman campaigned aggressively in nine states during the fall.[18]

After the election Minton and Truman predictably turned their attention to assessing how the new president was handling the series of crises that confronted him at home and abroad: civil rights, the economy, price increases by Big Steel, Cuba, and Berlin. Minton applauded Kennedy's actions against segregation. "He is dead right on the Negro question. It is time someone had a show down with the South."[19] Of the president's proposed tax cut in 1963 Minton opined, "I don't think he will get a satisfactory tax bill. He knocked hell out of Congress when he threw that big deficit at them and then said now we will make it up with a nice big tax cut! Is that possible?"[20] Kennedy's own fight with big steel companies, in which he forced them to rescind announced price increases, naturally evoked memories of an earlier crisis in the steel industry when Truman seized the mills and Minton, voting in the minority on the Court, supported the action. "I think of those battles you had with them [steel companies] one of which you lost in our Court. I still think Vinson's dissent in which Reed & I concurred stated the law correctly."[21]

Berlin was another common conundrum that confronted the two presidents. In 1948 Truman used the Berlin airlift to thwart the Soviet blockade of the city, and thirteen years later the Soviet Union again precipitated an international crisis by constructing a wall to halt the flow of refugees from the East to the West. "The damned commies haven't changed one bit," Truman wrote. "Berlin is as it was when the airlift made them back up." The Soviets only understand military superiority, he said, using his meeting at Potsdam with Churchill and Stalin on the status of Poland to illustrate the point: "Old Stalin had agreed with me that they should have free elections and so had the British Prime Minister. Churchill then made a remark that the Pope would not be pleased if Poland happened to be mistreated. Stalin put his elbow on the table, pulled his big mustache and said, 'Mr. Prime Minister, how many divisions has the Pope?'"[22]

As befitting their long-standing friendship, Minton and Truman also sprinkled their letters with nostalgia for their Senate days, concern about each other's well-being, and unabashed admiration for the other. "I just had to write and tell you what a wonderful appearance you made with Ed Murrow," begins a Minton letter in early 1958. "Your grasp of the present situation and your excursion in the history recent & ancient was marvelous."[23] Responding, Truman noted that he had received between fifteen hundred and two thousand letters about the Murrow show, all but four of them favorable. He noted, "That four turned out to be Baptist and Methodist preachers who didn't like damn and hell. That's what they scare their members with when they are trying to increase their paying customers. But no farm boy should use those Biblical terms for educational purposes."[24]

Truman's respect for Minton is spelled out in a statement, written in the third person, he composed for Gordon R. Owen, a Purdue University graduate student who was writing his dissertation on Minton. Truman sent Minton a copy of the statement, which read in part: "Sherman Minton is among the greatest men Truman has been associated with in his forty years in public life. Senator Minton has a keen mind—one of the keenest—he has a true sense of honor and he acts on that basis, both publicly and privately. When Truman became the President of the United States, he appointed Sherman Minton to the Supreme Court, his top notch appointment after the Chief Justice."[25]

Minton's correspondence with Justices Douglas, Frankfurter, and Black, in particular, had much the same flavor as Truman's in that the exchanges were congenial, candid, and solicitous. Many of the Minton-Douglas letters contain the added feature of ribaldry. Minton picked up many of his so-called stories on his trips to the county courthouse and delighted in passing them on in all their spicy detail to Douglas. One of his tamer stories concerned "one old nestor" who wanted to be a delegate to a convention, but was urged to go as an alternate by the county chairman, who claimed alternates were just as important as delegates: "But the old nestor insisted he knew what an alternate was and he knew the difference. Finally the chairman said, 'What is the difference?' The old boy said, 'Did you ever see a couple of dogs fastened?' 'Yes,' said the chairman. 'Do you remember that bunch of little dogs circling around the stuck dogs?' 'Yes,' said the chairman. 'Well, them was alternates.'"[26]

In one letter Minton, complimenting Douglas on a television appearance, wrote, "You were great. A time or two you had that twinkle in your eye like you would like to tell them a couple of good stories." Minton had none of his own to offer this time, noting, "I never hear anymore because I don't get down town. You know Gertrude doesn't know many stories!!!"[27]

Besides stories, Minton and Douglas swapped tales about travel, politics, football, and the brethren. When Burton retired Douglas wrote: "We all hated to see Harold Burton leave. He is, as you said, a warm and loveable person—probably the best true Christian who sat on this Court for a long, long time."[28]

Douglas's remarks about Chief Justice Warren were in stark contrast. He wrote Minton after Warren lashed out at Frankfurter in open court for giving an extemporaneous summary of his dissent, accusing him of degrading the Court with his "lecture." Douglas said, "I've never been a Felix fan, as you know," but Douglas thought it was Warren not Frankfurter who had degraded the Court. "It's a nasty spectacle. Perhaps the old boy is off his rocker."[29] Responding, Minton wrote, "I was sad after reading your letter and to learn that all is not too well with the finest group of men I ever worked with." He added that he was against handing down opinions orally from the bench. "We are just talking to ourselves. I must say Felix is not the only lecturer. Do you suppose the Chief's not only edgy about Felix but is under too much strain?"[30] A few days later Douglas reported on another Warren transgression: "The CJ fired that good colored barber we had because someone said the police had picked him up drunk on weekends. He never drank around here. I never thought it was my business what an employee did on weekends. The CJ thinks the Court is a Bureau in Sacramento, and that he runs it. He's headed for tragedy. We all got here on our own. I don't know of a soul who respects him any more. I have defended him in public and in private. But no more. The Washington press is, I think, now laying in wait for the old boy to pop off once more. The truth is, I think, that Earl Warren is a cheap politico with a Christer complex. It's sad, but true."[31]

Frankfurter also complained to Minton about Warren. He wrote, "John Harlan is no doubt right in finding the C.J. a 'martinet' but it's too late in the day for me to knuckle under where my deep convictions are involved."[32] Minton had asked whether Warren had prevailed upon Frankfurter "to give up your method of 'dismissing as improvidently granted,'" a reference to Frankfurter's practice of refusing to vote on cases that he felt the Court should not have accepted for review.[33] Frankfurter said he would never cease to "dismiss as improvidently granted," and added: "Indeed the more the Chief forgets, as he increasingly does, that he is not Governor of California but only *primus inter pares,* the more important do I deem it to emphasize the *pares*."[34]

Minton's correspondence with Frankfurter, in particular, made him feel close to the fraternity because Frankfurter almost always touched on some Court-related subject in his letters. The exchanges were therapeutic for Minton, who had lamented to Frankfurter on the first anniversary of his retirement: "When that first Monday in Oct. rolls around I miss joining the Court. I feel sorta left out." After a trip to Washington Minton wrote that he was sorry the two of them were unable to spend more time together, because "I needed a little visit with you to make me feel that I still belonged."[35]

Retirement did not mellow Minton's fervent belief in judicial restraint, and he was clearly bothered by a number of decisions from the increasingly activist Warren Court. In Frankfurter, who generally adhered to a passive role, Minton found a sympathetic ear to his protestations that the high court was getting into areas beyond its jurisdiction. "Some time when you have the leisure tell me what the Federal question is in Schware v. New Mexico & Konigsberg v. Calif.?" Minton asked.[36] In these two cases a divided Court placed constitutional limitations on the almost absolute power organized bar associations had to regulate admissions to their ranks. "As to *Konigsberg*, that 'made me puke' (I'm quoting Holmes) and you read my *narrow* ground in *Schware*," Frankfurter responded.[37]

Minton also wrote that there "seems to be no end to the FELA [Federal Employers' Liability Act] cases." He added: "You all seem to have reached the position in the law of negligence where a railroad employee has the urgent call of nature the railroad company is negligent if it does not furnish him a safe good car to crap in—To your credit you are still dissenting to this kind of law."[38]

The Court's decision to overturn a ban on the film *Lady Chatterly's Lover* by the regents of the University of the State of New York would not have been unanimous had Minton still been a justice. Writing to Frankfurter he said, "As you might have guessed I would have been against the Court in Lady Chatterly's Lover." Minton supported the state court, which banned the movie's showing because it portrayed adultery as proper conduct for individuals under certain conditions. That made sense to Minton: "Adultery has been outlawed since Moses brought the tablets down from the mountain. N.Y. public policy is against it. Adultery is an absolute ground for divorce, it is also a crime. To say that this policy couldn't be carried out by N.Y. preventing the teaching of adultery as a way of life because the Constitution makes teaching adultery something protected by it, seems ridiculous to me. I suppose a gangster school set up to teach crime would be protected!"[39]

Minton and Frankfurter also kept each other informed about the books they were reading, which were mainly histories and biographies. Minton, upon reading Alpheus T. Mason's biography of Chief Justice Harlan F. Stone, told Frankfurter he was concerned about the author's access to "raw material. Lots goes on off the bench that should be as secret as the secret relations between man & wife."[40]

Exchanges between the two men contained occasional levity. They enjoyed kidding each other about Indiana senator William Jenner, a Joseph McCarthy ally. As head of the Senate's Internal Security Committee, Jenner had reacted vindictively to a series of high court decisions that favored the individual over the security powers of government officials by proposing a bill to limit the Court's appellate jurisdiction in the internal security area. At the time Jenner was blustering with his legislation, which was never enacted, Minton noted in a letter to Frankfurter that he was going to a party for a lawyer in Bedford, Indiana, "the home town of your friend Senator Jenner." He said he was sorry to admit it, "but Jenner correctly reflects the political thinking of Indiana. It is now the most reactionary, isolationist state in the union."[41] In another letter Minton, responding in kind to a Frankfurter prank, threatened to sue him for libel for scribbling Minton's name on a list of people attending a dinner for Jenner. "You know I would be as apt to attend that affair as you & Dean Acheson would a clam bake for John Foster Dulles."[42]

Although their philosophies on the Court hardly indicated affinity, Minton and Black never let judicial differences weaken the strong personal bond they had formed as firebrand New Deal senators. Minton, congratulating Black on his twenty-five years as a justice, wrote, "One of my cherished memories is having served with you briefly in the Senate & the Court." He added: "What a joy it was to your friends to vote for your confirmation and to see you go on after that dastardly attack on you to become one of the greatest of justices & put to shame the lousy bastards that attacked you."[43]

Responding, Black said, "It was quite a boost to get your letter about my twenty-fifth anniversary on the Court. It brought back cherished memories of our long years of unbroken friendship and affection." Looking out the door of his study, Black said, he could see two pictures of Minton, Schwellenbach, and himself taken at a hearing of the lobby committee. He wrote: "Those were interesting days and I doubt if any three men in public life ever worked any better together than we did. It has always been a regret to me that we could not have been together again on the Court. And of course I have regretted that ill health made your stay on the Court so short."[44]

Because of their long involvement in politics, though, the two men well understood that things do not always turn out as they should. In reporting to Black on how Hoosier Democrats fared in 1958 Minton noted the capricious nature of elections in the rock-ribbed Republican state. Although the party's candidate for United States senator, Vance Hartke, was not especially strong, he "got a 242,000 majority—the largest ever given a candidate statewide in Indiana." Minton added, "It pays to be at the right place at the right time in politics as I once discovered."[45] Black felt the same was true of Kennedy in 1960, whose good fortune, in part, was due to his opponent. Writing to Minton, Black said: "My own belief is that if Kennedy wins, as he well may, it will be largely due to rather widespread dislike or distrust of Nixon, and to the fact that Kennedy has made a better impression on the public in his campaign."[46]

Minton, never in the Black camp on the Court, nonetheless told his friend that he would have joined him in *Engel v. Vitale,* which found state-composed prayers in the public schools unconstitutional. Black, replying that he had no doubt about Minton's support, said the press and some politicians confused the issue for many. Black's opinion did not contain "one word that could justify a statement that we were trying to outlaw prayer," he wrote. "We said and meant that prayer is too holy, too personal to be dependent to any extent at all on election numbers."[47]

Although Minton was not close to Warren ideologically on the Court, the two were drawn together by their backgrounds in politics and especially by their love of football and baseball. Invariably their correspondence included comments about whatever sport happened to be in season. When Minton accepted the brief court of claims assignment, Warren wrote him, "It will be good to have you back in Washington for a while, and I am looking forward to seeing some football games with you."[48]

Baseball was a major topic of discussion in the letters between Minton and Harry Wallace. Minton demonstrated his prognosticating prowess in the spring of 1957 when he called Wallace's home team the best in baseball and "you could be going all the way."[49] The Braves were indeed the game's best in 1957, winning not only the National League pennant, but also beating Minton's team, New York, in the World Series. "While I am always a Yankee rooter I did not feel bad about the Braves winning," Minton wrote to Wallace. "In fact I found myself rooting for them that last game."[50]

In late 1957 Wallace undertook the task of writing about Minton's seven years on the Supreme Court. His thorough examination of Minton's work on the Court was published in 1959 in the *Indiana Law Journal*. Minton had told Wallace he was delighted "you care to write about what is to be written about me. Too bad for you there isn't more to write about. All we dealt with were Communists, Negroes & Jehovah's Witnesses. We seem to have gotten in trouble with each of them."[51] Wallace expanded his work on Minton into a full-blown biography, although it was never published. Commenting on the manuscript after its completion, Minton said he liked it and complimented Wallace for "a whale of a job. If it doesn't sell it will be the fault of the subject."[52]

On 30 September 1959 Minton wrote Wallace about his appraisal of the World Series that was to start the next day. "I see the Sox are favored to win the Series. Why I don't know. They do have some good pitching & a strong defense. Have the Sox the power to make some runs? I will be pulling for Nellie Fox, Aparicio, Lollar, Smith, Kluszewski et al & I hope they can produce some runs."[53]

Later that afternoon in his home the sixty-eight-year-old Minton suffered his second heart attack. This seizure, the result of a blood clot near the heart, exacerbated his already poor condition and permanently altered how he lived his remaining years.

After spending several weeks in a New Albany hospital he returned home, but it was clear that his retirement activities, traveling in particular, would be sharply curtailed. Plans that he and Gertrude had for traveling to Mexico and going around the world again now were out of the question. Within three months Minton reported to friends that he could sit up most of the time, and Gertrude was taking him for short rides, weather permitting. He resumed reading, watching television, and entertaining his grandchildren, whom he called "the joy of my life." In spite of such progress, he had great difficulty walking and had trouble going to sleep. "I get around so badly," he wrote to Truman. "Since I was sick I have lost a great deal of the use of my legs. And I have my sleeping all turned around."[54]

Minton was well enough by the fall of 1960, a year after the attack, to toddle up to Bloomington, as he put it, for a couple of football games and attend a party at the New Albany Country Club in honor of his seventieth birthday. More than a hundred people attended the celebration, including federal judges F. Ryan Duffy, Earl Major, and John Hastings, and Minton's brother Roscoe, a Fort Worth, Texas, county commissioner. The centerpiece at the party was a huge cake in the shape of the Supreme Court building. Truman, unable to attend because of prior commitments, sent a telegram of congratulations. He called Minton "a great senator, a great judge and a great justice."[55] "Thanks for your birthday telegram but most of all for your friendship over the years," Minton wrote him in reply. "The older I get the more appreciative I am of it."[56] Throughout 1960 Minton expressed the hope of traveling to Independence to see Truman, but he never made it. Less than a year after the birthday party Minton was dealt yet another serious blow to his health that ended forever the possibility of such a trip.

In the summer of 1961 Minton, already in the hospital recovering from an ankle fracture, was stricken by a cerebral hemorrhage while sitting on the hospital porch. For several days his condition was listed as "very grave," and he was confined to an oxygen tent. He survived this threat, but it left him a semi-invalid. In a letter to Truman he said, "I am now confined to my house almost entirely. I am unable to sleep. I am up all night and try to sleep in the day time. I am writing this at 2:30 a.m."[57] Although the handwriting was shaky, his words showed him to be an interested and knowledgeable observer of current events.

Writing to Truman in the spring of 1963 Minton worried about the slide in Kennedy's popularity, noting that "the Gallup Poll shows a loss of 10% since January." Minton thought the Republicans, with the aid of the press, had "driven Kennedy from the heights of success in Oct. in Cuba to the depths to where Cuba is now referred to as a mess." He added, "I think I approve of his policy toward Cuba since the Bay of Pigs which was the root of all our trouble."[58] In another letter he urged Truman to "give the test ban treaty your hearty endorsement. The argument that no good can come out of the Russians isn't quite true. I can't see where the treaty will do much but it is a step away from war as the President says."[59] Commenting on the 1964 presidential race in a letter to Black, Minton said he expected Goldwater would win Indiana, but felt neither party's campaign had gotten off the ground. "I am prejudiced against [William] Miller & I think he is a phony," Minton said. "Goldwater is always having to explain what he means but does his explanations go down?"[60] Black, in his response, said he was reluctant to make a prediction, but it "does look to me as if the South is likely to go Republican."[61]

During the fall of 1964 Minton was back in the hospital after suffering yet another heart attack. Despite the latest setback he persisted in keeping up with two of his great loves—politics and baseball. Cong. Winfield K. Denton of Indiana recalled visiting Minton in the hospital: "Although he was in an oxygen tent I found him listening to a ballgame and when I entered his room he immediately roused to discuss politics and the campaign. Such an indomitable spirit is not often found."[62]

After being released from the hospital shortly before the election, Minton wrote to Frankfurter that he still believed Lyndon B. Johnson could not carry Indiana "or any other state if he has any more Jenkins cases," a reference to the scandal over the arrest of Walter Jenkins, a senior aide to Johnson, for "indecent gestures" in a Washington YMCA washroom. The letter also included Minton's assessment of Arthur Goldberg, who succeeded Frankfurter in 1962: "Mr. J. Goldberg is a walking Constitutional Convention! Wow what an activist he is!" Reporting on his health to Frankfurter, whose own condition was fragile, Minton said he was able to get around in the house with a walker and "with the aid of our yard man to walk on crutches each day about three or four blocks."[63]

The two New Dealers, however, did live long enough to witness the dawning of Johnson's Great Society, but the end came to both in early 1965. Frankfurter, eighty-two, died of a heart attack on 22 February. In the early morning hours of 9 April, Sherman "Shay" Minton, seventy-four, died in his sleep at a New Albany hospital, where he had been admitted a week earlier suffering from intestinal bleeding. His wife Gertrude was with him when he died. A funeral Mass at Holy Trinity Catholic Church in New Albany for Minton, who had converted to Catholicism a few years before his death, was attended by hundreds of friends and associates, including Chief Justice Warren, Justices Black and Clark, retired Justice Reed, and Indiana governor Roger Branigin. Following burial, New Albany attorney

MARY ANNE CALLANAN COLLECTION

Sherman Minton in 1964 outside his birthplace in Georgetown, Indiana.

John A. Cody, Jr., who had practiced law with Minton and was one of his closest friends, hosted these dignitaries and others at his house for lunch. He inquired about their beverage preference, offering ice tea, soft drinks, or something stronger. Warren replied for the group that "Shay" would have wanted them to have the hard stuff, and so they did in a farewell toast to their friend.

Many salutes and gestures were offered in Minton's memory; the flag on the state capitol was lowered to half-staff; numerous bar associations and courts adopted memorial resolutions; and members of Congress, including Republicans, eulogized him on the floor of the House and Senate. A year after his death, as is traditional, a memorial service was held at the Supreme Court.

Solicitor General Thurgood Marshall, who as counsel for the National Association for the Advancement of Colored People won a unanimous decision from the Court in the historic school desegregation cases, presided over the occasion. He read a tribute prepared by Leon Wallace, dean of the Indiana University Law School and father of Harry Wallace, Minton's biographer. Wallace's tribute described Minton as a man of ambition, sensitivity, and conviction who had an "abiding faith in the people and a belief that the government is 'we the people.'" In his remarks Chief Justice Warren, noting Minton's own impoverished beginnings, said, "To his dying day, he believed that government is designed to relieve such undeserved distress as far as possible."[64]

Two Indiana attorneys, Alan T. Nolan of Indianapolis and Marshall E. Hanley of Muncie, drawing upon their intimate relationships with Minton, delivered stirring remembrances. Nolan and Hanley had been Minton law clerks on the Seventh Circuit, but both were close to him long before serving him in a professional capacity. Nolan's bond developed from the close friendship his parents, Val and Jeannette, had with Minton. Hanley was captivated by Minton, when, at the age of fourteen, he heard Minton speak at a rally during the 1934 senatorial campaign. He recalled that event in his eulogy: "He is a big and powerful man; his words thunder across the crowd. That night I find a hero." As his law clerk, Hanley continued, "He shares with me his experiences in government and scholarship in the law. He counsels me on all matters. He does not hesitate to point out my many mistakes, but he never fails to say a kind word on even the smallest task he thinks well done." Of his last visit with Minton at his home in New Albany, Hanley said: "Thirty years now have passed, and my feeling of youthful hero-worship has nurtured to respect, later to admiration, and now is one of deepest affection. His legs no longer carry him among the lovely trees of his yard high above the Ohio River where we have strolled and talked so often for so many years past. He now must sit in his library. But his mind is alert and his concern for his fellow man is the subject of his conversation. He talks of our profession in a troubled world, of the work of this Court and of its members whom he loves, of civil rights, of religious freedom, of old friends and of young grandchildren."[65]

Nolan said the memorial was the fitting and proper thing to do, but "Sherman Minton would not have approved of these proceedings today. In spite of a lifetime of high distinction, he was an unpretentious man. He was a man without a sense of his own importance and was utterly unable to take himself too seriously." Minton was serious about politics and public life. According to Nolan, "He considered politics as the means by which the people go about the business of attempting to perfect themselves. He thought of public office as the agency of the community for carrying out this attempt at perfection." He added that while Minton was a partisan and had an advocate's instinct toward life, "his partisanship and advocacy were always accompanied by high good humor, and they were never mean or harsh or personal." Because Minton was well motivated, principled, and an exceptionally able man,

Nolan said, "He put into life, and into our lives, vastly more than he took out."[66]

Nolan's statement as well as any captured the essence of Sherman Minton. The record is replete with evidence of how he enriched the lives of others through selfless acts of kindness, compassion, and thoughtfulness. These he bestowed irrespective of a person's politics, status, or race. Minton was especially attentive to those in the political arena, even after his days in active politics had long ended.

Replying to Minton's warm letter about White's retirement from the Senate in 1948, Wallace H. White, Jr., a Maine Republican, said, "I can not begin to tell you how deeply I appreciate the kindly things you have said." He added that "those on your side of the aisle . . . have shown me a kindness that I did not have any right to expect and for which I shall always be deeply grateful. You always treated me with marked consideration and I shall think of you always with pleasure and gratitude for our acquaintance."[67]

When Democratic senator Tom Connally of Texas decided not to enter the primary for renomination, Minton wrote to express his regret at the decision, adding, "I have no doubt but what you could have won, but the sacrifice should not have been asked—you should have been returned without opposition. Since the vagaries of politics decreed otherwise, Texas and the Nation lose by your departure."[68] Connally, in thanking Minton for his generous comments, said he believed he could have been reelected, but mounting an "arduous campaign . . . to combat the tidal waves of lies, misrepresentations and demagoguery" was "too high a price to pay for re-election to six more years of headaches and heavy responsibilities in the Senate."[69]

Similarly, another Texas politician, Lyndon B. Johnson, was grateful for Minton's considerate letter after Johnson's defeat in 1941 for the United States Senate. In his reply Johnson said, "Others could have said the same words, perhaps, but when they come from you they fill my heart with inspiration and encouragement." He added, "You have been through the mill and you know the reactions—and they are many."[70]

Minton sent a solicitous letter to venerable Nebraska senator George W. Norris, the progressive Republican who was a staunch supporter of Roosevelt and the New Deal, following his defeat for reelection in 1942. "Though unsuccessful at the polls, you are still the All American Senator," Minton wrote. "Your record of achievement made in forty years of clean, honest, honorable service in the advancement of the highest ideals in public life will live forever."[71]

When friends suffered a death in the family or other personal calamities Minton provided solace. In gratitude for one such letter of comfort, Claude Pepper of Florida, who served with Minton in the Senate, wrote: "Shay, several times have I read over your moving letter upon the passing of my father. It is one of those tender and understanding letters that makes one feel better, and I greatly thank you."[72] Another senator, Clyde L. Herring of Iowa, whose son was missing in action in World War II, wrote to Minton, "Of all the hundreds of letters I have received . . . none was more beautifully phrased or more consoling than the hand-written message which you have sent to me."[73] Later Herring was able to report to Minton that his son was in a German prison camp that had an excellent infirmary, regular rations, a good library, theater, and church services. "Your faith in his safety helped more than you know at a time when I was beginning to slip a bit," Herring said.[74]

Minton extended such consideration and comfort to those from all walks of life. He was, according to Dilsey Scott, a New Albany woman who worked at the Minton home after he retired, "a helping man clear to the day he died. I could take my troubles to that man day or night. Nothing in my life I wouldn't go to him about."[75] Bud Ricke, of New Albany, recalled that his father, Ed, while delivering mail in Silver Hills, would stop his car by the Minton house at

EBONY

Sherman Minton with his Supreme Court messenger, Olyus Hood.

the top of the hill to eat lunch. "Minton would come out and bring my father something to drink. I think it was water, but I'm not for sure."[76] In 1934 Minton maneuvered through a maze of adoption procedures in a matter of days for friends Ruth and Wayne Walts in his hometown of Georgetown.[77] The baby girl was named Darlene, but to Minton she was "Candy Doll," and he accorded her special treatment. On Christmas Eve 1940, for example, he sent her a "Greetings from Santa Claus" telegram that read: "I have a list of all the toys you wanted me to bring, and I will do my very best to bring you everything."[78]

Likewise, Minton gave special treatment to Olyus Hood, of Upper Marlboro, Maryland, a member of Minton's Supreme Court office staff. No title could adequately describe Hood's role. He had official duties as messenger, receptionist, and driver, but his personal relationship with the boss was the one that mattered most. "Hood, you're just like a member of the family," Minton told him. "That's going a long way for a white man," Hood said.

The Mintons made Hood feel like part of the family when he stayed at their home after driving them back to New Albany from Washington. "I slept upstairs in the guest room, and it was none of that Southern-style stuff," Hood recalled. "We ate in the kitchen. He sat at the head of the table, me the other end."

On the road in the 1950s, however, lodging and eating were not that simple. The Mintons were welcomed to stay and eat where they pleased, but not Hood, and that was unacceptable to Minton. On one trip back to New Albany, Hood said, they pulled into a tourist home near Cincinnati. Minton went in and came back to report: "We can stay here Hood, but they won't let you stay." Minton got in the car and said, "Drive on. We don't need Ohio." After crossing the border into Kentucky, they stopped at a restaurant. Again, Minton went in and came back with the same message. Hood recalled what happened next: "So, I told him, 'Judge, you're getting all excited for nothing. I was born this way. You know what color I am. Don't worry about it. We got sandwiches here. We got lemonade.' Oh, no, he said, I'm going to make them feed you. After a while a waitress came out and took my order. She came back, and the fish smelled kind of antique, so I threw it under the car and had myself a couple of them sandwiches . . . and some coffee."

When he returned to the car Minton asked what happened, and Hood said he was served and he had fish.

"By God, I'm glad, I'm glad," Minton said. "Now I know where you can sleep."

Hood asked, "Where's that?"

"New Albany, Indiana," Minton responded.[79]

Minton was just as protective of the well-being of his gardener, William Short, a disabled World War I veteran who had no family of his own. When a flood in 1945 drove Short from his small cottage in New Albany, the Mintons took him and his belongings in until the waters receded. "Most of his possessions consisted of three dogs and some ten or twelve old radio cabinets with no operative parts in any of them," Minton wrote in an essay about Short.[80] Minton interceded in Short's behalf to expedite his claim for a disability pension, which was about to be granted when Short was struck and killed by a car in the fall of 1951. Although busy with the start of a new Supreme Court term, Minton, by wire, phone, and letter, directed the details of Short's funeral, burial, and disposition of his property. About Short, Minton said, "From the humblest station in life, he bore himself always as a gentleman. Our lives were enriched by his, and his tragic death was a distressing thing."[81]

Minton's simple gestures of kindness enriched the life of a young girl in Bloomington, Indiana, who used to sit on her front steps to catch a glimpse of him when he was the tall, handsome, college football star. "You don't remember me," Mary White wrote to Minton upon his appointment to the Supreme Court, "but I was that little girl—and when you went by, you always spoke." She added, "I have followed your career with interest, ever since then, and now I cannot resist writing you to tell you that I am very proud of my great football hero who was always kind to me when I was a little girl."[82]

After White met her hero on a trip to Washington in 1950, she wrote to tell him that it was "like having a long-cherished dream come true. The years have changed you from the great Shay Minton of college days to the great Justice Minton of the Supreme Court. But to one who used to sit on the steps and watch you pass, you are, and will always be, admired by me not so much for what you have become in your life, as for what you are in your heart!"[83]

NOTES

Chapter 1

1. *Indianapolis Times*, 18 Sept. 1949.

2. Ibid.

3. President Franklin D. Roosevelt was expected to make Senate Majority Leader Joseph T. Robinson of Arkansas his first Supreme Court nominee, but Robinson died before Roosevelt could make the announcement.

4. Joseph Alsop and Turner Catledge, *The 168 Days* (Garden City, N.Y.: Doubleday, Doran and Co., Inc., 1938), 299.

5. James A. Farley, *Jim Farley's Story: The Roosevelt Years* (New York: Whittlesey House, 1948), 97–98. Also cited in Alsop and Catledge, *168 Days*, 298, and Harold L. Ickes, *The Secret Diary of Harold L. Ickes*, 3 vols. (New York: Simon and Schuster, 1953–54), 2:182, 183.

6. Alsop and Catledge, *168 Days*, 303.

7. *New York Times*, 22 Aug. 1938.

8. A more detailed discussion of Minton's efforts on behalf of McNutt's presidential aspirations is in Chapter 5.

9. Private Papers of Sherman Minton, Mary Anne Callanan Collection, Bethesda, Md. (hereafter cited as Minton Papers, Callanan Collection).

10. Farley, *Jim Farley's Story*, 367. Minton's consideration for the 1944 vice presidential nomination is also discussed in George Edward Allen's *Presidents Who Have Known Me* (New York: Simon and Schuster, 1950), 125. A thorough examination of the maneuvering by Democratic party bosses to get Wallace off the ticket and Truman on it is in

Alfred Steinberg's *The Man from Missouri: The Life and Times of Harry S. Truman* (New York: G. P. Putnam's Sons, 1962), 199–218.

11. Steinberg, *Man from Missouri*, 205.

12. Harry S. Truman to Lewis B. Schwellenbach, 10 Aug. 1944, Minton Papers, Callanan Collection.

13. Sherman Minton to Franklin D. Roosevelt, 27 Feb. 1941, Minton Papers, Harry S. Truman Library, Independence, Mo.

14. Minton to Truman, 11 Oct. 1944, ibid.

15. Examples of speculative articles are: *New Albany Tribune*, 16 June, 6 July 1945; *Indianapolis News*, 24 July, 15 Sept. 1945; *Indianapolis Star*, 19 Aug. 1945; *New York Times*, 20 Sept. 1945.

16. *Indianapolis Star*, 10 Sept. 1945.

17. *Indianapolis News*, 16 Sept. 1949.

18. Minton to Hugo L. Black, 15 Sept. 1945, Hugo L. Black Papers, Manuscript Division, Library of Congress, Washington, D.C.

19. Black to Minton, 19 Sept. 1945, Minton Papers, Callanan Collection.

20. Minton to Black, 20 Sept. 1945, Black Papers.

21. David Howard Corcoran, "Sherman Minton: New Deal Senator" (Ph.D. diss., University of Kentucky, 1977), 375.

22. *New York Times*, 4 Apr. 1948. Details on Minton's role in investigating the coal strike and the board's report are in Chapter 6.

23. Alan T. Nolan, interview by author, 17 July 1991. Nolan, an Indianapolis attorney, was a law clerk for Minton on the Seventh Circuit Court of Appeals.

24. Minton to Truman, 17 July 1948, Minton Papers, Truman Library.

25. Robert G. Scigliano, *The Supreme Court and the Presidency* (New York: The Free Press, 1971), 142, 143.

26. Henry J. Abraham, *Justices & Presidents: A Political History of Appointments to the Supreme Court*, 3d rev. ed. (New York: Oxford University Press, 1992), outlines four primary reasons for presidential selections to the Supreme Court: objective merit, personal friendship, "representativeness," and political and ideological compatibility. He says all four Truman appointees fit into the personal and political friendship category.

27. Richard Kirkendall, "Tom C. Clark," in Leon Friedman and Fred L. Israel, eds., *The Justices of the United States Supreme Court, 1789–1969: Their Lives and Major Opinions*, 5 vols. (New York: R. R. Bowker Co., in association with Chelsea House Publishers, 1969–78), 4:2667.

28. Robert S. Allen and William V. Shannon, *The Truman Merry-Go-Round* (New York: Vanguard Press, 1950), 388.

29. Harold L. Ickes, "Tom Clark Should Say 'No Thanks,'" *The New Republic*, 15 Aug. 1949, p. 11. Years later, Truman called Clark "that damn

fool from Texas" and said his appointment was "my biggest mistake."

30. *New York Times*, 12 Sept. 1949.

31. Minton to Cong. Winfield K. Denton, 19 Sept. 1949, Minton Papers, Callanan Collection.

32. *Indianapolis Star*, 15 Sept. 1949.

33. Frances Kelly, interview by author, 20 Mar. 1992. Kelly was Minton's secretary during his tenure in the Senate, on the Seventh Circuit Court of Appeals, and the Supreme Court.

34. *Indianapolis Star*, 16 Sept. 1949.

35. *Indianapolis News*, 16 Sept. 1949.

36. Minton to Paul V. McNutt, 19 Sept. 1949, Paul V. McNutt Mss, Manuscripts Department, Lilly Library, Indiana University, Bloomington.

37. Minton to Denton, 19 Sept. 1949, Minton Papers, Callanan Collection.

38. *Indianapolis Times*, 15 Sept. 1949.

39. *New York Times*, 16 Sept. 1949.

40. *Indianapolis News*, 16 Sept. 1949.

41. *New York Times*, 16 Sept. 1949.

42. "Mr. Justice Minton," *The New Republic*, 26 Sept. 1949, p. 9.

43. "Politics and People," *The Nation*, 24 Sept. 1949, pp. 292–93.

44. *Washington Post*, 16 Sept. 1949.

45. Harold L. Ickes, "Justice Rutledge," *The New Republic*, 26 Sept. 1949, p. 20.

46. An article in *United States Law Week* 18 (11 Oct. 1949), noted that Minton's decision upholding the price discrimination system by Staley Manufacturing Company was reversed by the Supreme Court. It added that his decision in Standard Oil "apparently represents judicial deference to the ruling of a superior tribunal rather than an indication of his own political views." (p. 3097).

47. Minton to Black, 7 June 1946, Black Papers.

48. *Indiana Law Journal* 24, no. 2 (winter 1949): 202.

49. Elizabeth Anne Hull, "Sherman Minton and the Cold War Court" (Ph.D. diss., New School for Social Research, 1977), 81, 82.

50. "Gentleman from Indiana," *Newsweek*, 26 Sept. 1949, p. 21.

51. *New York Times*, 16 Sept. 1949.

52. *Hearing before the Committee of the Judiciary, United States Senate, Eighty-First Congress, First Session, on the Nomination of Sherman Minton, of Indiana, to be Associate Justice of the Supreme Court of the United States, September 27, 1949* (Washington, D.C.: Government Printing Office, 1949), 3.

53. Minton's relationship with the press and his controversial libel proposal are discussed in Chapter 4.

54. *Hearing before the Committee of the Judiciary*, 7.
55. Ibid., 5.
56. Ibid., 11.
57. Ibid., 2, 12.
58. Ibid., 12.
59. Ibid., 13.
60. Ibid., 16.
61. Ibid., 17.
62. Ibid., 19, 20.
63. James A. Thorpe, "The Appearance of Supreme Court Nominees before the Senate Judiciary Committee," *Journal of Public Law* 2 (1969): 371–402. The article provides a thorough discussion of the evolution of the practice. Starting with the appearance in 1968 of Justice Abe Fortas, nominated to succeed Chief Justice Earl Warren, committee deliberations into Court nominations have become forums for scoring partisan points and attracting wide and often dramatic—as in the case of the Clarence Thomas hearings in 1991—coverage in the news media.
64. Minton to Claude G. Bowers, 18 Oct. 1949, Minton Papers, Callanan Collection.
65. Minton to Kurt Pantzer, 27 Sept. 1949, ibid.
66. Minton to Harley Kilgore, 1 Oct. 1949, ibid. The letter was published in its entirety in several newspapers, including the *New York Times*, 4 Oct. 1949.
67. *Chicago Daily Tribune*, 5 Oct. 1949.
68. *New York Times*, 6 Oct. 1949.
69. *Indianapolis Times*, 12 Oct. 1949.
70. *Indianapolis News*, 8 Oct. 1949.

Chapter 2

1. The genealogy portion of this chapter is based on an ancestry chart compiled by Mary Anne Callanan and other documents, including a letter stating the circumstances of Jonathan Minton's death, in the Private Papers of Sherman Minton, Mary Anne Callanan Collection, Bethesda, Md. (hereafter cited as Minton Papers, Callanan Collection); David H. Corcoran, "The Preconditions for Greatness: A Case Study of Sherman Minton" (paper, Special Collections, Indiana Room, New Albany-Floyd County Public Library, New Albany, Ind.); Harry L. Wallace, "Hoosier Justice" (unpublished biography made available to the authors); Sister Mary Louise Donnelly, *Arnold Livers Family in America* (Lyvers, Lievers) (Burke, Va.: Donnelly, 1977); *Abstracts of Entries of Government Lands in Floyd County, Ind.*; marriage and death records

in the New Albany-Floyd County City-County Building; and census data from 1850 to 1900.

2. The account of the transience of the Minton family is drawn primarily from Wallace, "Hoosier Justice."

3. Minton's recollections about Georgetown and his youth are in a speech he delivered 11 Nov. 1957, which is in the Minton Papers, Callanan Collection.

4. Statement by Grant Berg in an interview with Gordon Owen, cited in Gordon Owen, "The Public Speaking of Sherman Minton" (Ph.D. diss., Purdue University, 1962), 35.

5. *Louisville Times*, 14 Sept. 1950.

6. Berg interview with David H. Corcoran, cited in Corcoran, "Preconditions for Greatness," 15.

7. Recounted by Homer McAfee and Jesse Burkhart in interviews cited in ibid.

8. Information on this phase of Minton's life is derived mainly from Wallace, "Hoosier Justice" and Corcoran, "Preconditions for Greatness."

9. An account of Bryan's visit to New Albany is in Gerald O. Haffner, *New Mown Hay and Other Cuttings from Hoosier History* (New Albany: Indiana University Southeast, 1978), 122–26.

10. Statement by Roscoe Minton to Owen, cited in Owen, "Public Speaking of Sherman Minton," 34.

11. Wallace, "Hoosier Justice," Chapter 2, p. 10.

12. *Louisville Courier-Journal*, 13 June 1959, in Gerald O. Haffner, "A Hoosier Country Doctor: Dr. Harry K. Engleman's Medical Ledger, 1911–1917," *Indiana Magazine of History* 85 (June 1989): 152 n. 3.

13. *Louisville Courier-Journal*, 18 Sept. 1949.

14. Information on Minton's life at this point is from Wallace, "Hoosier Justice."

15. *New Albany Tribune*, 23 July 1959.

16. Owen, "Public Speaking of Sherman Minton," 37.

17. Ibid., 39.

18. *Louisville Courier-Journal*, 18 Sept. 1949.

19. Prof. Albert Kohlmeier to Gordon Owen, 23 May 1962, cited in Owen, "Public Speaking of Sherman Minton," 40.

20. Ibid., 39.

21. *Vista*, New Albany High School Yearbook, Class of 1910, p. 34.

22. Ibid., 49.

23. Minton's letter of apology is in a display case of memorabilia at New Albany High School.

24. Statement by Walter Heazlitt in interview with Corcoran, 28 Oct. 1967, cited in Corcoran, "Preconditions for Greatness," 27.

25. *Vista*, 18.

26. Official transcript, Indiana University, certified by C. E. Harrell, registrar, 17 Oct. 1961, cited in Owen, "Public Speaking of Sherman Minton," 43.

27. "Sherman Minton's Greatest Sports Thrill," *Indiana Alumni Magazine* 19, no. 3 (Dec. 1956): 18.

28. "The Minton Story," ibid., 12, no. 3 (Nov. 1949): 26.

29. Wallace, "Hoosier Justice," Chapter 4, p. 4.

30. Letter from James W. Ryan to the Senate Judiciary Committee, 26 Sept. 1949, Minton Papers, Callanan Collection.

31. "Minton Story," 26.

32. Ibid.

33. Wallace, "Hoosier Justice," Chapter 4, p. 11.

34. Sherman Minton to Gov. Samuel M. Ralston, 18 Mar. 1916, Samuel M. Ralston Manuscripts, Lilly Library, Indiana University, Bloomington. Minton later joined Stotsenburg's law firm in New Albany. The interim senatorial appointment went to Thomas Taggart, who was defeated in the fall election by James E. Watson.

35. Owen, "Public Speaking of Sherman Minton," 45.

36. Kurt Pantzer speech 15 June 1951, Minton File, New Albany-Floyd County Public Library and Pantzer Manuscripts, Indiana State Library, Indianapolis, p. 12. Pantzer delivered the speech at the dedication of Minton's portrait at the United States Court of Appeals, Seventh Circuit, Chicago.

37. Minton speech, 26 July 1955, New Albany, Minton File, New Albany-Floyd County Public Library.

38. "Statement of the Training and Military Service of Sherman Minton," War Department, 20 Aug. 1943, Minton Papers, Callanan Collection.

39. Pantzer speech, p. 13.

40. *Indianapolis Times*, 4 Oct. 1952.

41. Ibid.

Chapter 3

1. The Third District consisted of ten counties: Clark, Crawford, Dubois, Floyd, Harrison, Lawrence, Orange, Perry, Scott, and Washington. Most of these counties comprise the present-day Ninth Congressional District.

2. *Indianapolis Star*, 13 June 1934.

3. Harry L. Wallace, "Hoosier Justice" (unpublished biography made available to the authors), Chapter 5, p. 14.

4. For an in-depth analysis of party history in Indiana see Frank James Munger, "Two-Party Politics in the State of Indiana" (Ph.D. diss., Harvard University, 1955), 1–60.

5. The Klan helped nominate and elect Jackson as governor. During Jackson's term Stephenson was sent to prison for second-degree murder. When Stephenson was not pardoned by Governor Jackson as expected, he provided testimony that led to Jackson's indictment by the Marion County Grand Jury for failing to report large campaign contributions given to him by Stephenson. Several witnesses, including Stephenson and former Governor McCray, testified against Jackson. There was not much doubt about his guilt, but the trial judge reluctantly dismissed the case because of a legal technicality. For a more complete discussion of the Klan's involvement in Indiana politics see James H. Madison, *Indiana through Tradition and Change: A History of the Hoosier State and Its People, 1920–1945* (Indianapolis: Indiana Historical Society, 1982), 55–75.

6. *Bedford Daily Times-Mail*, 29 Aug. 1957.

7. A lengthy discussion of the political role of the American Legion in Indiana is in Richard Morris Clutter, "The Indiana American Legion, 1919–1960" (Ph.D. diss., Indiana University, 1974). Also see Robert Rex Neff, "The Early Career and Governorship of Paul V. McNutt" (Ph.D. diss., Indiana University, 1963), 74–76 and Munger, "Two-Party Politics in the State of Indiana," 283–85.

8. *Indianapolis Star*, 13 June 1934.

9. Munger, "Two-Party Politics in the State of Indiana," 283 n. 33, 284.

10. Neff, "The Early Career and Governorship of Paul V. McNutt," 74.

11. Madison, *Indiana through Tradition and Change*, 79–80.

12. Sherman Minton to Paul V. McNutt, 11 Mar. 1931, Paul V. McNutt Mss, Lilly Library, Indiana University, Bloomington.

13. McNutt to Minton, 20 Mar. 1931, ibid.

14. *South Bend Tribune*, 22 June 1932.

15. Neff, "Early Career and Governorship of Paul V. McNutt," 123.

16. Ibid., 127.

17. Farley kept a daily log of all his meetings and conversations. Throughout 1937 and 1938 there are regular entries in which he reports his conversations with Roosevelt about McNutt's 1932 transgressions as well as the threat of McNutt's presidential ambitions. Private Papers of James A. Farley, reels 2, 3, 4, Library of Congress, Washington, D.C.

18. Baker, a pacifist, had been Woodrow Wilson's secretary of war.

19. Neff, "Early Career and Governorship of Paul V. McNutt," 126.

20. *Indianapolis Star*, 13 June 1934.

21. Wallace, "Hoosier Justice," Chapter 7, p. 5.
22. *Newark (Ind.) Evening News*, 27 Oct. 1934.
23. Neff, "Early Career and Governorship of Paul V. McNutt," 161.
24. *New Albany Weekly Ledger*, 20 July 1934.
25. Ibid.
26. Ibid.
27. Ibid., 23 Feb. 1934.
28. Irving Leibowitz, *My Indiana* (Englewood Cliffs, N.J.: Prentice Hall, [c. 1964]), 119.
29. Ibid.
30. Neff, "Early Career and Governorship of Paul V. McNutt," 305.
31. Milton S. Mayer, "Men Who Would Be President: III Pretty Boy McNutt," *The Nation*, 30 Mar. 1940, pp. 415–18.
32. Madison, *Indiana through Tradition and Change*, 97.
33. Munger, "Two-Party Politics in the State of Indiana," 170.
34. Wilson Democratic Club to Paul V. McNutt, telegram, 3 Apr. 1933, Paul V. McNutt Papers, box 4, folder 47, file A7012, Indiana State Archives, Commission on Public Records, Indiana State Library, Indianapolis.
35. Leibowitz, *My Indiana*, 119.
36. Neff, "Early Career and Governorship of Paul V. McNutt," 372.
37. Madison, *Indiana through Tradition and Change*, 35–36.
38. *New Albany Weekly Ledger*, 8 June 1934.
39. Ibid.
40. Wallace, "Hoosier Justice," Chapter 7, p. 8.
41. Neff, "Early Career and Governorship of Paul V. McNutt," 413.
42. Wallace, "Hoosier Justice," Chapter 7, p. 8.
43. *Indianapolis Star*, 13 June 1934.
44. Minton to McNutt, 19 Sept. 1949, McNutt Mss, Lilly Library.
45. Minton to Val Nolan, 29 Apr. 1938, Nolan Mss, ibid. In a corroborating story on 27 July 1934 the *Gary Post-Tribune* reported that Greenlee did not know until six hours before the convention that Minton would get McNutt's support.
46. Gordon Owen, "The Public Speaking of Sherman Minton" (Ph.D. diss., Purdue University, 1962), 55.
47. *New Albany Tribune*, 18 June 1934.
48. Wallace, "Hoosier Justice," Chapter 7, p. 11.
49. *Fort Wayne Journal-Gazette*, 28 Oct. 1934.
50. *New Albany Weekly Ledger*, 17 Aug. 1934.
51. Ibid., 14 Sept. 1934.
52. *Indianapolis News*, 17 Sept. 1934.
53. The same story appeared in several Democratic newspapers. One example was the *Madison Daily Herald*, 27 Oct. 1934.

54. Neff, "Early Career and Governorship of Paul V. McNutt," 416–17.

55. M.G. French to McNutt, 29 Sept. 1934, box 75, folder 780, file A7038, McNutt Papers, Indiana State Archives.

56. *Fort Wayne Journal-Gazette*, 28 Oct. 1934.

57. Neff, "Early Career and Governorship of Paul V. McNutt," 417.

58. *Fort Wayne Journal-Gazette*, 28 Oct. 1934.

59. *Greenfield Hancock Democrat*, 4 Oct. 1934.

60. *Fort Wayne Journal-Gazette*, 28 Oct. 1934.

61. *Greenfield Hancock Democrat*, 4 Oct. 1934. Early in his Senate term, Minton bowed to the pressure of his fellow veterans and voted to override Roosevelt's veto of a veterans' pension bill.

62. *Indianapolis Times*, 13 Sept. 1934.

63. Rolland E. Friedman to McNutt, 13 Sept. 1934, box 75, file A7038, McNutt Papers, Indiana State Archives.

64. Zaharakos to Greenlee, 15 Sept. 1934, ibid.

65. Thomas Taylor to McNutt, 12 Sept. 1934, ibid.

66. Wallace, "Hoosier Justice," Chapter 7, p. 19.

67. *Greenfield Hancock Democrat*, 4 Oct. 1934.

68. Madison, *Indiana through Tradition and Change*, 70. (His source is U.S. Senate, *Senatorial Campaign Expenditures, Hearings before a Special Committee Investigating Expenditures in Primary and General Elections*, Part 3 [69th Cong., 1st sess., 1926], 2033–34.)

69. Newspaper clipping from family scrapbook, Private Papers of Sherman Minton, Mary Anne Callanan Collection, Bethesda, Md.

70. *Monticello White County Democrat*, 14 Sept. 1934.

71. Ibid.

72. *New Albany Weekly Ledger*, 5 Oct. 1934.

73. Ibid., 14 Sept. 1934.

74. Ibid., 21 Sept. 1934.

75. Ibid., 2 Nov. 1934.

76. *New Albany Tribune*, 7 Nov. 1934.

77. Minton to McNutt, 5 Jan. 1935, file 7048, #1013, McNutt General Correspondence, McNutt Papers, Indiana State Archives.

78. *Christian Science Monitor*, 7 Nov. 1934.

Chapter 4

1. *Boston Herald*, 14 June 1935.

2. Virginia Van Der Veer Hamilton, *Hugo Black: The Alabama Years* (Baton Rouge: Louisiana State University Press, 1972), 246, 248.

3. *New York Times*, 17 Aug. 1935.

4. William E. Leuchtenburg, *Franklin D. Roosevelt and the New Deal, 1932–1940* (New York: Harper and Row, 1963), 156.
5. *New York Times*, 5 Apr. 1936.
6. *Congressional Record*, 74th Cong., 2d sess., 1936, vol. 80, pt. 4:4384.
7. Ibid., 4:4578–79.
8. *New York Times*, 24 Mar. 1938.
9. Richard Polenberg, *Reorganizing Roosevelt's Government: The Controversy over Executive Reorganization, 1936–1939* (Cambridge, Mass.: Harvard University Press, 1966), 76.
10. *New York Times*, 21 Mar. 1938.
11. Ibid., 24 Mar. 1938.
12. Harry L. Wallace, "Hoosier Justice" (unpublished biography made available to the authors), Chapter 12, p.15.
13. *New York Times*, 28 Apr. 1938.
14. *Congressional Record*, 75th Cong., 3d sess., 1938, vol. 83, pt. 6:5912–13.
15. Ibid.
16. *Chicago Tribune*, 30 Apr. 1938.
17. *New York Times*, 3 May 1938.
18. *Washington Post*, 14 Nov. 1949.
19. Sherman Minton to William Allen White, 16 May 1938, Private Papers of Sherman Minton, Mary Anne Callanan Collection, Bethesda, Md. (hereafter cited as Minton Papers, Callanan Collection).
20. White to Minton, 20 May 1938, ibid.
21. "Freedom of the Press" speech, 13 Aug. 1938, ibid. Minton delivered the speech before the American Press Society at the Astor Hotel in New York City, and it was carried on radio station WEAF.
22. *New York Times*, 6 May 1938.
23. Ibid., 7 May 1938.
24. Ibid.
25. *New York Herald-Tribune*, 19 May 1938.
26. *Congressional Record*, 74th Cong., 2d sess., 1936, vol. 80, pt. 1:498.
27. Ibid., 1:500.
28. Minton to Hugh E. Willis, 14 Jan. 1936, Minton Papers, Callanan Collection.
29. Willis to Minton, 17 Jan. 1936, ibid.
30. *Congressional Record*, 74th Cong., 2d sess., 1936, vol. 80, pt. 1:500.
31. "Supreme Court and the T.V.A.," NBC radio speech, 24 Feb. 1936, Minton Papers, Callanan Collection.
32. Ibid.

33. David E. Lilienthal to Minton, 7 Mar. 1936, ibid.

34. Minton speech before the Federal Bar Association, 4 Mar. 1936, Mayflower Hotel, Washington, D.C., ibid.

35. *New York Times*, 24 Jan. 1937. Minton's proposal was not unprecedented. In 1923 Sen. William E. Borah of Idaho introduced a bill that would have required a seven-vote majority of the Court, and the House of Representatives once passed a bill to require a two-thirds majority.

36. Wallace, "Hoosier Justice," Chapter 11, p. 28.

37. *New York Times*, 19, 20 Jan. 1937.

38. Leuchtenburg, *Franklin D. Roosevelt and the New Deal*, and Joseph Alsop and Turner Catledge, *The 168 Days* (Garden City, N.Y.: Doubleday, Doran and Co., Inc., 1938), give an account of the conception of the Court-packing proposal.

39. Alsop and Catledge, *168 Days*, 67.

40. *New York Times*, 16 Feb. 1937.

41. "A Larger Supreme Court," NBC radio speech, 15 Feb. 1937, Minton Papers, Callanan Collection.

42. *New Albany Tribune*, 21 July 1937.

43. *Congressional Record*, 75th Cong., 1st sess., 1937, vol. 81, pt. 6:6985–88.

44. *New Albany Tribune*, 21 July 1937.

45. F. E. Hoffman to Minton, 14 May 1937, U.S. Senate, 75th Cong., Special Committee on Lobbying, box 198, National Archives, Washington, D.C.

46. Minton to Hoffman, 18 May 1937, ibid.

47. Dorothea Garber to Minton, 15 Feb. 1937, box 190, ibid.

48. Nathan M. Ely to Minton, 19 May 1937, box 198, ibid.

49. Minton to Ely, 24 May 1937, ibid.

50. Thomas F. Konop to Minton, 19 Feb. 1937, box 190, ibid.

51. Abram Simmons to Minton, 23 Feb. 1937, box 189, ibid.

52. *Congressional Record*, 75th Cong., 1st sess., 1937, vol. 81, pt. 3:2948, 2949, 2950.

53. "Reorganization of Federal Judiciary" speech, 9 July 1937, Minton Papers, Callanan Collection.

54. Minton to Evan Stotsenburg, 20 July 1937, ibid.

55. Alsop and Catledge, *168 Days*, 300.

56. Thomas L. Stokes, "Sen. Minton Emerges as Oratorical Star in His Stirring Defense of Court Bill," Scripps-Howard Newspapers Alliance, Minton Papers, Callanan Collection.

57. *Indianapolis News*, 13 July 1937.

58. *Philadelphia Record*, 20 July 1937.

59. *Indianapolis Times*, 14 Aug. 1937.

60. Leuchtenburg, *Franklin D. Roosevelt and the New Deal*, 186.

61. *Congressional Record*, 75th Cong., 3d sess., 1938, vol. 83, pt. 2:1931–45.

62. *Indianapolis News*, 6 Mar. 1940.

63. *New York Times*, 6 Mar. 1940.

64. "The American Forum of the Air," radio speech, 24 Mar. 1940, Minton Papers, Callanan Collection.

65. *Congressional Record*, 76th Cong., 3d sess., 1940, vol. 86, pt. 3:2635.

66. *Indianapolis News*, 14 Mar. 1940.

67. *Indianapolis Times*, 8 Apr. 1940.

68. "Neutrality," CBS radio speech for National Press Club program, 30 Sept. 1939, Minton Papers, Callanan Collection.

69. *Indianapolis Times*, 17 Jan. 1940.

70. Minton speech, Young Democrats of Indiana Convention, 25 May 1940, Evansville, Minton Papers, Callanan Collection.

71. Minton speech, Southern Indiana Labor Day Association, 2 Sept. 1940, Mount Carmel, Ill., ibid.

72. See note 70 above. Minton's sons, Sherman Jr. and John, served in the navy during World War II. John also served in the Korean War.

73. *New York Times*, 7 Aug. 1940.

74. Ibid., 8 Aug. 1940.

75. The letter from Democrat Hattie W. Caraway of Arkansas was noncommittal. It read: "I thank you for your letter of May 20th regarding Senator Minton. I will be glad to bear in mind what you have to say about him. With best wishes, I am." Original letters to William A. Kunkel Jr., Minton Papers, Callanan Collection.

76. Minton to William G. McAdoo, 7 Jan. 1939, ibid.

Chapter 5

1. Sherman Minton to William A. Kunkel Jr., 20 June 1939, Private Papers of Sherman Minton, Mary Anne Callanan Collection, Bethesda, Md. (hereafter cited as Minton Papers, Callanan Collection).

2. The account of the settlement is taken from the Henry Morgenthau diaries, book 259 on microfilm 70 and book 262 on microfilm 71, at the Franklin D. Roosevelt Library, Hyde Park, N.Y.

3. David Howard Corcoran, "Sherman Minton: New Deal Senator" (Ph.D. diss., University of Kentucky, 1977), 40.

4. Minton to James A. Farley, 10 Aug. 1936, Minton Papers, Callanan Collection.

5. James C. Penman to Pleas E. Greenlee, 19 Jan. 1935, Pleas E. Greenlee Papers, in Paul V. McNutt Papers, Executive Secretary,

1933–1937, Mer thru Mo (Minton), Drawer 85, Folder 1, Indiana State Archives, Indiana Commission on Public Records, Indiana State Library, Indianapolis.

6. Greenlee to Minton, 28 Feb. 1935, ibid.

7. Greenlee to Minton, 19 Feb. 1935, ibid.

8. Greenlee to Minton, 31 May 1935, ibid.

9. Greenlee to Minton, 7 May 1935, ibid.

10. Minton to Greenlee, 15 Jan. 1935, ibid.

11. Greenlee to Minton, 24 Apr. 1935, ibid.

12. Hugh A. Barnhart to Minton, 9 Sept. 1936, Hugh A. Barnhart Papers, Indiana Division, Indiana State Library.

13. Barnhart to Minton, 20 Jan. 1938, ibid.

14. Barnhart to Minton, 20 July 1939, ibid.

15. Minton to Barnhart, 2 June 1937, ibid.

16. Minton to Barnhart, 11 Dec. 1937, ibid.

17. Minton to Greenlee, 21 Feb. 1935, Greenlee Papers.

18. Wayne Coy to Franklin D. Roosevelt, 9 Aug. 1935, Minton Papers, Roosevelt Library.

19. Interview conducted with Minton by Robert Rex Neff. Cited in Neff, "The Early Career and Governorship of Paul V. McNutt (Ph.D. diss., Indiana University, 1963), 422.

20. Minton to James A. Woodburn, 3 Feb. 1936, James A. Woodburn Mss., Manuscripts Department, Lilly Library, Indiana University, Bloomington.

21. Minton speech, 14 Feb. 1936, Shelbyville, Ind., Minton Papers, Callanan Collection.

22. Minton to Val Nolan, 21 June 1939, Nolan Mss., Manuscripts Department, Lilly Library. Minton tells Nolan in this letter that he has had no word about Nolan's possible appointment as a United States district court judge. Minton began working on the position for his friend in mid-1938, but it never occurred.

23. *New York Times*, 22 May 1936.

24. Iwan Morgan, "Factional Conflict in Indiana Politics during the Later New Deal Years, 1936–1940," *Indiana Magazine of History* 79 (Mar. 1983): 35.

25. *Indianapolis Star*, 15 July 1937.

26. John D. Barnhart and Donald F. Carmony, *Indiana: From Frontier to Industrial Commonwealth*, 4 vols. (New York: Lewis Historical Publishing Co., 1954), 2:485.

27. A thorough discussion of Capehart's rise to power and the Cornfield Conference is contained in William B. Pickett's *Homer E. Capehart: A Senator's Life, 1897–1979* (Indianapolis: Indiana Historical Society, 1990).

28. "Senator Minton's Campaign Address, 1938," Minton Papers, Callanan Collection.

29. Minton WIRE radio speech, 6 Nov. 1938, Indianapolis, ibid.

30. *Indianapolis Times*, 27 July 1934.

31. Minton to Nolan, 1 Apr. 1935, Nolan Mss.

32. *Indianapolis Times*, 9 July 1940.

33. Minton to Woodburn, 3 Feb. 1936, Woodburn Mss.

34. *Congressional Record*, Senate, 76th Cong., 1st sess., 1939, vol. 84, pt. 8:8927.

35. Ibid.

36. James H. Madison, *Indiana through Tradition and Change* (Indianapolis: Indiana Historical Society, 1982), 99.

37. Ibid., 100.

38. Cited in I. George Blake, *Paul V. McNutt: Portrait of a Hoosier Statesman* (Indianapolis: Central Publishing Co., 1966), 238.

39. *New Albany Tribune*, 22 May 1936.

40. *Indianapolis Star*, 9 Dec. 1936.

41. *New York Times*, 24 Feb. 1938. Party officials denied that the cost of the event came from the Two Per Cent Club, maintaining that twenty-five friends of McNutt paid for the event.

42. Farley memorandum, 14 Dec. 1939, Private Papers of James A. Farley, Library of Congress, Washington, D.C.

43. Roosevelt to Minton, 29 Oct. 1940, Minton Papers, Roosevelt Library.

44. *Indianapolis Star*, 3 Oct. 1940.

45. Ibid., 3 Nov. 1940.

46. Ibid., 24 Oct. 1940.

47. *Vincennes Sun-Commercial*, 20 Oct. 1940.

48. *Indianapolis Times*, 3 Oct. 1940.

49. *Indianapolis Star*, 18 Oct. 1940.

50. *Terre Haute Tribune*, 24 Oct. 1940.

51. *Indianapolis News*, 18 Oct. 1940.

52. *New Albany Tribune*, 18 Oct. 1940.

53. *Indianapolis Star*, 19 Oct. 1940.

54. *Gary Post-Tribune*, 25 Oct. 1940.

55. Ibid.

56. *New Albany Tribune*, 17 Oct. 1940.

57. *Muncie Evening Press*, 31 Oct. 1940.

58. *New Albany Tribune*, 5 Nov. 1940.

59. Election figures are from *Who's Who And What's What in Indiana Politics* (Indianapolis: James E. Perry, Publisher, 1944), 346.

60. Minton to George W. Norris, 25 Nov. 1940, Minton Papers, Callanan Collection.

61. Minton to Josephus Daniels, 20 Nov. 1940, ibid.
62. Sherman Minton to Roscoe Minton, 13 Nov. 1940, ibid.
63. Minton to William G. McAdoo, 9 Nov. 1940, ibid.
64. Minton to Clarence R. McNabb, 14 Nov. 1940, ibid.
65. Minton to F. Ryan Duffy, 13 Nov. 1940, ibid.
66. Sherman Minton to Roscoe Minton, 13 Nov. 1940, ibid.

Chapter 6

1. Sherman Minton to Lister Hill, 6 Dec. 1940, Private Papers of Sherman Minton, Mary Anne Callanan Collection, Bethesda, Md. (hereafter cited as Minton Papers, Callanan Collection).
2. Hill to Franklin D. Roosevelt, 26 Nov. 1940, File 4241, Franklin D. Roosevelt Library, Hyde Park, N.Y.
3. James Rowe to Roosevelt, 3 Jan. 1941, PS File, ibid.
4. *New York Times*, 8 Jan. 1941.
5. *Indianapolis Star*, 8 Jan. 1941.
6. Ibid.
7. William A. Kunkel, Jr., Fort Wayne, Ind., telegram to Roosevelt, 8 Jan. 1941, File 4241, Roosevelt Library.
8. Lewis B. Schwellenbach to Minton, 1 Feb. 1941, Minton Papers, Callanan Collection.
9. Minton memorandum to Roosevelt, 17 Mar. 1941, ibid.
10. Minton memorandum to Roosevelt, 15 Mar. 1941, President's Personal File, Roosevelt Library.
11. Exchange of memoranda between Minton and Roosevelt and William McReynolds and Roosevelt, filed under Memorandum for Sherman Minton, 15 Apr. 1941, Minton Papers, Callanan Collection.
12. Minton memorandum to Roosevelt, 25 Jan. 1941, ibid.
13. Ibid., 27 Feb. 1941, Minton Papers, Harry S. Truman Library, Independence, Mo.
14. Rowe memorandum to Roosevelt, 28 Apr. 1941, File 4241, Roosevelt Library.
15. *Louisville Times*, 25 Oct. 1960.
16. Presidential memorandum for the attorney general, 29 Apr. 1941, Roosevelt Library.
17. Minton to Roosevelt, 7 May 1941, PS File, ibid.
18. Aline Treanor to Minton, 18 May 1941, Minton Papers, Callanan Collection. Minton and Treanor's friendship dated to their undergraduate days at Indiana University, and, as a senator, Minton sponsored Treanor's appointment to the Seventh Circuit in 1938.
19. Evan Evans to Minton, 14 May 1941, Minton Papers, Callanan Collection.

20. William Sparks to Minton, 8 May 1941, ibid.

21. Schwellenbach telegram to Harry S. Truman, 27 May 1941, ibid.

22. The memorandum confirming this transaction notes that the picture was handed to Miss Frances Kelly, secretary to Sen. Sherman Minton. Memorandum for Miss Lehand, 28 May 1941 and attachment, 29 May 1941, President's Personal File 2235, Roosevelt Library.

23. Reported in an interview between Jim St. Clair and Alan T. Nolan, Minton law clerk on the Seventh Circuit, 17 July 1991, Indianapolis, Ind.

24. *Chicago Tribune*, 8 Oct. 1941.

25. Minton to James A. Farley, 10 May 1941, Minton Papers, Callanan Collection.

26. Minton to Theodore Bilbo, 12 May 1941, ibid.

27. James Rowe to Minton, 14 June 1941, ibid.

28. Rayman L. Solomon, *History of the Seventh Circuit, 1891–1941* (Published under the auspices of the Bicentennial Committee of the Judicial Conference of the United States, 1981).

29. Nolan interview.

30. Elizabeth Anne Hull, "Sherman Minton and the Cold War Court" (Ph.D. diss., New School for Social Research, 1977), 35.

31. Solomon, *History of the Seventh Circuit*, 161.

32. Evan Evans to Minton, 29 Oct. 1945, Private Papers of Evan Evans, George A. Evans Collection, Whitefish Bay, Wis. (hereafter cited as Evans Papers).

33. Data from *Congressional Record*, 23 Nov. 1942, and reported in a letter from Evans to Minton, 7 Dec. 1942, Minton Papers, Callanan Collection.

34. Robert H. Jackson to Minton, 21 Dec. 1942, ibid.

35. Minton to Roosevelt. No date shows on the letter, but Roosevelt's response to Minton was dated 26 Nov. 1941, President's Personal File, 2235, Roosevelt Library.

36. Minton to Harry S. Truman, 25 June 1942, Minton Papers, Callanan Collection.

37. Truman to Minton, 21 Apr. 1944, ibid.

38. Minton to Truman, 11 Oct. 1944, ibid.

39. Minton to Truman, 11 Jan. 1945, Senatorial Papers, Truman Library.

40. Truman to Minton, 26 Jan. 1945, ibid.

41. Minton to Truman, 16 Mar. 1945, ibid.

42. Truman to Minton, 11 May 1945, ibid.

43. *Time*, 4 June 1945, p. 23.

44. Hugo L. Black to Minton, 20 Sept. 1945, Minton Papers, Callanan Collection.

45. Evans to Minton, 3 Jan. 1946, Evans Papers.

46. Carl A. Hatch memorandum to Truman, Mar. 1946, Senatorial Papers, Truman Library.
47. Truman to Hatch, 23 Mar. 1946, ibid.
48. Minton to Truman, 22 May 1946, ibid.
49. Truman to Minton, 25 May 1946, ibid.
50. Thomas E. Baker, "Frederick Moore Vinson," in Kermit L. Hall, ed., *The Oxford Companion to the Supreme Court of the United States* (New York: Oxford University Press, 1992), 898.
51. Hugo L. Black to Minton, 11 June 1946, Minton Papers, Callanan Collection.
52. *Indianapolis Times*, 31 July 1945.
53. Minton to Truman, 23 Oct. 1947, Senatorial Papers, Truman Library.
54. Minton to Truman, 26 Nov. 1948, Minton Papers, Callanan Collection.
55. Minton to Truman, 29 Jan. 1949, ibid.
56. Truman to Minton, 1 Feb. 1949, ibid.
57. Minton to Truman, 20 Apr. 1949, Senatorial Papers, Truman Library.
58. Although James Noland publicly endorsed John Hurt's appointment, he later fought against the appointment. Private Papers of John Hurt, Martinsville, Ind.
59. *Indianapolis Times*, date unknown. From John Hurt's private collection of clippings.
60. Minton to Truman, 25 May 1949, Senatorial Papers, Truman Library.
61. Truman to Minton, 2 June 1949, ibid.
62. *New Albany Tribune*, 29 July 1949.
63. Alexander Campbell to Hurt, 14 July 1949, Private Papers of John Hurt.
64. Several years after losing out on the appointment, Hurt visited Washington, D.C., on business. He called Minton who invited him to his Supreme Court office. Hurt later recalled that the two had a very friendly visit over a glass of whiskey. No mention was ever made of Minton's successful attempt to prevent Hurt's appointment as U.S. district attorney.
65. Minton to Hatch, 3 May 1949, Minton Papers, Callanan Collection.

Chapter 7

1. *Indianapolis News*, 7 Oct. 1941.
2. Abner J. Mikva, "Sherman Minton: The Supreme Court Years, Lecture on the 100th Anniversary of His Birth," Indiana University Southeast, New Albany, Ind., 14 Oct. 1990, p. 1.

3. Casper W. Ooms, "Honorable Sherman Minton, Judge" (tribute to Justice Minton upon presentation of his portrait at the session of the Judicial Conference and Bar Association of the Seventh Circuit, 15 June 1951), 22.

4. David N. Atkinson, "Mr. Justice Minton and the Supreme Court, 1949–1956" (Ph.D. diss., University of Iowa, 1969), 161–62.

5. "Taxes," *Tax Magazine*, Oct. 1949, pp. 873–74.

6. Ooms, "Honorable Sherman Minton," 33.

7. *Adler* v. *Northern Hotel Co.*, 175 F2d 619, 622 (7th Cir. 1942). Hereafter in this chapter all citations from the Federal Reporter, 2d series are from the Seventh Circuit.

8. *McCarthy* v. *Pennsylvania R. Co.*, 156 F2d 877, 880 (1946).

9. *Schreiber et al.* v. *United States*, 129 F2d 836, 840 (1942).

10. *United States ex rel. Hack* v. *Clark, U.S. Attorney General et al.*, 159 F2d 552, 554 (1947).

11. *Marshall Field & Co.* v. *National Labor Relations Board*, 135 F2d 391, 395 (1943).

12. Elizabeth Anne Hull, "Sherman Minton and the Cold War Court" (Ph.D. diss., New School for Social Research, 1977), 47.

13. For a discussion of Minton's decisions regarding rulings of administrative agencies see Atkinson, "Mr. Justice Minton and the Supreme Court," 322–44.

14. *Interlake Iron Corporation* v. *National Labor Relations Board*, 131 F2d 129, 133 (1942).

15. "Fourth Truman Appointee Confirmed," *United States Law Week* 18 (11 Oct. 1949): 3097.

16. *United States* v. *New York Great Atlantic and Pacific Tea Co.*, 173 F2d 79 (1949).

17. Ibid., 82, 83, 88.

18. *Cargill, Inc.* v. *Board of Trade of City of Chicago et al.*, 164 F2d 820, 823 (1947).

19. Evan Evans to Sherman Minton and Earl Major, 2 Dec. 1947, Private Papers of Evan Evans, George A. Evans Collection, Whitefish Bay, Wis. (hereafter cited as Evans Papers).

20. *A. E. Staley Mfg. Co. et al.* v. *Federal Trade Commission*, 144 F2d 221 (1944).

21. Ibid., 224.

22. Harry L. Wallace, "Hoosier Justice" (unpublished biography made available to the authors), Chapter 20, p. 17.

23. *Standard Oil Co.* v. *Federal Trade Commission*, 173 F2d 210, 216 (1949).

24. Two years later, when Minton was on the Supreme Court, his *Standard Oil* decision was reversed by a 3 to 5 majority (*Standard Oil Co.* v. *Federal Trade Commission*, 340 US 231 [1950]). Minton, who did not participate in the decision, must have been perplexed about the

reversal of his *Standard Oil* opinion because it was based on the Supreme Court ruling five years earlier that overturned his *Staley* opinion. Nonetheless, this was one instance where Minton should have been pleased by reversal.

25. *Zangerle & Petersen Co.* v. *Venice Furniture Novelty Mfg. Co.*, 133 F2d 266, 269 (1943).

26. *E. Edelman & Co.* v. *Auto Parts & Gear Co.*, 127 F2d 897, 898–99 (1942).

27. *General Industries Co.* v. *20 Wacker Drive Bldg. Corporation et al.*, 156 F2d 474, 478 (1946).

28. *California Fruit Growers Exchange* v. *Sunkist Baking Co.*, 166 F2d 971, 973–74 (1948).

29. "Recent Cases," *George Washington Law Review* 589 (June 1948): 592.

30. *Quaker Oats Co.* v. *General Mills, Inc.*, 134 F2d 429, 430–31 (1943).

31. *Horlick's Malted Milk Corporation* v. *Horlick*, 143 F2d 32 (1944).

32. *Consumer Petroleum Co.* v. *Consumer Co. of Illinois*, 169 F2d 153 (1948).

33. Minton made two radio addresses, one in 1939 and one in 1940, defending the NLRA. In both speeches Minton harshly criticized the "minority of chiselers that made it necessary to pass the National Labor Relations Act" and staunchly defended the NLRB, which he said had "performed a most difficult task in a highly satisfactory manner."

34. Wallace, "Hoosier Justice," Chapter 21, p. 2.

35. Hull, "Sherman Minton and the Cold War Court," 58.

36. *National Labor Relations Board* v. *W. A. Jones Foundry & Machine Co.*, 123 F2d 552, 555 (1941).

37. *Rapid Roller Co.* v. *National Labor Relations Board*, 126 F2d 452, 459 (1942).

38. *National Labor Relations Board* v. *William Davies Co., Inc.*, 135 F2d 179, 181 (1943).

39. *National Labor Relations Board* v. *Sunbeam Electric Mfg. Co.*, 133 F2d 856, 860 (1943).

40. *National Labor Relations Board* v. *American Car & Foundry Co.*, 161 F2d 501, 503 (1947).

41. Rayman L. Solomon, *History of the Seventh Circuit, 1891–1941* (Published under the auspices of the Bicentennial Committee of the Judicial Conference of the United States, 1981), 163.

42. For a discussion of judicial interpretation of NLRB powers see Charles Oscar Gregory, *Labor and the Law* (New York: W. W. Norton Co., 1946), 589–633.

43. *National Labor Relations Board* v. *Marshall Field & Co.*, 129 F2d 169, 171 (1942).

44. *Marshall Field & Co.* v. *National Labor Relations Board*, 394.

45. *National Labor Relations Board* v. *William Davies Co., Inc.*, 182.

46. *Western Cartridge Co.* v. *National Labor Relations Board*, 139 F2d 855, 858 (1943).

47. *National Labor Relations Board* v. *Sheboygan Chair Co.*, 125 F2d 436, 439 (1942).

48. The following are examples of cases where Minton denied relief to workers' appeals because he thought they were not guaranteed by the statute: *Walling, Adm'r of Wage and Hour Div., Dept. of Labor* v. *Swift & Co.*, 131 F2d 249 (1942); *Walling, Administrator of Wage and Hour Division of United States Dept. of Labor* v. *T. Buettner & Co.*, 133 F2d 306 (1943); *Jumps et al.* v. *Leverone et al.*, 150 F2d 876 (1945); *Cederblade et al.* v. *Parmelee Transp. Co.*, 166 F2d 554 (1948).

49. *Chicago, Burlington and Quincy Railroad Company* v. *Chicago*, 166 US 226 (1897).

50. *Gitlow* v. *People of New York*, 268 US 652 (1925).

51. 302 US 319 (1937).

52. David J. Bodenhamer, *Fair Trial: Rights of the Accused in American History* (New York: Oxford University Press, 1992), 99.

53. Hull, "Sherman Minton and the Cold War Court," 50–51.

54. Evans to William Sparks and Minton, 9 Dec. 1946, Evans Papers.

55. *Andrews* v. *Hotel Sherman, Inc., et al.*, 138 F2d 524, 528 (1943).

56. *Lutwak et al.* v. *United States*, 344 US 604, 619 (1953).

57. *Powell* v. *Alabama*, 287 US 45 (1932).

58. *United States ex rel. Adams* v. *Ragen*, 172 F2d 693, 696 (1949).

59. *Wood* v. *Howard*, 157 F2d 807, 808 (1946).

60. *Sweet* v. *Howard, Warden*, 155 F2d 715, 717 (1946).

61. *United States ex rel. Feeley* v. *Ragen*, 166 F2d 976, 980 (1948).

62. Ibid., 981.

63. *Lanning* v. *National Ribbon & Carbon Paper Mfg. Co.*, 125 F2d 565, 568 (1942).

64. *Wiggington* v. *Order of United Commercial Travelers of America*, 126 F2d 659, 662 (1942).

65. *Erie Railroad Co.* v. *Tompkins*, 304 US 64 (1938).

66. *United States* v. *Johnson*, 142 F2d 588, 591 (1944).

67. *Tovar* v. *Jarecki, Collector of Internal Revenue*, 173 F2d 449, 450 (1949).

68. *Kasual* v. *George F. Nord Bldg. Corporation*, 129 F2d 173, 176 (1942).

69. *Montgomery Ward & Co., Inc.* v. *McGraw-Hill Pub. Co., Inc.*, 146 F2d 171, 176 (1944).

70. *United States* v. *Knauer*, 149 F2d 519, 522 (1945).

71. Evans to Minton, 25 Mar. 1946, Evans Papers.

72. Hull, "Sherman Minton and the Cold War Court," 55.

73. The story of Minton's boosting Truman's career is found in Chapter 1.

Chapter 8

1. From Cert notes, *Youngstown*, n.d., WODP, Box 220, cited in Howard Ball and Phillip J. Cooper, *Of Power and Right: Hugo Black, William O. Douglas, and America's Constitutional Revolution* (New York: Oxford University Press, 1992), 133.

2. *Louisville Times*, 14 Nov. 1956.

3. *Youngstown Sheet & Tube Co. et al.* v. *Sawyer*, 343 US 579, 587 (1952).

4. Sherman Minton review of *Mr. Justice Black: The Man and His Opinions*, by John P. Frank, *Indiana Law Journal* 24 (winter 1949): 302.

5. Sherman Minton to Felix Frankfurter, ca. Nov. 1953, cited in H. N. Hirsch, *The Enigma of Felix Frankfurter* (New York: Basic Books, 1981), 189.

6. Howard Ball, *The Vision and the Dream of Justice Hugo L. Black: An Examination of a Judicial Philosophy* (University: University of Alabama Press, c. 1975), 2–13.

7. "A Larger Supreme Court," NBC speech by Sherman Minton, 15 Feb. 1937, Private Papers of Sherman Minton, Mary Anne Callanan Collection, Bethesda, Md. (hereafter cited as Minton Papers, Callanan Collection).

8. For Frankfurter's strategies with other justices see Hirsch, *Enigma of Felix Frankfurter*, 177–89.

9. Maeva Marcus, *Truman and the Steel Seizure Case: The Limits of Presidential Power* (New York: Columbia University Press, 1977), 205.

10. David N. Atkinson, "Mr. Justice Minton and the Supreme Court, 1949–1956" (Ph.D. diss., University of Iowa, 1969), 67.

11. Ibid., 167.

12. "A Larger Supreme Court."

13. Story told to David N. Atkinson by Justice Minton's secretary in an interview, 30 Jan. 1968, cited in Atkinson, "Mr. Justice Minton and the Supreme Court," 109.

14. "A Larger Supreme Court."

15. David McCullough states that Truman announced to members of his staff in mid-November 1951 that he did not intend to run again, but he swore them to secrecy, which they kept for five months. David McCullough, *Truman* (New York: Simon and Schuster, 1992), 874.

16. Sherman Minton to Fred M. Vinson, 12 Mar. 1952, Frederick M. Vinson Papers, Margaret I. King Library, University of Kentucky, Lexington.

17. Harry S. Truman to Minton, 8 Apr. 1952, Minton Papers, Callanan Collection.

18. Marcus, *Truman and the Steel Seizure Case*, 228.
19. Ibid.
20. Ibid., 231.
21. That Truman's anti-Communist strategies were driven by a concern about the outcome of the presidential election is argued persuasively by Michal R. Belknap in *Cold War Political Justice: The Smith Act, the Communist Party, and American Civil Liberties* (Westport, Conn.: Greenwood Press, 1977), 6, 49–50.
22. Ibid., 47.
23. Ronald Gene Marquat, "The Judicial Justice: Mr. Justice Minton and the Supreme Court" (Ph.D. diss., University of Virginia, 1962), 58–59, cited in Frances Howell Rudko, *Truman's Court: A Study in Judicial Restraint* (Westport, Conn.: Greenwood Press, 1988), 31.
24. *Dennis* v. *United States*, 339 US 162, 164 (1949).
25. *Frazier* v. *United States*, 335 US 497 (1948); *United States* v. *Wood*, 299 US 123 (1936).
26. Stanley F. Reed, who concurred with the majority, indicated that he read "the Court's decision to mean that Government employees may be barred for implied bias when circumstances are properly brought to the court's attention which convince the court that Government employees would not be suitable jurors in a particular case." *Dennis* v. *United States* (1949), 168, 172–73.
27. Frankfurter to the Conference *re Dennis* v. *United States*, 339 US 162 (1949), 11 Jan. 1950, Sherman Minton Papers, Harry S. Truman Library, Independence, Mo.
28. *Dennis* v. *United States* (1949), 172.
29. Justice Minton's file *re Dennis* v. *United States*, 339 US 162 (1949), undated, Minton Papers, Truman Library.
30. *Dennis et al.* v. *United States*, 341 US 494 (1951).
31. *Schenck* v. *United States*, 249 US 47, 52 (1919).
32. Belknap, *Cold War Political Justice*, 133.
33. *Dennis et al.* v. *United States* (1951), 510, 509.
34. Minton to Vinson, 15 June 1961, Vinson Papers.
35. Kermit Hall, *The Magic Mirror: Law in American History* (New York: Oxford University Press, 1989), 314.
36. C. Herman Pritchett, *Civil Liberties and the Vinson Court* (Chicago: University of Chicago Press, 1954), 240.
37. Bernard Schwartz, *A History of the Supreme Court* (New York: Oxford University Press, 1993), 258.
38. For a detailed chronicle of the Court's handling of the Rosenbergs' case and Douglas's role in it see James F. Simon, *Independent Journey: The Life of William O. Douglas* (New York: Harper and Row, 1980), 298–313.

39. A former Douglas law clerk, William Cohen, defends Douglas's behavior in "Justice Douglas and the *Rosenberg* Case: Setting the Record Straight," *Cornell Law Review* 70 (1985): 211–52. Cohen says that Douglas's votes to deny review in the Rosenberg cases were not inconsistent. Rather, they were based on the issues raised, and each case presented a different issue.

40. Harry L. Wallace letter to the author, 4 Oct. 1993.

41. Elizabeth Anne Hull, "Sherman Minton and the Cold War Court" (Ph.D. diss., New School for Social Research, 1977), 129.

42. Atkinson, "Mr. Justice Minton and the Supreme Court," 101.

43. Felix Frankfurter to Minton, 20 Aug. 1954, Minton Papers, Callanan Collection.

44. William O. Douglas to Minton, 16 June 1960, ibid.

45. Minton to Douglas, 17 Oct. 1951, William O. Douglas Papers, Manuscript Division, Library of Congress, Washington, D.C.

46. Alfred H. Kelly and Winfred A. Harbison, *The American Constitution: Its Origins and Development*, 5th ed. (New York: W. W. Norton, 1976), 833–37, provides a general summary of the history of the federal loyalty programs.

47. *Bailey* v. *Richardson*, 341 US 918 (1951).

48. *Joint Anti-Fascist Refugee Committee* v. *McGrath, Attorney General et al.*, 341 US 123 (1951).

49. Pritchett, *Civil Liberties and the Vinson Court*, 99.

50. *Adler et al.* v. *Board of Education of the City of New York*, 342 US 485 (1952).

51. Ibid., 492.

52. Ibid., 493.

53. Ibid., 511.

54. Ibid.

55. *New York Sun*, 4 May 1952, cited in Richard Kirkendall, "Sherman Minton," in Leon Friedman and Fred L. Israel, eds., *The Justices of the Supreme Court, 1789–1969: Their Lives and Major Opinions*, 5 vols. (New York: R. R. Bowker Co., in association with Chelsea House Publishers, 1969–78), 4:2705.

56. Minton to Kurt Pantzer, n.d., Minton Papers, Truman Library.

57. John P. Frank, "The United States Supreme Court: 1951–1952," *University of Chicago Law Review* 20, no. 1 (autumn 1952): 23.

58. George D. Braden to Minton, 19 Mar. 1952, Private Papers of George D. Braden, Truman Library.

59. Minton to Braden, 20 Mar. 1952, ibid.

60. Minton to Edmund M. Hanrahan, 10 Apr. 1952, and Minton to George J. Pickett, 7 Mar. 1952, Minton Papers, Truman Library.

61. Minton's unpublished dissent in *re Cole* v. *Young*, 351 US 536 (1956), ibid.

62. *Wieman et al.* v. *Updegraff et al.*, 344 US 183 (1952).

63. Leo Pfeffer, *This Honorable Court: A History of the United States Supreme Court* (Boston: Beacon Press, 1965), 370.

64. *Shaughnessy, District Director of Immigration and Naturalization* v. *United States ex rel. Mezei*, 345 US 206 (1953).

65. John P. Frank, "Fred Vinson and the Chief Justiceship," *University of Chicago Law Review* 21, no. 2 (winter 1953): 231–32.

66. *United States ex rel. Knauff* v. *Shaughnessy, Acting District Director of Immigration and Naturalization*, 338 US 537, 540, 548 (1949).

67. Clark, attorney general when Knauff was denied entry to the country, did not participate, and Douglas was out during most of the 1949–50 term recuperating in Arizona from a back injury sustained in a horseback-riding accident.

68. *United States ex rel. Knauff* v. *Shaughnessy*, 544.

69. Ibid., 543.

70. Ibid., 551–52.

71. Ibid., 548.

72. *Chicago Sun Times*, 23 Jan. 1950.

73. Minton to Russell Stewart, 28 Jan. 1950, Minton Papers, Truman Library.

74. Mark Ethridge to Minton, 31 Jan. 1950, ibid.

75. Minton to Myron Harris, 28 Jan. 1950, ibid.

76. Braden to Minton, 17 Mar. 1950, Braden Papers.

77. Minton to Braden, 29 Mar. 1950, ibid. The *Knauff* opinion was not the last step in Ellen Knauff's attempts to enter the country. The *St. Louis Post Dispatch* publicized her case extensively and many measures were taken in her behalf. These measures included intervention by the White House, by Congress, and even by the Supreme Court when Justice Jackson issued an order preventing the Immigration Service from returning her to Germany until the Supreme Court could consider her petition. Although Knauff did get a hearing, the Immigration Service refused to grant her permission to enter the country. Subsequently, the House of Representatives passed a bill to enable her to remain in the country, and the chairman of the House Judiciary Committee advised the attorney general that he would be in contempt of the House if Knauff was deported while congressional action was pending. Finally the Board of Immigration Appeals reversed the order of exclusion, and on 1 Nov. 1951 Knauff was admitted to the country after spending more than three years on Ellis Island.

78. *Brock* v. *North Carolina*, 344 US 424, 427–28 (1953).

79. *Lutwak et al.* v. *United States*, 344 US 604, 619 (1953).

80. David J. Bodenhamer, *Fair Trial: Rights of the Accused in American History* (New York: Oxford University Press, 1992), 78–79.

81. *Schwartz* v. *Texas*, 344 US 199, 203, 201 (1952).

82. Gerald T. Dunne, *Hugo Black and the Judicial Revolution* (New York: Simon and Schuster, 1977), 271.

83. *Harris* v. *United States*, 331 US 145 (1946).

84. *Trupiano et al.* v. *United States*, 334 US 699 (1948).

85. *United States* v. *Rabinowitz*, 339 US 56 (1950).

86. Dunne, *Hugo Black and the Judicial Revolution*, 274.

87. *United States* v. *Rabinowitz*, 65–66.

88. *Trupiano et al.* v. *United States*, 699.

89. *United States* v. *Rabinowitz*, 65–66.

90. Ibid., 70.

91. Frankfurter to Minton, 25 Jan. 1950, Felix Frankfurter Papers, Manuscript Division, Library of Congress.

92. Minton to Braden, 20 Mar. 1950, Braden Papers.

93. *United States* v. *Rabinowitz*, 63.

94. "Search and Seizure in the Supreme Court: Shadows on the Fourth Amendment," *University of Chicago Law Review* 28, no. 4 (summer 1961): 684, 686.

95. George D. Braden, "Mr. Justice Minton and the Truman Bloc," *Indiana Law Journal* 26 (1951): 155.

96. John P. Frank, "The United States Supreme Court, 1949–50," *University of Chicago Law Review* 18, no. 1 (autumn 1950): 52.

97. Minton to Erwin G. Gjerde, 28 Mar. 1950, Minton Papers, Truman Library.

98. Theodore A. Werntz to Minton, 22 Feb. 1950, ibid.

99. Frank, "United States Supreme Court, 1949–1950," p. 51.

100. Atkinson, "Mr. Justice Minton and the Supreme Court," 162.

101. Braden to Minton, 12 Sept. 1950, Braden Papers.

102. Minton to Braden, 20 Sept. 1950, ibid.

103. Frank, "United States Supreme Court, 1949–1950," p. 52.

104. John E. Miller to Minton, 11 Feb. 1950, Minton Papers, Callanan Collection.

105. Sherman Minton to Sherman Minton, Jr., 17 May 1950, Private Papers of Sherman Minton, Sherman Minton, Jr., Collection, Indianapolis, Ind.

106. Minton to Frankfurter, 17 June 1950, Frankfurter Papers.

107. Vinson to Minton, 18 July 1950, Vinson Papers.

108. Minton to Vinson, 24 July 1950, ibid.

109. Interview with Minton law clerk, cited in Atkinson, "Mr. Justice Minton and the Supreme Court," 148.

110. *Alabama Great Southern Railroad Co. et al.* v. *United States et al.*, 340 US 216 (1951).

111. Louis L. Jaffe, "The Supreme Court, 1950 Term," *Harvard Law Review* 65 (1951–52): 111.

112. John P. Frank, "The United States Supreme Court: 1950–1951," *University of Chicago Law Review* 19, no. 2 (winter 1952): 184.

113. William O. Douglas, *The Court Years, 1939–1975: The Autobiography of William O. Douglas* (New York: Random House, 1980), 246.

114. *McLaurin* v. *Oklahoma State Regents for Higher Education et al.*, 339 US 637 (1950).

115. *Sweatt* v. *Painter et al.*, 339 US 629 (1950).

116. *Henderson* v. *United States et al.*, 339 US 816 (1950).

117. *Barrows et al.* v. *Jackson*, 346 US 249 (1953).

118. *Shelley* v. *Kraemer*, 334 US 1 (1948).

119. *Pierce, Governor of Oregon et al.* v. *Society of Sisters*, 268 US 510 (1925).

120. Minton Papers, Truman Library, cited in Hull, "Sherman Minton and the Cold War Court," 210.

121. *Terry et al.* v. *Adams et al.*, 345 US 461 (1953).

122. Ibid., 484–85.

123. Frankfurter to Minton, 29 Apr. 1953, Frankfurter Papers.

124. Minton to Frankfurter, 29 Apr. 1953, ibid.

125. Minton to Robert H. Jackson, 28 Mar. 1953, Minton Papers, Callanan Collection.

126. Hugo L. Black to Minton, 22 Dec. 1959, ibid.

127. Minton to Vinson, 22 Aug. 1953, Vinson Papers.

128. Vinson to Minton, 24 Aug. 1953, Minton Papers, Callanan Collection.

129. Minton to Vinson, 17 June 1951, Vinson Papers.

130. *New Albany Tribune*, 8 Sept. 1953.

131. Minton to Roberta Vinson, 13 Sept. 1953, Vinson Papers.

132. Mark V. Tushnet, *Making Civil Rights Law: Thurgood Marshall and the Supreme Court, 1936–1961* (New York: Oxford University Press, 1994).

Chapter 9

1. David N. Atkinson, "Mr. Justice Minton and the Supreme Court, 1949–1956" (Ph.D. diss., University of Iowa, 1969), 160.

2. Sherman Minton to Homer Bone, 28 Nov. 1953, Private Papers of Sherman Minton, Mary Anne Callanan Collection, Bethesda, Md. (hereafter cited as Minton Papers, Callanan Collection).

3. Sherman Minton to Harry S. Truman, 16 Jan. 1953, Post-Presidential Office Files, Harry S. Truman Library, Independence, Mo.

4. Atkinson, "Mr. Justice Minton and the Supreme Court," 153.

5. Felix Frankfurter to Minton, 8 Oct. 1953, Minton Papers, Callanan Collection.

6. Minton to Frankfurter, 9 Oct. 1953, ibid.

7. *Leyra* v. *Denno, Warden*, 347 US 556, 584 (1954).

8. *United States* v. *Morgan*, 346 US 502, 516–17, 519–20 (1954).

9. *Toolson* v. *New York Yankees, Inc., et al.*, 346 US 356 (1953).

10. *Federal Baseball Club of Baltimore, Inc.* v. *National League of Professional Baseball Clubs et al.*, 259 US 200 (1922).

11. *United States* v. *International Boxing Club of New York, Inc., et al.*, 348 US 236, 251 (1955).

12. *United States* v. *Employing Plasterers Association of Chicago et al.*, 347 US 186 (1954).

13. Ibid., 190.

14. *National Labor Relations Board* v. *Jones & Laughlin Steel Corp.*, 301 US 1 (1937).

15. James W. Ely, Jr., *The Guardian of Every Other Right: A Constitutional History of Property Rights* (New York: Oxford University Press, 1992), 129.

16. *Phillips Petroleum Co.* v. *Wisconsin et al.*, 347 US 672 (1954).

17. Elizabeth Anne Hull, "Sherman Minton and the Cold War Court" (Ph.D. diss., New School for Social Research, 1977), 287.

18. *Washington Post*, 17 Jan. 1956.

19. Abner J. Mikva, "Sherman Minton: The Supreme Court Years, Lecture on the 100th Anniversary of His Birth," Indiana University Southeast, New Albany, Ind., 14 Oct. 1990.

20. Richard Kluger, *Simple Justice: The History of Brown* v. *Board of Education and Black America's Struggle for Equality* (New York: Alfred A. Knopf, 1976), 679.

21. Cited in Bernard Schwartz, *A History of the Supreme Court* (New York: Oxford University Press, 1993), 287.

22. Kluger, *Simple Justice*, 682.

23. Schwartz, *History of the Supreme Court*, 295.

24. Letter from a former Minton law clerk to the author, 7 Oct. 1993.

25. *Brown* v. *Board of Education of Topeka et al.*, 347 US 483, 494 (1954).

26. Allan Morrison, "Justice Minton's Biggest Decision," *Ebony*, Dec. 1956, p. 98.

27. *Louisville Times*, 14 Nov. 1956.

28. Kluger, *Simple Justice*, 741.

29. Homer Bone to Minton, 19 May 1954, Minton Papers, Callanan Collection.

30. Frankfurter to Minton, 20 Aug. 1954, ibid.

31. Minton to Frankfurter, 25 Aug. 1954, Felix Frankfurter Papers, Manuscript Division, Library of Congress, Washington, D.C.

32. Atkinson, "Mr. Justice Minton and the Supreme Court," 169.

33. *Bell* v. *United States*, 349 US 81 (1955).

34. Ibid., 84.

35. Harry S. Truman to Minton, 6 Nov. 1961, Minton Papers, Callanan Collection.

36. Minton to Harry L. Wallace, 6 July 1955, Private Papers of Harry L. Wallace, Milwaukee, Wis.

37. Minton to Frankfurter, 10 July 1955, Frankfurter Papers.

38. Minton to Truman, 27 Dec. 1955, Post-Presidential Office Files, Truman Library.

39. Atkinson, "Mr. Justice Minton and the Supreme Court," 112–13.

40. Ibid., 113.

41. *United States ex rel. Toth* v. *Quarles, Secretary of the Air Force*, 350 US 11 (1955).

42. Ibid., 44.

43. *Griffin et al.* v. *Illinois*, 351 US 12 (1956).

44. Ibid., 27–29.

45. *Cole* v. *Young et al.*, 351 US 536 (1956).

46. Minton's unpublished dissent in *re Cole* v. *Young*, 351 US 536 (1956), Minton Papers, Truman Library.

47. *Southern Pacific Co.* v. *Gileo et al.*, 351 US 493 (1956); *Reed* v. *Pennsylvania Railroad Co.*, 351 US 502 (1956).

48. *Reed* v. *Pennsylvania Railroad Co.*, 506, 510.

49. Frankfurter to Minton, 11 June 1956, Minton Papers, Callanan Collection.

50. Tom C. Clark to Minton, 3 May 1956, ibid.

51. Minton to Hugo L. Black, 18 May 1956, Hugo L. Black Papers, Manuscript Division, Library of Congress.

52. "An Echo Fades," *Time*, 17 Sept. 1956, p. 31.

53. Carl A. Hatch to Minton, 29 Aug. 1956, Minton Papers, Callanan Collection.

54. Minton to Hatch, 4 Sept. 1956, ibid.

55. Memorial Proceedings before the United States Supreme Court, 384 US v, xxv (1966).

56. Truman to Minton, 28 Jan. 1950, original copy, Minton Papers, Callanan Collection.

57. *Louisville Courier-Journal*, 27 Jan. 1950.

58. *Indianapolis Times*, 25 Jan. 1950.

59. "An Echo Fades," 31.

60. *New York Times*, 8 Sept. 1956.

61. Ibid.

62. In 1972 a group of law school deans and professors of law, history, and political science evaluated all the Supreme Court justices. Minton, along with seven other justices, including Vinson and Burton, were rated as failures. Roy M. Mersky and Albert P. Blaustein, "Rating the Supreme Court Justices," *American Bar Association Journal* 58 (Nov. 1972): 1183–89.

63. The most thorough examinations of Minton's seven years on the Supreme Court are the dissertations of David N. Atkinson and Elizabeth Anne Hull, and Harry L. Wallace's "Mr. Justice Minton: Hoosier Justice on the Supreme Court," *Indiana Law Journal* 34 (spring 1959).

64. Roy M. Mersky and Gary R. Hartman, "Ranking of the Justices," in Kermit L. Hall, ed., *The Oxford Companion to the Supreme Court of the United States* (New York: Oxford University Press, 1992), 708.

65. Minton to Frankfurter, 18 Jan. 1960, Frankfurter Papers.

66. Hull, "Sherman Minton and the Cold War Court," 308.

67. Earl Warren, "Proceedings in the Supreme Court in Memory of Mr. Justice Minton," 384 US v, xxv (1966).

68. Nicholas Katzenbach, ibid., xxi.

69. Minton to Frank McHale, 19 Sept. 1956, Minton Papers, Callanan Collection.

70. Morrison, "Justice Minton's Biggest Decision," 99.

71. Atkinson, "Mr. Justice Minton and the Supreme Court," 168–69.

72. Ibid., 170.

73. Minton generally did not like concurring opinions and wrote only three in his seven-year career on the Court.

74. Hull, "Sherman Minton and the Cold War Court," 311.

75. Harold H. Burton to Minton, 7 Sept. 1956, Minton Papers, Callanan Collection.

76. *New York Times*, 8 Sept. 1956.

Chapter 10

1. Sherman Minton to Felix Frankfurter, 9 June 1956, Felix Frankfurter Papers, Manuscript Division, Library of Congress, Washington, D.C.

2. *Louisville Times*, 13 Nov. 1956.

3. Sherman Minton to William O. Douglas, 20 Mar. 1959, William O. Douglas Papers, Manuscript Division, Library of Congress.

4. Earl Major to Minton, 28 May 1958, Private Papers of Sherman Minton, Mary Anne Callanan Collection, Bethesda, Md. (hereafter cited as Minton Papers, Callanan Collection).

5. After Minton's death the Indiana University board of trustees designated the law school's moot courtroom in his honor. An oil portrait of Minton hangs in the facility.

6. *Louisville Courier-Journal*, 22 Dec. 1956.

7. *Louisville Times*, 19 Dec. 1956.

8. *Louisville Courier-Journal*, 5 May 1962.

9. Sherman Minton to Harry S. Truman, 24 Aug. 1956, Minton Papers, Callanan Collection.

10. Minton to Truman, 2 Sept. 1958, ibid.

11. Truman to Minton, 6 Sept. 1958, ibid.

12. Minton to Truman, 11 Nov. 1958, ibid.

13. Truman to Minton, 28 Nov. 1958, ibid.

14. Truman to Minton, 9 Apr. 1960, ibid.

15. Ibid.

16. Minton to Truman, 7 May 1960, ibid.

17. Minton to Truman, 16 July 1960, ibid.

18. Truman to Minton, 30 Aug. 1960, ibid.

19. Minton to Truman, 29 July 1963, Post-Presidential Office File, Harry S. Truman Library, Independence, Mo.

20. Minton to Truman, 17 Feb. 1963, ibid.

21. Minton to Truman, 1 May 1962, ibid.

22. Truman to Minton, 6 Nov. 1961, Minton Papers, Callanan Collection.

23. Minton to Truman, 7 Feb. 1958, ibid.

24. Truman to Minton, 27 Mar. 1958, ibid.

25. Truman to Minton, 19 July 1961, Post-Presidential Office File, Truman Library.

26. Minton to Douglas, 17 June 1958, Douglas Papers.

27. Minton to Douglas, 4 Jan. 1959, ibid.

28. Douglas to Minton, 18 Oct. 1958, Minton Papers, Callanan Collection.

29. Douglas to Minton, 27 Apr. 1961, Douglas Papers.

30. Minton to Douglas, 4 May 1961, ibid.

31. Douglas to Minton, 8 May 1961, ibid.

32. Frankfurter to Minton, 10 Aug. 1957, Minton Papers, Callanan Collection.

33. Minton to Frankfurter, 6 Aug. 1957, Frankfurter Papers.

34. Minton to Frankfurter, 15 Oct. 1957, ibid.

35. Minton to Frankfurter, 3 Jan. 1958, ibid.

36. Minton to Frankfurter, 6 Aug. 1957, ibid.

37. Frankfurter to Minton, 10 Aug. 1957, Minton Papers, Callanan Collection.

38. Minton to Frankfurter, 6 Aug. 1957, Frankfurter Papers.

39. Minton to Frankfurter, 21 July 1959, ibid.

40. Minton to Frankfurter, 6 July 1957, ibid.

41. Minton to Frankfurter, 8 Aug. 1957, ibid.

42. Minton to Frankfurter, 15 July 1958, ibid.

43. Minton to Hugo L. Black, 29 June 1962, Hugo L. Black Papers, Manuscript Division, Library of Congress.

44. Black to Minton, 15 July 1962, Minton Papers, Callanan Collection.

45. Minton to Black, 18 Nov. 1958, Black Papers.

46. Black to Minton, 28 Oct. 1960, ibid.

47. Black to Minton, 15 July 1962, Minton Papers, Callanan Collection.

48. Earl Warren to Minton, 15 Nov. 1957, ibid.

49. Minton to Harry L. Wallace, 26 Mar. 1957, Personal Papers of Harry L. Wallace, Milwaukee, Wis.

50. Minton to Wallace, 17 Oct. 1957, ibid.

51. Ibid.

52. Minton to Wallace, 13 Oct. 1962, ibid.

53. Minton to Wallace, 30 Sept. 1959, ibid.

54. Minton to Truman, 28 Mar. 1960, Minton Papers, Callanan Collection.

55. *Indianapolis Star*, 21 Oct. 1960.

56. Minton to Truman, 23 Oct. 1960, Minton Papers, Callanan Collection.

57. Minton to Truman, 17 Feb. 1963, Post-Presidential Office File, Truman Library.

58. Minton to Truman, 5 Apr. 1963, ibid.

59. Minton to Truman, 29 July 1963, ibid.

60. Minton to Black, undated, Black Papers.

61. Black to Minton, 17 Sept. 1964, ibid.

62. *Congressional Record*, 89th Cong., 1st sess., 1965, vol. 111, pt. 6:7922.

63. Minton to Frankfurter, 22 Oct. 1964, Frankfurter Papers.

64. *Indianapolis Star*, 3 May 1966.

65. Marshall E. Hanley eulogy, Private Papers of Alan T. Nolan, Indianapolis, Ind.

66. Alan T. Nolan eulogy, ibid.

67. Wallace H. White, Jr., to Minton, 12 July 1948, Minton Papers, Callanan Collection.

68. Minton to Tom Connally, 16 Apr. 1952, ibid.

69. Connally to Minton, 6 May 1952, ibid.
70. Lyndon B. Johnson to Minton, 12 July 1941, ibid.
71. Minton to George W. Norris, 5 Nov. 1942, ibid.
72. Claude Pepper to Minton, 20 Mar. 1946, ibid.
73. Clyde L. Herring to Minton, 9 Apr. 1943, ibid.
74. Herring to Minton, undated, ibid.
75. Dilsey Scott, interview with the authors, 5 May 1993.
76. Bud Ricke, interview with the authors, 8 July 1992.
77. Ruth Walts, interview with the authors, 16 June 1992.
78. Telegram, Private Papers of Ruth Walts, Georgetown, Ind.
79. Olyus Hood, interview with the authors, 18 Mar. 1992.
80. Sherman Minton, "The Most Unforgettable Character I've Met," essay, Minton Papers, Callanan Collection.
81. Minton to Nell Brown, 8 Nov. 1951, ibid.
82. Mary White to Minton, 25 Nov. 1949, ibid.
83. White to Minton, 6 May 1950, ibid.

BIBLIOGRAPHY

Authors' Interviews

David N. Atkinson, Kansas City, Mo.; David J. Bodenhamer, Indianapolis, Ind.; George D. Braden, Scarborough, Maine; Marilyn Bryant, Georgetown, Ind.; Mary Anne Callanan, Bethesda, Md.; Donald F. Carmony, Bloomington, Ind.; John A. Cody, Jr., New Albany, Ind.; Margaret Conner, New Albany, Ind.; Richard T. Conway, Washington, D.C.; James W. Ely, Jr., Nashville, Tenn.; Robert H. Ferrell, Bloomington, Ind.; William Goen, Salem, Ind.; Raymond Gray, Nashville, Ind.; Lillian Harris, Spencer, Ind.; Olyus Hood, Upper Marlboro, Md.; John Hurt, Martinsville, Ind.; Frances Kelly, Arlington, Va.; James Madison, Bloomington, Ind.; Keith Mann, Palo Alto, Calif.; Abner J. Mikva, Washington, D.C.; John Minton, Chevy Chase, Md.; Sherman Minton, Jr., Indianapolis, Ind.; Alan T. Nolan, Indianapolis, Ind.; Alice O'Donnell, Washington, D.C.; Gordon R. Owen, Las Cruces, N. Mex.; Bud Ricke, New Albany, Ind.; Dilsey Scott, New Albany, Ind.; Rayman L. Solomon, Evanston, Ill.; Lawrence Taylor, Dallas, Tex.; Harry L. Wallace, Milwaukee, Wis.; Ruth Walts, Georgetown, Ind.

Unpublished Sources

Manuscript Collections Consulted

Indiana Historical Society Library.
Papers of Carleton B. McCulloch.
Indiana State Archives.
Papers of Pleas E. Greenlee.
Papers of Paul V. McNutt.
Indiana State Library, Indiana Division.
Papers of Hugh A. Barnhart.
Papers of Raymond E. Willis.
Margaret I. King Library, University of Kentucky.
Papers of Alben Barkley.
Papers of Stanley F. Reed.
Papers of Fred M. Vinson.
Library of Congress, Manuscript Division.
Papers of Hugo L. Black.
Papers of Harold H. Burton.
Papers of William O. Douglas.
Papers of James A. Farley.
Papers of Felix Frankfurter.
Papers of Robert H. Jackson.
Papers of William G. McAdoo.
Papers of Wiley B. Rutledge.
Papers of Lewis B. Schwellenbach.
Lilly Library, Indiana University.
Papers of Paul V. McNutt.
Papers of Val Nolan.
Papers of Samuel M. Ralston.
Papers of James A. Woodburn.
Franklin D. Roosevelt Presidential Library.
Papers of Sherman Minton.
Papers of Henry Morgenthau, Jr.
Harry S. Truman Library.
Papers of Sherman Minton.
Papers of Harry S. Truman.
Private Papers of George D. Braden.

Private Collections

Private Papers of Sherman Minton. Mary Anne Callanan Collection, now located at Lilly Library, Indiana University.
Private Papers of Sherman Minton. Harry L. Wallace Collection.

Dissertations

Atkinson, David N. "Mr. Justice Minton and the Supreme Court, 1949–1956." Ph.D. diss., University of Iowa, 1969.
Clutter, Richard. "The Indiana American Legion, 1919–1960." Ph.D. diss., Indiana University, 1974.
Corcoran, David Howard. "Sherman Minton: New Deal Senator." Ph.D. diss., University of Kentucky, 1977.
Hull, Elizabeth Anne. "Sherman Minton and the Cold War Court." Ph.D. diss., New School for Social Research, 1977.
Marquat, Ronald Gene. "The Judicial Justice: Mr. Justice Minton and the Supreme Court." Ph.D. diss., University of Virginia, 1962.
Munger, Frank O. "Two Party Politics in the State of Indiana." Ph.D. diss., Harvard University, 1955.
Neff, Robert Rex. "The Early Career and Governorship of Paul V. McNutt." Ph.D. diss., Indiana University, 1963.
Owen, Gordon. "The Public Speaking of Sherman Minton." Ph.D. diss., Purdue University, 1962.

Other Library and Archival Sources

Filson Club, Louisville, Ky.
The National Archives.
Papers of Special Committee on Lobbying.
New Albany-Floyd County Public Library, Indiana Room.
U.S. Department of Justice, Federal Bureau of Investigation.
U.S. Senate Historical Office.

Other Unpublished Material

Abstracts of Entries of Government Lands in Floyd County, Ind.; marriage and death records and census data from 1850 to 1900, New Albany-Floyd County City-County Building; Corcoran, David H.," The Preconditions for Greatness: A Case Study of Sherman Minton," special collection, Indiana Room, New Albany-Floyd County Public Library; Hearing before the Committee of the Judiciary, United States Senate, September, 1949; Mikva, Abner J., "Sherman Minton: The Supreme Court Years, Lecture on the 100th Anniversary of His Birth," Indiana University Southeast, New Albany, Ind., 14 Oct. 1990; Minton's letter of apology, display case of memorabilia, New Albany High School; Ooms, Casper W., "Honorable Sherman Minton, Judge," tribute to Justice Minton upon presentation of his portrait at the Judicial Conference and Bar Association of the Seventh Circuit, 15 June 1951; Wallace, Harry L., "Hoosier Justice," Minton biography made available to the authors (no date).

Published Sources

Books

Abraham, Henry J. *Justices & Presidents: A Political History of Appointments to the Supreme Court*. 3d rev. ed. New York: Oxford University Press, 1992.

Allen, George Edward. *Presidents Who Have Known Me*. New York: Simon and Schuster, 1950.

Allen, Robert S., and William V. Shannon. *The Truman Merry-Go-Round*. New York: Vanguard Press, 1950.

Alsop, Joseph, and Turner Catledge. *The 168 Days*. New York: Doubleday, Doran and Co., Inc., 1938.

Ball, Howard. *The Vision and the Dream of Justice Hugo L. Black: An Examination of a Judicial Philosophy*. University: University of Alabama Press, c. 1975.

Ball, Howard, and Phillip Cooper. *Of Power and Right: Hugo Black, William O. Douglas, and America's Constitutional Revolution*. New York: Oxford University Press, 1992.

Barnhart, John E., and Donald F. Carmony. *Indiana: From Frontier to Industrial Commonwealth*. 4 vols. New York: Lewis Historical Publishing Co., Inc., 1954.

Belknap, Michal R. *Cold War Political Justice: The Smith Act, the Communist Party, and American Civil Liberties*. Westport, Conn.: Greenwood Press, 1977.

Blake, I. George. *Paul V. McNutt: Portrait of a Hoosier Statesman*. Indianapolis: Central Publishing Co., 1966.

Bodenhamer, David J. *Fair Trial: Rights of the Accused in American History*. New York: Oxford University Press, 1992.

Donnelly, Sister Mary Louise. *Arnold Liver's Family in America* (Lyvers, Lievers). Burke, Va.: Donnelly, 1977.

Douglas, William O. *The Court Years, 1939–1975: The Autobiography of William O. Douglas*. New York: Random House, 1980.

Dunne, Gerald T. *Hugo Black and the Judicial Revolution*. New York: Simon and Schuster, 1977.

Ely, James W., Jr. *The Guardian of Every Other Right: A Constitutional History of Property Rights*. New York: Oxford University Press, 1992.

Farley, James A. *Jim Farley's Story: The Roosevelt Years*. New York: Whittlesey House, 1948.

Gregory, Charles Oscar. *Labor and the Law*. New York: W. W. Norton Co., 1946.

Haffner, Gerald O. *New Mown Hay and Other Cuttings from Hoosier History*. New Albany: Indiana University Southeast, 1978.

Hall, Kermit. *The Magic Mirror: Law in American History*. New York: Oxford University Press, 1989.

Hamilton, Virginia Van Der Veer. *Hugo Black: The Alabama Years*. Baton Rouge: Louisiana State University Press, 1972.

Hirsch, H. N. *The Enigma of Felix Frankfurter*. New York: Basic Books, 1981.

Ickes, Harold L. *The Secret Diary of Harold L. Ickes*. 3 vols. New York: Simon and Schuster, 1953–54.

Leuchtenburg, William E. *Franklin D. Roosevelt and the New Deal, 1932–1940*. New York: Harper and Row, Publishers, 1963.

Madison, James H. *Indiana through Tradition and Change: A History of the Hoosier State and Its People, 1920–1945*. Indianapolis: Indiana Historical Society, 1982.

Marcus, Maeva. *Truman and the Steel Seizure Case: The Limits of Presidential Power*. New York: Columbia University Press, 1977.

Miller, Merle. *Plain Speaking: An Oral Biography of Harry S. Truman*. New York: G. P. Putnam's Sons, 1973.

Pfeffer, Leo. *This Honorable Court: A History of the United States Supreme Court*. Boston: Beacon Press, 1965.

Pickett, William B. *Homer E. Capehart: A Senator's Life, 1897–1979*. Indianapolis: Indiana Historical Society, 1990.

Polenberg, Richard. *Reorganizing Roosevelt's Government*. Cambridge, Mass.: Harvard University Press, 1966.

Pritchett, Herman C. *Civil Liberties and the Vinson Court*. Chicago: University of Chicago Press, 1954.

Rudko, Frances. *Truman's Court: A Study in Judicial Restraint*. Westport, Conn.: Greenwood Press, 1988.

Schwartz, Bernard. *A History of the Supreme Court*. New York: Oxford University Press, 1993.

Scigliano, Robert G. *The Supreme Court and the Presidency*. New York: The Free Press, 1971.

Simon, James F. *Independent Journey: The Life of William O. Douglas*. New York: Harper and Row, 1980.

Solomon, Rayman L. *History of the Seventh Circuit, 1891–1941*. Washington, D.C.: Published under the auspices of the Bicentennial Committee of the Judicial Conference of the United States, 1981.

Steinberg, Alfred. *The Man from Missouri: The Life and Times of Harry S. Truman*. New York: G. P. Putnam's Sons, 1962.

Tushnet, Mark. *Making Civil Rights Law: Thurgood Marshall and the Supreme Court, 1936–1961*. New York: Oxford University Press, 1994.

Vista, New Albany High School Yearbook, Class of 1910.

Who's Who and What's What in Indiana Politics. Indianapolis: James E. Perry, Publisher, 1944.

Articles

"An Echo Fades." *Time* (17 Sept. 1956).

Baker, Thomas E. "Frederick Moore Vinson." In *The Oxford Companion to the Supreme Court of the United States*, ed. Kermit L. Hall. New York: Oxford University Press, 1992.

Braden, George D. "Mr. Justice Minton and the Truman Bloc." *Indiana Law Journal* 26 (1951).

Cohen, William. "Justice Douglas and the Rosenberg Case: Setting the Record Straight." *Cornell Law Review* 70 (1985).

"Fourth Truman Appointee Confirmed." *The United States Law Week* (11 Oct. 1949).

Frank, John P. "Fred Vinson and the Chief Justiceship." *University of Chicago Law Review* 21, no. 2 (winter 1954).

_______. "Mr. Justice Black: The Man and His Opinions." *Indiana Law Journal* 24 (winter 1949).

_______. "The United States Supreme Court." *University of Chicago Law Review* 18, no. 1 (autumn 1950).

_______. "The United States Supreme Court: 1950–1951." *University of Chicago Law Review* 19, no. 2 (winter 1952).

_______. "The United States Supreme Court: 1951–1952." *University of Chicago Law Review* 20, no. 1 (autumn 1952).

"Gentleman from Indiana." *Newsweek* (26 Sept. 1949).

Haffner, Gerald O. "A Hoosier Country Doctor: Dr. Harry K. Engleman's Medical Ledger, 1911–1917." *Indiana Magazine of History* 85 (June 1989).

Ickes, Harold L. "Justice Rutledge." *The New Republic* (26 Sept. 1949).

_______. "Tom Clark Should Say 'No Thanks.'" *The New Republic* (15 Aug. 1949).

Jaffe, Louis L. "The Supreme Court, 1950 Term." *Harvard Law Review* 65 (1951–52).

Katzenbach, Nicholas. "Proceedings in the Supreme Court in Memory of Mr. Justice Minton, Monday, May 2, 1966." 382 US v, xxi (1966).

Kirkendall, Richard. "Tom C. Clark" and "Sherman Minton."In *The Justices of the United States Supreme Court, 1789–1969*, eds. Leon Friedman and Fred L. Israel. 5 vols. New York: R. R. Bowker Co. in association with Chelsea House Publishers, 1969–78.

Mayer, Milton. "Men Who Would Be President: Pretty Boy McNutt." *The Nation* (30 Mar. 1940).

Mersky, Roy M., and Albert P. Blaustein. "Rating the Supreme Court Justices." *American Bar Association Journal* 58 (Nov. 1972).

Mersky, Roy M., and Gary R. Hartman. "Ranking of the Justices." In *The Oxford Companion to the Supreme Court of the United States*, ed. Kermit L. Hall. New York: Oxford University Press, 1992.

"The Minton Story." *Indiana Alumni Magazine* (Nov. 1949).

"Mr. Justice Minton." *The New Republic* (26 Sept. 1949).

Morgan, Iwan. "Fractional Conflict in Indiana Politics during the Later New Deal Years, 1936–1940." *Indiana Magazine of History* 79 (Mar. 1983).

Morrison, Allan. "Justice Minton's Biggest Decision." *Ebony* (Dec. 1956).

"Politics and People." *The Nation* (24 Sept. 1949).

"Recent Cases." *The George Washington Law Review* 16 (June 1948).

"Search and Seizure in the Supreme Court: Shadows on the Fourth Amendment." *University of Chicago Law Review* 28, no. 4 (summer 1961).

"Sherman Minton's Greatest Sports Thrill." *Indiana Alumni Magazine* (Dec. 1956).

"Taxes." *Tax Magazine* (Oct. 1949).

Thorpe, James A. "The Appearance of Supreme Court Nominees before the Senate Judiciary Committee." *Journal of Public Law* 2 (1969).

Wallace, Harry L. "Mr. Justice Minton—Hoosier Justice on the Supreme Court." *Indiana Law Journal* 146 (winter 1959).

Warren, Earl. "Proceedings in the Supreme Court in Memory of Mr. Justice Minton, May 2, 1966." 384 US v, xxv (1966).

Newspapers

Bedford Daily Times-Mail.

Boston Herald.

Chicago Sun Times.

Chicago Tribune.

Christian Science Monitor.

Fort Wayne Journal-Gazette.

Gary Post-Tribune.

Hancock Democrat.

Indianapolis News.

Indianapolis Star.

Indianapolis Times.

Louisville Courier-Journal.

Louisville Times.

Monticello White County Democrat.

Muncie Evening Press.

New Albany Tribune.
New Albany Weekly Ledger.
New York Herald-Tribune.
New York Times.
Newark Evening News.
Philadelphia Record.
Terre Haute Tribune.
Vincennes Sun-Commercial.
Washington Post.

Congressional Record

Congressional Record. 1936. 74th Cong., 2d sess. 16 Jan., 26, 30 Mar.
Congressional Record. 1937. 75th Cong., 1st sess. 31 Mar., 9 July.
Congressional Record. 1938. 75th Cong., 2d sess. 15 Feb., 28 Apr.
Congressional Record. 1939. 76th Cong., 1st sess. Vol. 84, pt. 8.
Congressional Record. 1940. 76th Cong., 2d sess. 11 Mar.
Congressional Record. 1965. 89th Cong. 13 Apr.

Court Cases

Adler et al. v. *Board of Education of the City of New York*, 342 US 485 (1952).
Adler v. *Northern Hotel Co., Inc., et al.*, 175 F2d 619 (1942).
Alabama Great Southern Railroad Co. v. *United States*, 340 US 216 (1951).
Andrews v. *Hotel Sherman*, 138 F2d 524 (1943).
Bailey v. *Richardson*, 341 US 918 (1951).
Barrows v. *Jackson*, 346 US 249 (1953).
Bell v. *United States*, 349 US 81 (1955).
Brock v. *North Carolina*, 344 US 424 (1953).
Brown v. *Board of Education*, 347 US 483 (1954).
California Fruit Growers Exchange v. *Sunkist Baking Co.*, 166 F2d 971 (1948).
Cargill, Inc. v. *Board of Trade of City of Chicago*, 164 F2d 820, 823 (1947).
Cederblade et al. v. *Parmelee Transp. Co.*, 166 F2d 554 (1948).
Chicago, Burlington and Quincy Railroad Company v. *Chicago*, 166 US 226 (1897).
Chimel v. *California*, 395 US 752 (1969).
Christopher v. *American News Co.*, 171 F2d 275 (1948).
Cole v. *Young et al.*, 351 US 536 (1956).

Consumer Petroleum Co. v. *Consumer Co. of Illinois*, 160 F2d 153 (1948).
Dennis v. *United States*, 339 US 162 (1950).
Dennis et al. v. *United States*, 341 US 494 (1951).
E. Edelman & Co. v. *Auto Parts & Gear Co.*, 127 F2d 897 (1942).
Erie Railroad Co. v. *Tompkins*, 304 US 64 (1938).
Federal Baseball Club v. *National League*, 259 US 200 (1922).
Frazier v. *United States*, 335 US 497 (1948).
General Industries Company v. *20 Wacker Drive Bldg. Corporation et al.*, 156 F2d 474 (1946).
Gitlow v. *New York* 268 US 652 (1925).
Griffin et al. v. *Illinois*, 351 US 12 (1956).
Harris v. *United States*, 331 US 145 (1947).
Henderson v. *United States et al.*, 339 US 816 (1950).
Horlick's Malted Milk Corporation v. *Horlick*, 143 F2d 32 (1944).
Interlake Iron Corp. v. *National Labor Relations Board*, 131 F2d 129, 133 (1942).
Joint Anti-Fascist Refugee Committee v. *McGrath*, 341 US 123 (1951).
Jumps et al. v. *Leverone et al.*, 150 F2d 876 (1945).
Kasual v. *George F. Nord Bldg. Corporation*, 129 F2d 173 (1942).
Lanning v. *National Ribbon and Carbon Paper Mfg. Co.*, 125 F2d 565 (1942).
Leyra v. *Denno*, 347 US 556 (1954).
Lutwak et al. v. *United States*, 344 US 604 (1953).
McCarthy v. *Pennsylvania R. Co.*, 156 F2d 877 (1946).
McLaurin v. *Oklahoma State Regents*, 339 US 637 (1950).
Marshall Field and Co. v. *National Labor Relations Board*, 135 F2d 391 (1943).
Montgomery Ward & Co., Inc. v. *McGraw-Hill Pub. Co., Inc.*, 146 F2d 171 (1944).
National Labor Relations Board v. *American Car and Foundry Co.*, 161 F2d 501 (1947).
National Labor Relations Board v. *Laughlin Steel Corporation*, 301 US 1 (1937).
National Labor Relations Board v. *Marshall Field & Co.*, 129 F2d 169 (1942).
National Labor Relations Board v. *Sheboygan Chair Co.*, 125 F2d 436 (1942).
National Labor Relations Board v. *Sunbeam Electric Mfg. Co.*, 133 F2d 856 (1943).
National Labor Relations Board v. *W. A. Jones Foundry & Machine Co.*, 123 F2d 552 (1941).

National Labor Relations Board v. *William Davies Co.*, 135 F2d 179 (1943).
Quaker Oats Co. v. *General Mills, Inc.*, 134 F2d 429 (1943).
Palko v. *Connecticut*, 302 US 319 (1937).
Phillips Petroleum Company v. *Wisconsin*, 347 US 672 (1954).
Pierce v. *Society of Sisters*, 268 US 510 (1925).
Powell v. *Alabama*, 287 US 45 (1932).
Rapid Roller Co. v. *National Labor Relations Board*, 126 F2d 452 (1942).
Reed v. *Pennsylvania Railroad Company*, 351 US 502 (1956).
Sax v. *National Labor Relations Board*, 171 F2d 769 (1948).
Schenck v. *United States*, 249 US 47 (1919).
Schreiber et al. v. *United States*, 129 F2d 836 (1942).
Schwartz v. *Texas*, 344 US 199 (1952).
Securities and Exchange Commission v. *Vacuum Can Co. et al.*, 157 F2d 530 (1946).
Shaughnessy, District Director of Immigration and Naturalization v. *United States ex rel. Mezei*, 345 US 206 (1953).
Shelley v. *Kraemer*, 334 US 1 (1948).
Southern Pacific Co. v. *Gileo et al.*, 351 US 493 (1956).
A. E. Staley Mfg. Company et al. v. *Federal Trade Commission*, 144 F2d 221 (1944).
Standard Oil Company v. *Federal Trade Commission*, 173 F2d 210 (1949).
Standard Oil Co. v. *Federal Trade Commission*, 340 US 231 (1951).
Sweatt v. *Painter*, 339 US 629 (1950).
Sweet v. *Howard, Warden*, 155 F2d 715 (1946).
Terry et al. v. *Adams et al.*, 345 US 461 (1953).
Toolson v. *New York Yankees, Inc., et al.*, 346 US 356 (1953).
Toth v. *Quarles*, 350 US 11 (1955).
Tovar v. *Jarecki, Collector of Internal Revenue*, 173 F2d 449 (1949).
Trupiano et al. v. *United States*, 334 US 699 (1948).
United States ex rel. Adams v. *Ragen*, 172 F2d 693 (1949).
United States ex rel. Feeley v. *Ragen*, 166 F2d 976 (1948).
United States ex rel. Hack v. *Clark, U.S. Attorney General et al.*, 159 F2d 552 (1947).
United States ex rel. Knauff v. *Shaughnessy*, 338 US 537 (1950).
United States v. *Employing Plasterers Association of Chicago, et al.*, 347 US 186 (1954).
United States v. *Johnson*, 142 F2d 588 (1944).

United States v. *Knauer*, 149 F2d 519 (1945).
United States v. *Morgan*, 346 US 502 (1954).
United States v. *New York Great Atlantic and Pacific Tea Company*, 173 F2d 79 (1949).
United States v. *One 1946 Plymouth Sedan Automobile*, 167 F2d 3 (1948).
United States v. *Rabinowitz*, 339 US 56 (1950).
United States v. *Wood*, 299 US 123 (1936).
Walling, Admin'r of Wage and Hour Div., Dept. of Labor v. *Swift & Co.*, 131 F2d 249 (1942).
Walling, Administrator of Wage and Hour Division of United States Dept. of Labor v. *T. Buettner & Co.*, 133 F2d 305 (1943).
Western Cartridge Co. v. *National Labor Relations Board*, 139 F2d 858 (1943).
Wieman et al. v. *Updegraff et al.*, 344 US 183 (1952).
Wiggington v. *Order of United Commercial Travelers of America*, 126 F2d 659 (1942).
Wood v. *Howard*, 157 F2d 807 (1946).
Youngstown Sheet and Tube v. *Sawyer*, 343 US 579 (1952).
Zangerle & Petersen Co. v. *Venice Furniture Novelty Mfg. Co.*, 133 F2d 266 (1943).

Photographic Archival Sources

Private Collection of Mary Anne Callanan.
Indianapolis Times Archives.
Harry S. Truman Library.
United States Supreme Court.

INDEX

Designer: Dean Johnson Design, Inc., Indianapolis, Indiana
Typeface: Palatino
Typographer: Douglas & Gayle Limited, Indianapolis, Indiana
Paper: 60-pound Booktext Natural
Printer: BookCrafters, Chelsea, Michigan